This page intentionally left blank so the reader may write any initial notes or handwritten bookmarks. Subsequential pages have a small amount of room at the bottom of said page for further handwritten notes.

Operating System Design
FYSOS: The Virtual File System

Benjamin David Lunt

About the Author

Benjamin David Lunt has been programming computers since 1984 and has always enjoyed the hardware side of the spectrum. He has programmed many different types of programs, mostly for DOS and other minimal operating systems, as well as a few programs for the Windows family.

Many years ago, he started to read up on the Universal Host Controller Interface (UHCI) and got hooked on the USB concept. He has been programming for USB ever since. One of the more known projects has been the USB support for the Bochs Emulator (https://bochs.sourceforge.io/).

Programming is not Ben's only line of work. He has been in the building trade since 1991, and enjoys remodeling homes.

He also enjoys hunting, fishing, and is an active member of his local church's scouting program.

Ben recently became a grandfather for the first time and is very much enjoying that new adventure in his life. If he knew grandchildren would be so enjoyable, he would have had them first.

Credits

Publisher
*CreateSpace Independent
            Publishing Platform*

Editor
Benjamin David Lunt

Book Designer
Benjamin David Lunt

Cover Designer
Benjamin David Lunt

Production Team
Forever Young Software

Technical Review
Benjamin David Lunt

This book is dedicated to my daughter, son,
and three grandchildren.

Larissa and Colby
John and Maya
Chelsea, Benji, and Austin

First Published: April 2014
1st Edition: 20140415
1st Edition Update: 20220209

Contents

Part 1

Part 2

Introduction

The series as a whole
This book is part of a whole, a series of books describing how to design and write an operating system. The operating system in question is called *FYSOS, aka Konan*. Throughout this book you may see references to this as a whole. I will try to make this book as independent of the whole series as possible, but there may be times when I refer to another book in the series.

Currently, this series, *Operating System Design*, includes:
Volume 1 -- The System Core
Volume 2 -- The Virtual File System
Volume 3 -- Media Storage Devices
Volume 4 -- Input and Output Devices
Volume 5 -- Misc. System Services
Volume 6 -- The Graphical User Interface
Volume 7 -- The Network Interface
Volume 8 -- The Universal Serial Bus

At the writing of this edition, six books have been written, highlighted above. The other two books in the series will be completed when time and interest allow.

Who is this series for?
Have you ever wanted to write your own Operating System? Have you ever wondered how and where to start? How does the computer know where my code is? How do I make the computer do what I want? Have you ever wondered about these things?

Within the pages of each book in this series, and with the freely available code and data, I will take you through the process of creating a minimal, though fully functional operating system. I will discuss the boot process, where and how to get your operating system loaded and executed, how to detect and interact with the hardware, as well as creating a user interface.

I will also discuss the pros and cons of the process of writing and testing your code. What kind of hardware to use for testing, and what software you will need to create your own operating system.

Each book in the series should be independent of another. It is not required that you have another book in the series to use this or any other book within the series.

This book, *FYSOS: The Virtual File System*, includes information on a subject that I am most fond of--file systems. Other books in this series will be released and/or updated when time and interest allow.

The subject in this book is the Virtual File System. This is the part of your operating system that is the communication link between your kernel and the media that is attached. This Virtual File System creates an anonymous link allowing any type of file system to be used, independent of the Kernel and the physical medium the file system resides on.

The first few chapters will focus on how to make this link independent of the file systems of the media, a communication link no matter the format of the media. Then I will discuss the benefits and faults of a few file systems, from simple to more complicated. Other subjects within this book will be, for example, the way file names may be stored and the format they use, along with file recovery, journals, and other topics pertaining to file systems.

How to use this book?

There are small icons displayed in this book from time to time. These icons indicate that this paragraph or text box is of difference than the main text. Here are these icons and their descriptions:

 Indicates that the source listing is freely available on-line.

Indicates that this is a note-box of significant importance.

 Indicates that this is a note-box or "please note this" item.

Indicates that this is an "off the subject" note and is of interest only.

There may also be some places where I may ask you to enter text into the DOS prompt or text editor. The actual text to be entered will have a shaded background while a specified key will be italic and enclosed in brackets. Here is an example on loading the file *demo.com* with DEBUG.

At the C:\ prompt enter the following:

```
C:\>DEBUG demo.com<enter>
```

There are numeric values throughout the text. When a value other than decimal is given, sometimes it will have the decimal value in parentheses just after it. For example, if I have the value 0FFh, if the subject calls for it, I will proceed it with the following: (255d) – meaning 255 in decimal format.

Things to know before reading this book

When I use a physical memory address, I always use a number of leading zeros depending on the memory access size I am currently using. If I am discussing something in 16-bit, I use five digits to indicate the address. Since in 16-bit real mode, the CPU has a 20-bit address bus, this 20-bit address can be shown in five hex digits.

For example, if I were pointing to offset 0x123 in memory, I would use

```
0x00123
```

to describe this address. Four bits per hex digit, times five digits, is twenty bits. All addresses in 16-bit real mode will have this notation.

When I am discussing memory addresses in 32-bit protected mode, I will use the same notation except that it will have eight digits on the right side of the 'x'.

Since I use C and Assembly to build all of the projects in this series, I will assume that you know enough about these two languages and I will use them throughout this book. If you are not familiar with C, please study up on C before dwelling deep into this book. If you are not familiar with Assembly, you may be able to use this book without any knowledge of Assembly. However, any operating system writing and understanding will require some Assembly language knowledge.

Throughout this book I will use the terms "system software" and "your driver" often. These two terms relate to the software that you are writing whether it be BIOS code, an Operating System, or simply a driver for an already created Operating System. When I use these two terms, I am talking about the code you are writing.

Abbreviations

The following abbreviations might be used throughout this book.

CRLF	Carriage Return Line Feed pair. ASCII pair 13/10.
DOS	Disk Operating System (Usually referring to MS-DOS®)
FreeDOS	A freeware clone of MS-DOS found at www.freedos.org
i.e.	Latin for *id est*, or *in other words*.
e.g.	Latin for *exempli gratia*, *for the sake of example* or *for example*.
FAT	File Allocation Table. Microsoft's FAT file system
FYSFS	The FYSOS' file system
LEANFS	A file system used in FreeDOS
NTFS	The Windows NT series of file systems
EXT2/3/4	The Linux file system
SFS	Simple File System
LBA	Logical Block Address
CHS	Cylinder / Head / Sector
BCD	Binary Coded Decimal

NULL	A pointer value of zero
VFS	Virtual File System
FPB	File Pointer Block
DPB	Disk Parameter Block
DLE	Device List Entry
BPB	BIOS Parameter Block
Super Block	Data, stored on the disk, specially used to introduce a file system.

When declaring an amount of memory or data, or when describing bits, I will use the following notation:

MSb	Most significant bit. The left most or highest bit.
LSb	Least significant bit. The right most or lowest bit.
MSB	Most significant byte.
LSB	Least significant byte.
Bit	A single bit of either 0 or 1.
Bits 7:5	Declares a series of three bits, bits 7, 6, and 5.
Nibble	A 4-bit field, the low or high 4 bits of a byte.
Byte	A single byte of 8 bits.
Word	Two consecutive bytes totaling 16 bits.
Dword	Four consecutive bytes totaling 32 bits.
Qword	Eight consecutive bytes totaling 64 bits.
Page	Four Kilobytes of aligned memory.
K	Kilobyte. 1024 bytes. 100k = 100 * 1024
M	Megabyte. 1024 kilobytes. 100M = 100 * 1024 * 1024
G	Gigabyte. 1024 megabytes. 1G = 1024 * 1024 * 1024

Please note that even though most modern hard drives will use the term Gigabytes or Terabytes for its capacity, they are referring to the decimal form. For example, if the manufacturer indicates that its capacity is 100 Gigabytes, the actual capacity is 100,000,000,000 bytes, not 107,374,182,400 as you might think. They did this solely for advertisement. Makes it look like more space than is actually there.

When declaring variables and/or labels with a size in the C/C++ code throughout this series, I use type defines such as

```
bit8u  variable0;
bit16s variable1;
bit32u variable2;
bit64s variable3;
```

bit8u simply is an 8-bit byte and is unsigned, while bit16s is a 16-bit word and is signed. For more information on these types, please see `ctype.h` in the `\utils\include\` directory.

When I write a numeric value, I will use the decimal form unless otherwise noted, or it is obvious that a different form is better for the current context. All decimal numbers will be in the form of 1234567890, while all hexadecimal numbers will use the form of 0x01234567, the standard C form with a preceding 0x, or will have a trailing 'h' as in 01234567h. All binary numbers will be in the form of 11001100b and have a trailing 'b'. Hexadecimal or Binary numbers might have an underscore within the number sequence as 0101_0101b. This is to help the eye see the bit positions easier. For example, a 32-bit dword in binary form could be 01010101111001001100100100101001b. This is difficult to count where bit 23 might be. However, the same binary representation of 0101_0101_1110_0100_1100_1001_0010_1001b is much easier to find a numbered bit.

Definitions

The following words may be used within this book. I list their meaning here to clarify what is intended.

The words *should, shall, will,* or *must* are used to indicate mandatory requirements. This means that it is mandatory for a device or function when this term is used.

The words *may, might,* or *can* are used to indicate that it is recommended or is a possibility for a device when this term is used. The word *may* is usually referred to as, *is permitted to*. The word *can* is usually referred to, *is capable of*.

The word *Host* is referring to the code, operating system, driver, or whatever code is currently requesting access to the media.

Little-endian is used to indicate that a value larger than a byte is stored lowest byte first, then the next lowest byte, and so on. This is considered the Intel format.

Big-endian is just the opposite. The highest byte is stored first, then the next highest, and so on. This is considered the IBM format.

An example of the little-endian format would be if the value of 0x01234567 were to be written to memory, it would be written as shown below.

```
0x00000000  67 45 23 01
```

with the lowest byte written to the lower memory byte, the next lowest byte written to the next byte in memory, and so on.

Tables

Most tables within this book will have the first column as an offset column, and the second as a size column. The offset is the zero-based offset from the start of the object described, while the size is shown in bytes, unless otherwise noted.

What you will need to use this book?

I am going to use an Intel compatible processor, capable of 16-bit real mode, 32-bit protected mode, or 64-bit long mode code, and at least one empty IDE hard drive. This will be sufficient for this book, though you may want to have multiple hard drives available and maybe a few USB thumb drives available.

The code will be written in 32-bit protected mode code written in 32-bit C and/or 32-bit and/or 16-bit assembly. Instructions on obtaining a C compiler and an assembler are in Appendix B.

This book does little if any actual hardware interaction. I will discuss the format of the media on the hardware. Therefore, there are no hardware requirements for this book. You simply need a media source to be able to format to the different file systems within this book, to study how they work. The actual writing of the media is outside of the purpose of this book, though there are a few utilities included to help write to the media device you have chosen.

There is no platform requirement to this book either. All you will need is the available media and a way to write to it as explained above. However, I use a Win98 DOS Command Line style platform and all example source code and will assume a similar platform.

I may refer to code within the FYSOS operating system throughout this book. If I do, there will be comments and descriptions in the code of this book to give similar or exact results, and documented accordingly.

What is in the repository?

As mention, there is a freely available repository of source code and data included with this book. It contains all of the source code within this book except the small snippets, which are just a few lines of code rather than a complete program. Please see Appendix A for more information.

A code listing will have a small image of a disk at its beginning, declaring that the repository contains this listing.

Also included in the repository are all utilities mentioned in the text. You can find these utilities in the \main\filesys\utils directory.

See Appendix A for a complete listing of the repository's contents.

Prerequisite to using this book

It is not required that you know much or anything about the format of a file system. As mentioned before, you will only need a host machine capable of writing to a blank media device, such as a floppy, hard drive, or USB thumb drive. For a better understanding of the first few chapters of this book, it is recommended, though not required, that you have read Volume 1 of this series, "FYSOS: The System Core".

What is not discussed in this book

I will not discuss the actual process of reading and writing to the media via the media's hardware. This will be for another book in this series. The intent of this book is to discuss the possibilities of the ways you can format your media for use within your operating system. After all, all media must have some form of known format to be able to use it. Volume 3, "FYSOS: Media Storage Devices" explains in detail the process used to read and write such media devices.

Final word before we get started

All of the information in this book and the code in the repository is accurate to the best of my knowledge. The information contained comes from my own research and development. If there is ever a discrepancy, the associated specification takes precedence. If there is an error in the accuracy of this book's information, you use it at your own risk. I have done my best to be as accurate as possible, but I give no warranty, either expressed or implied, to the correctness of this book. However, if you do find an error, please let me know, so that I may correct it in a later edition. I may then list your name as a contributor in a later edition.

Enough with the pleasantries, shall we get started?

Part 1

In Part 1 I will discuss the link between your operating system and the found media, a way to be independent of the format of the media, and show the functions you will need to create this link.

I will also discuss directories, sometimes called folders, what makes a file system simple or complex, and how to make a stable file system.

Chapter 1 – The File System Overview

An operating system needs a link between the user application and the file systems that reside on the media of the computer it resides on. An operating system could have each file system coded within its kernel, but that could take up a lot of valuable space and what happens when that file system changes or a new file system is introduced to the system? Therefore, it is much better to have the file system code separate from the kernel. This way, when a file system is updated or a new one is introduced, the only thing that needs to be updated/installed is a file system driver.

However, now you need a standard link of communication between the kernel and the driver. The kernel needs to be able to call a standard set of routines, completely independent of the file system, while the file system needs to be completely independent of the physical media it resides on.

The design goal of this book

This is where the first few chapters of this book come in. I will explain the connection needed to do this. Then later chapters will detail specific file systems and give advantages and disadvantages to each so that you have an idea of what you can do if you decide to create your own.

I will show details within these file systems that make it a good file system or give it limits such as file name lengths. I will also detail ways to store file names and other details about a file within that file system.

I will also show enhancements to file systems that can help in file recovery and a system crash, leaving the file system in a stable state.

Other things to know and consider

File systems can be from as simple as a file name, a date and time, and a pointer or pointers to where the file data resides on the media, to extensive information about that file. Some file systems are designed for specific types of media and may not work well on other types.

Another thing to consider is that some file systems are patented and/or proprietary and may be illegal to use in some cases. For example, part of the Microsoft FAT file system is patented and goes against that patent if you implement that specific part. More on this later.

Implementation and Design

In Part 1, I will show what your kernel needs to communicate with a file system and what that file system driver needs to communicate with the kernel. I will call this the Virtual File

System within the remainder of this book. I will then describe some of the items within a simple file system to a larger file system, directories within these file systems, and other information pertaining to data integrity and recovery.

Part 2 will show in detail a couple of the most common file systems used, two hobby file systems created by fellow coders, and a file system I wrote for the purpose of FYSOS and this book.

Other than the obvious "for the fun of it" answer, you might want to implement a file system of your own so that you can learn what it takes to create and use a file system. Nothing is a better way to learn than hands on learning.

Tested devices

Since very little of the information in this book is specific to a specific hardware device, the information in this book and the implementation of it, can be used on most any platform and device as long as you have an available media device and a way to read and write to it.

The process of reading and writing of this media device within your operating system is enough information to warrant another book within this series. Therefore, it is my intent to describe the process of the data on the device within this book and the process of writing to it within a different book.

Shall we begin?

Chapter 2 – The Virtual Link

The kernel needs a known fixed way to communicate with the file system driver, so that no matter the file system it is working with, it can communicate data transfers. The file system also needs a way to communicate with the kernel. This is the Virtual File System Link.

When the kernel finds a new media device, such as a hard drive, it parses the partitioning scheme to find partitions, also called Volumes, each volume possibly containing a file system. The kernel then creates a memory block to hold information about this Volume. This memory block is called a Disk Parameter Block, or DPB.

Some of the information it gathers could be how to read or write to the media device, where it is physically located on the device called a Starting LBA, as well as other information.

Once a volume is found, the kernel needs to detect the file system on the volume and once detected, load a suitable file system driver and store its location within this DPB.

When a user application makes a call to access this file system, it passes an identifier. For example, the standard C fopen() library function may do something like the following:

```
fopen("C:\\filename.txt", attrib);
```

The double backslash in the string above is not a typo. The C language uses the first backslash to indicate that the character following is a special character. If there was only one backslash, the C compiler would interpret the following 'f' character as the special character. Therefore, two backslashes are needed to represent a single backslash.

The identifier, in this case the C:, identifies which DPB it will use. Therefore, the kernel creates a Disk Parameter Block for each volume found.

We also need another block of memory to store information about an open file, such as current file size, file position, and access privileges, as well as other such information, one item being which BPB is being used by this open file. This memory block is called a File Pointer Block, or FPB.

Using these two blocks of memory, stored within the Virtual File System driver, we can now access any file on any volume using any file system, completely independent of one another.

See the figure on the next page for an example.

The kernel, or user application, using the FPB can identify which DPB is being used. Within this DPB, the kernel has stored a pointer to a file system driver.

Therefore, with any given open file, the kernel or user application, only needs to know the information with the FPB, sending commands to our Virtual File System, with one of the parameters a pointer to this FPB.

The Virtual File System will then, using this FPB, gather information from the corresponding DPB, pointed to be this FPB, and call the file system's driver, which is pointed to by a member in this DPB.

Figure 2-1: The Virtual File System Link

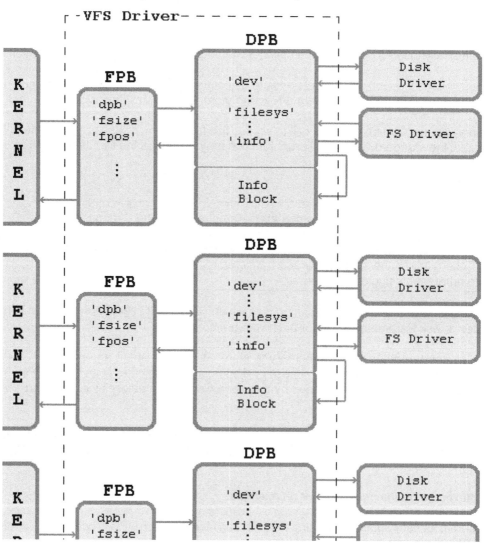

When access to the physical media is needed, the file system driver will use the information in the DPB to call a device driver to read and/or write physical sectors from/to the disk.

If you recall from Vol 1 of this series, *FYSOS: The System Core*, in Chapter 11, Listing 11-2, we created the Drive Parameter Block aka the 'DPB', and is detailed in the listing below.

Listing 2-1: Drive Parameter Block

```
; =-=-=-=-=-=-=-=-=-=-=-=-=-=-=-=-=-=-=-=-=-=-=-=-=-=-=-
; Drive Parameter Block
DPB            struct
  valid        byte      ; is entry valid/used (0 = not valid)
  ldrv         byte      ; 'A:' = 0, 'C:' = 2, 'D:' = 3
  name         dup 32    ; asciiz name of partition
  active       byte      ; is this an active mounted partition?
  access       dword     ; Access allowed (read/write/etc.)
  dev          dword     ; Pointer to the DEVICE_ENTRY member
  filesys      dword     ; Pointer to the File System driver
  fs_type      byte      ; File System type value
  base_lba     qword     ; Base LBA of partition
  size         qword     ; size of partition in sectors
  freespace    qword     ; running total of free sectors
  sect_size    word      ; sector size (512 bytes is default)
  info         dword     ; file system specific data pointer
  cur_path     dup MAX_PATH ; current directory on partition
  reserved     dup 1932 ; usually holds 'info' data above
DPB            ends
```

Therefore, whenever our kernel finds a media device and has scanned the media for partitions, it should create one of these DPBs for each partition it finds. This is called mounting the file systems.

At start up, your kernel may allocate memory and create room for 26 of these blocks, allowing for 26 partitions to be found using the letters 'A' through 'Z' for identification using the ldrv member. However, you can use the name member and have unlimited partitions and drive parameter blocks, allowing each partition to be named. It is completely up to you which technique you use.

Once this DPB is filled with the found data, all you have to do is pass an identifier and a filename to the Virtual File System driver and it will do the rest.

If you want to use the common volume naming technique of drive letters, you set the ldrv member to 0 for 'A:', 1 for 'B:', etc. You can then use the name member as a label for this volume. However, if you want to use another common volume naming technique, you set the `name` field to something like 'Part0' for the first partition found, 'Part1' for the next, and so on, ignoring the `ldrv` member.

The 'active' member is set to a value to indicate whether this partition is active and if so, the current state. The `access` field is used to indicate what type of access rights this volume has, such as read-only, for example.

The `dev` field is the pointer to the device driver to read and write to the device this volume was found on. You call the device driver with a few parameters, such as LBA, count of sectors, etc., using this field.

The `filesys` is the pointer to the file system driver for this volume. Once you have detected what file system this volume uses, you point this field to that driver. More on this field later.

The `base_lba` and `size` fields are set to the base LBA where this volume starts and the size in sectors it occupies. This way you can check to make sure the request is within the limits of this volume. The Virtual File System driver will use zero-based blocks or sectors based from this `base_lba` value for this volume.

The `info` field points to a block of memory specific for that file system. It usually points to the `reserved` field within this DPB, if there is enough room to hold all the information. This block of memory holds specific items for the file system to be able to access this file system and is formatted and filled at file system detection time. If the desired block of data is 1932 bytes or less, you may set it to point to the `reserved` field. If you need more memory for a specific file system, you can allocate that memory and point this field to it. When you unmount this file system, you can check this field to see if it points to the `reserved` field. If it does not, the memory it points to needs to be freed.

The other fields within this DPB may be used for various reasons within your VFS Driver.

Each time you call the file systems driver, using the `filesys` field, you send a pointer to this DPB block so that the file system driver has access to the items it needs to function along with the `dev` member to be able to call the device driver to read and write to the device. If I were using the C language to write my driver and I had a valid FPB (see the next section) filled with the information it needed, and a valid DPB, I would call the media device driver using the following source line.

```
fp->dpb.dev->driver(fp->dpb.dev, BLOCK_DEV_READ, lba, cnt, ptr);
```

By calling the disk driver in this fashion, you pass the service call number (BLOCK_DEV_READ), the starting sector number (lba), remembering this is zero based from the DPB's `base_lba` value, the count of sectors to read or write (cnt), and a pointer to the memory block to read from or write to (ptr).

At this point, the media device driver doesn't know where on the media the volume starts. Therefore, you have also passed a pointer to the Disk Parameter Block (DPB) to the driver (`fp->dpb.dev`). Now the disk driver has all the information it needs to correctly read or write to the disk. See later in this chapter on how to call the file system driver.

At this point, you have detected a media device, have a driver to read from and write to this device, have read in and parsed the partitioning scheme on the media, and now have a single DPB for each volume on this device. You may then read and detect what file system, if any, that resides on each volume found. The file system detection routine should format and modify the memory pointed to by the `info` pointer in the DPB, remembering that the format of this data is dependent of the file system found. You now have a filled DPB, the `dev` pointer pointing to the media device driver, and the `filesys` pointer pointing to the file system driver, for each volume found on this device.

The only part of all the information stored that is dependent upon the file system is the memory pointed to by the `info` member of the DPB. It is okay that this information is dependent upon, because the only item of the mentioned drivers to access it is the file system driver itself. This information is completely independent from all other aspects of the Virtual File System.

See Appendix F for file system detection.

Communication with the DPB

As stated earlier, now your Virtual File System code within your kernel can process any function on the mounted file systems by only a path and file name passed to it. For example, the function call:

```
fopen ("C:\\filename.txt", attrib);
```

is all that is required to open the file. The `C:` gives us the DPB needed to access the file system this file resides on.

Once we parse the file name, we can match the `C:` to the `ldrv` member of the DPB, or if used, the `Part0:` to the `name` field, and call the file system driver via the `filesys` member. See the next section on how to call this driver.

From this point on, I will use all C Language style memory structures and code listings. If at all possible, this part of your kernel should be in a high-level language to make it easier to code and possibly be portable if you so desire.

The File Pointer Block

When a program wants to access a file on the media, the operating system will return a file pointer used for all file access to that file. Therefore, we need to first create this File Pointer Block within the kernel's Virtual File System driver, fill it with information about the request, along with the dpb pointer, then call the file system driver to see if the request is successful. This File Pointer Block, or FPB, is used by all file system calls once a file is open, with each open file referencing one of these FPB's.

Listing 2-2: File Pointer Block

```
// =-=-=-=-=-=-=-=-=-=-=-=-=-=-=-=-=-=-=-=-=-=-=-=-=-=-=-=-
// File Pointer Block
struct FILE {
  bool   valid;
  bit8u  resv0[3];
  struct S_DPB *dpb;
  bit32u access;
  bit64u f_pos;
  bit64u f_size;
  bit64u prev_lba;
  bit64u parent;
  bit64u strtclst;
  bit32u root_index;
  bit32u dword;
  bit32u resv1;
};
```

The dpb member is the pointer to the Disk Parameter Block that contains the information this file will need to communicate with the kernel and the Virtual File System driver, which also contains the pointer to the file system driver for that file system.

The f_pos and f_size members are the current file's position and its current size in bytes. When the file is written to or read from, the position is updated so that the next time the file is accessed, it is accessed from the byte just after the last access.

The remaining members are used for directories and locations within these directories, root directory or not. See the chapter on directories for more information on these members.

The two reserved members are to align the data and size of this memory block.

Your Virtual File System driver should create as many of these blocks as desired at start up. You will need enough of these blocks to satisfy the number of open files your kernel wants to support. However, you can make this a growing number, simply adding more as the need arises.

When your driver requests to open a file, it can find a free File Pointer Block, fill it with the information it needs, and call the file system driver.

A suggestion would be to place a number of FPB's in the memory reserved for each app. Then the app uses its own FPB's. At app exit, the system can go through these FPBs and close any file that was not closed by the app. However, now there is more work needed to keep track of all the FPBs allocated to multiple apps, where as a single list of FPBs for the whole system is easier to manage. For now, use the easier technique of all FPBs in one list. Once you are comfortable with your abilities, you may want to use a more safe and secure way.

If the `fopen()` call is successful, the file system driver will have filled the remaining members of the FPB with the information it needs for each following request. The listing below shows a simple `fopen()` call. This code is in your Virtual File System driver and is called from the user application or operating system.

Listing 2-3: fopen()

```
// =-=-=-=-=-=-=-=-=-=-=-=-=-=-=-=-=-=-=-=-=-=-=-=-=-
// fopen(path, attrib)
struct FILE *fopen(const char *path, bit32u attrib) {
  struct FILE *fp;

  // find an empty FP struct in our FP list
  fp = find_free_fp();
  if (fp == NULL) {
    set_error(ERROR_NO_HANDLES);
    return NULL;
  }

  // get correct Disk Parameter Block
  fp->dpb = get_dpb_from_path(path);
  if (fp->dpb == NULL) {
    set_error(ERROR_INVALID_DPB);
    return NULL;
  }

  // now call the file system driver
  if (fp->dpb->file_sys(FOPEN, attrib, 0, TRUE,
                        path, fp) == FILE_SYS_SUCCESS)
    return fp;

  return NULL;
}
```

This function is better detailed in the next chapter.

Wrap Up

Now that you have a valid DPB for each volume found, you might detect what file system is on that volume and update the information pointed to by the `info` member within the DPB. Then when there is a request to access the file system, all you have to do is pass a pointer of this DPB to that file system driver, and it can handle the rest. This is your Virtual File System Link between the kernel and the file systems that reside on the media devices of the system.

A suggested sequence of events would be to find all media devices, create a Device List Entry for each (listed in Chapter 11 of Volume 1, "The System Core"), parse this device for partitions, creating a Disk Parameter Block for each found, detecting the installed file system on that partition, updating the information in the DPB, and continue scanning devices creating DPB's as you go.

The Device List Entry listed in Volume 1 of this series is simply a block of memory describing the device found and how to access it. It contains information needed to communicate with the hardware device, be it a PortIO ATA hard drive, a SATA drive, a USB external drive, or even a RAM disk. As far as the Virtual File System is concerned, it reads and writes sectors, nothing more, nothing less.

The figure on the next page shows an example of a system having only one disk and this disk having three volumes (partitions). This requires three Disk Parameter Blocks. However, the second and third volume each having the same file system type, being able to share the same file system driver. Since all three volumes are on the same disk, all three share the same media device driver.

Notice that the second two, which share a file system, the dependent information for each, having the same format but possibly different values, fits within the reserved area of the DPB, therefore not needing to be freed at unmount time. However, the first volume has a file system that needed more space for its dependent information, allocating another memory block, therefore needing to be freed at unmount time.

Figure 2-2: An Example Virtual File System Link

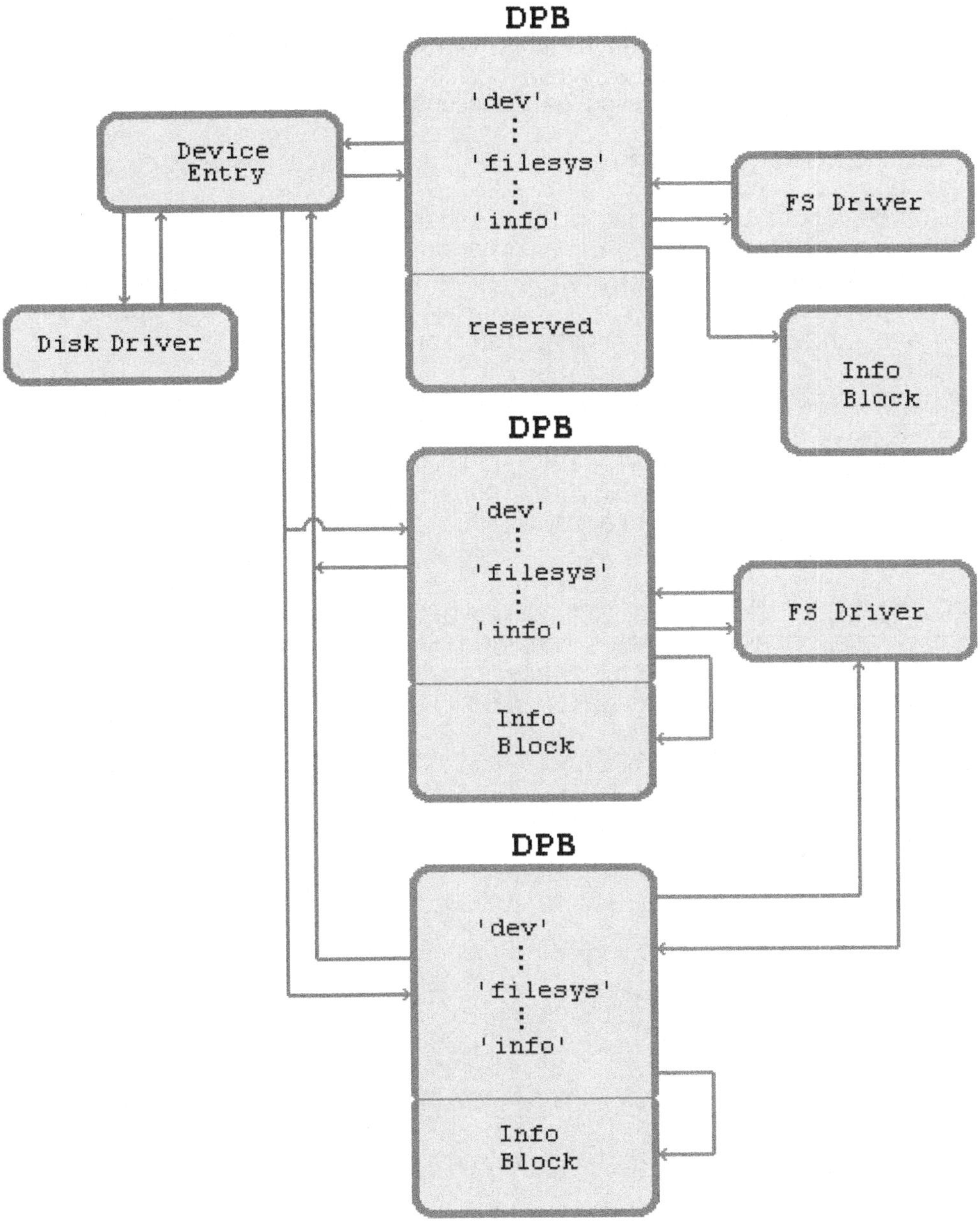

The next chapter will describe the function calls your Virtual System Driver will need to support to be able to function well and as described earlier in this chapter. However, before we proceed, Listing 2-4 below shows the steps needed to call a file system function.

Listing 2-4: Function Call

```
IF NOT FILE_POINTER
   GET FREE FILE_POINTER
   IF NOT FILE_POINTER
     RETURN ERROR: NO MORE FILE_POINTERS
   ENDIF
   EXTRACT PARTITION IDENTIFIER FROM PATH GIVEN
   IF NOT IDENTIFIER
     USE CURRENT DEFAULT PARTITION IDENTIFIER
   ENDIF
   USING IDENTIFIER, FIND ASSOCIATED DISK PARAMETER BLOCK
   IF NOT DPB
     RETURN ERROR: INVALID IDENTIFIER OR DPB
   ENDIF
   ASSIGN FOUND DPB TO FP->DPB
ENDIF

CALL FILE_SYSTEM DRIVER VIA FP->DPB->FILE_SYS, SENDING:
   SERVICE NUMBER,
   PARAMETER0, PARAMETER1, PARAMETER2,
   GIVEN PATH NAME AND/OR FILE NAME
   FILE_POINTER
RETRIEVE RETURN CODE
```

Chapter 3 – The Function Calls

The kernel and user programs need to call certain functions to be able to access the files on each volume. Some of these functions are used to open and close the file, move the file pointer, find a file, read or write, and retrieve other information from this file.

There are also other functions your Virtual File System driver will need that are separate from the user programs only accessible within this VFS driver.

To make sure that we are still independent of the installed file system, we need all information passed to be in the File Pointer Block, explained in the previous chapter, or the path name itself.

There are a few functions that you would think would be in your VFS driver that are actually within the STDIO library called from the user program. These functions include fopen(), fclose(), fseek(), and a few others. Most of these functions do call your underlining VFS, but are called within the Standard I/O Library. The fseek() function, however, doesn't call the underlining VFS. It simply sets the file's current position pointer and returns. It is up to the file system driver to make sure the file is end padded if the pointer is past the end of the file and a write is issued.

I will list most of the functions your VFS needs here and explain what they should do and the values they should return. I will also list those mentioned above that are within the user programs library.

The C Standard Library specifies certain parameters and other specifics that each function should expect, process, and return. You may follow these specifics or you may do your own. Therefore, please note that the specifics I describe here may or may not be per the C Standard Library specifications. These are just my recommendations of what a function should do.

All of these functions need to do all the work they can while in the VFS and then call the actual file system driver for that mounted file system if necessary. For example, as stated above, the fseek() function can do all that is needed within the stdio library or the VFS and simply return without calling the file system driver.

To call the file system driver, from the Virtual File System driver, use something similar to the following line.

```
fp->dpb->file_sys(FOPEN, attrib, 0, TRUE, path, fp);
```

Since the file_sys() call uses the same parameter count, size, and type, in order, each function must conform to these restrictions. However, most if not all of your functions can perform their duties with the amount of parameters the file_sys() function currently contains.

Within this book, my file_sys() function has the following prototype.

Listing 3-1: file_sys() Function Prototype
```
bool file_sys(bit32u serv_num,  // service call number
              bit64u param0,    // first parameter (64-bit)
              bit32u param1,    // second parameter (32-bit)
              bit64u param2,    // third parameter (64-bit)
              void *path,       // buffer pointer (ex: pathname)
              void *fp          // pointer to the FPB used
              );
```

Each file system function described within this chapter takes advantage of this protocol, sending Zero or NULL if the parameter is not used.

The following list of services are within your VFS driver or a standard library (<stdlib.h>) call. If the service needs to call the file system driver, it then uses the protocol shown above. Even though not shown in the list within this chapter, each function should return either an Integer (int) value, or a pointer value. If an integer value is returned, any negative number returned is considered an error being returned. If a pointer value is used, and a NULL value is returned, this is considered an unsuccessful function return, and the app should check the current error value.

```
int error_code = GetError();
```

Mount(struct DEV *device, bit64u base_lba)

This function mounts a file system. i.e.: you pass it the device information, which is the information to be able to read from the device, and the starting LBA of the partition, and this function will try to create a DPB for it. A DPB is first created, and the default values are stored. Then the function tries to detect the file system on the partition. If it is successful, it will point the file_sys member to a file system driver, loading a new one if necessary, fill the remaining members of the DPB and return a success. If it does not successfully detect the file system, it still returns a success, marks the DPB valid, but makes sure to mark as inactive.

If the VFS did not detect a file system, you still need to mount the partition so that the kernel and user programs can use it. One of these tasks might be to format it and write a file system to it.

UnMount(struct DPB *dpb)

This function unmounts a currently mounted DPB. It does not delete or clear the DPB, it simply marks it as inactive. There are a few reasons that this should be allowed. If you have mounted a file system and wish to re-format that partition, you need to unmount the partition to be able to remount it later. Remember to make sure that all file system processes for this DPB are processed before you unmount it, by first making a call to the file system driver, specifying that you are about to unmount this file system's host.

Get_DPB(const char logdrv)
Get_DPB(const char *name)

Get the VFS's DPB structure for the specified partition. Depending on whether you use a single char, 'A' through 'Z' as the partition indicator, or you use a name, such as 'PART0', the caller has passed this indicator as the only parameter. Your function should find the corresponding DPB and return a pointer to it, or if it is not found, return NULL. This function is usually only called from within your VFS and is seldom to never called from a user program or the kernel.

Since both types of calls, 'logdrv' and 'name', are valid, even if one is the default, make sure that every DPB's corresponding field is unique. If the default is to use the 'logdrv' technique and the 'name' call is used, it should never find two or more DPB's with the same value in either corresponding field.

Get_Current_DPB()

This function simply returns the current, default logical drive's DPB. For example, when you change to a drive on the command line, the VFS needs to remember which DPB you are using in case you do not specify the drive letter within the path name of a function. If successful, you should return a pointer to the current DPB, or return NULL if unsuccessful. In theory, this function should always return successful. However, don't assume it will.

Set_Current_DPB(struct S_DPB *dpb)

This function attempts to set the passed DPB as the current, default drive. If successful, it should return a pointer to the current DPB, or return NULL if unsuccessful.

This function should also take into account having only one physical floppy drive but show two logical floppy drives. See Appendix E for more information on this subject.

FindFirst(struct S_FILE_FIND *file_find)

This function, using the S_FILE_FIND structure passed to it, tries to find a file on the current or specified mounted DPB. The passed parameter may or may not have the drive specified in it. If it does, you need to use that DPB. If it does not, find the current DPB and use it.

If this function finds the file and it matches the attributes requested, it should return successful.

However, to be able to use the FindNext() function, this function should save the current location within the passed S_FILE_FIND structure so that it can pick up at this same place next time it calls the FindNext() function. See the FindNext() description below for a listing of this S_FILE_FIND structure.

FindNext(struct S_FILE_FIND *file_find)

This function is the same as the FindFirst() function above except that it uses the information you have already saved in the memory pointed to by the passed `file_find` parameter.

Storing all of the FindNext() or current location information in the passed S_FILE_FIND structure instead of a single place in the file system, as DOS did, allows you to be able to have multiple find instances without destroying the location of each other. This way, you can have two or more FileFind()'s going on at the same time and each maintaining their positions. To do this, the S_FILE_FIND structure contains a memory buffer used by the file system driver and is explained later in this chapter.

The FYSOS Virtual File System driver uses a S_FILE_FIND structure similar to the listing below.

Listing 3-2: File Find Structure

```
struct S_FILE_FIND {
  // is this a valid S_FILE_FIND struct
  bit8u  valid;              // (could use a crc instead?)

  // find next uses this, find first sets this
  bit8u  ldrive;

  // file name to search for, may use wildcards
  char   search[MAX_FILENAME_LEN+1];

  // attributes to look for, and attribute of file found
  bit32u sattrbs;        // attrib to search for
  bit32u attribute;      // attrib of file found

  // Time and Date of file found
  struct {
    bit8u hour;                          // time.hour
    bit8u min;                           // time.min
    bit8u sec;                           // time.sec
  } time;
  struct {
    bit16u year;                         // date.year
    bit8u  month;                        // date.month
```

```
    bit8u  day;                          // date.day
  } date;

  // file size of file found
  bit64u fsize;

  // file name of file found
  char   filename[MAX_FILENAME_LEN+1];

  // the next member is the memory block that is used by
  //  the file system driver to store the location and
  //  other information for the Find_Next() call.
  // the VFS does not know the format, only the file
  //  system driver does, therefore, just a memory block.
  bit8u  ftype_data[32];
};
```

The `ftype_data[]` member is used by the file system driver and needs to be large enough to hold the largest number of bytes used by any known file system. I currently use 32 bytes which is sufficient for any file system I support. This area stores information that the file system needs to be able to start where the last call left off.

Since this particular S_FILE_FIND structure's data, specifically the `ftype_data[]` member, will only be used on the file system it is mounted on, it can assume that the `ftype_data[]` memory block will always be valid for use by, and only by, the file system it resides on. The Kernel, Virtual File System driver, and User App should never modify any values within this 32-byte block.

CreateDir(const char *dir)
RemoveDir(const char *dir)
These two functions create a new directory or remove an existing directory in the current directory, or in another directory if a path is given in the `dir` parameter. These functions first call the FileFind() function to see if the directory exists, either function expecting an opposite response, and then calling the file system driver if that response is the expected one, returning unsuccessful if not.

GetCurrentDir(char *dir)
SetCurrentDir(const char *dir)
These functions return the current directory, or set the default to a new directory on the file system. The first, on a successful return, fills the memory pointed to by `dir` with the current directory path name, while the second uses the path pointed to by `dir` to attempt to change to a new directory, first calling FileFind() as before.

fopen(const char *dir, const bit32u attrib)

This function is located in the STDIO library, but then calls the VFS driver, which then calls the file system driver. The attribute passed indicates what it should do, whether it is opening an existing, truncating that existing, or creating a new file. If the open is successful, the function needs to return a valid File Pointer Block (FPB) pointer. The `dir` pointer will point to a string holding the file name and possibly a path to the file to open. It may or may not contain the drive identifier. If it does not, a call to GetCurrentDPB() is used before the call to the file system driver. Also, a call to FileFind() is made to see if the file already exists and its return compared to the attribute passed. This 'attrib' value simply states whether the file should be opened as an existing file, returning unsuccessful if it doesn't exist, truncates an existing file, creates a new file, or appends to an existing file, and also the type of file transfers, binary or text.

A type of Binary is used to read and write bytes as they are passed in the stream of data. The type of Text is indicated and used when the stream of data contains certain control characters such as a Carriage Return/Line Feed pair. It is up to your driver to read and write the pair, or only the Line Feed character whenever the CRLF pair is encountered.

fclose(struct FILE *fp)

This function is located in the STDIO library, calls the VFS, and if needed, calls the file system driver to purge any writes. This function should return successful or unsuccessful.

fread(void *buf, const bit32u count, struct FILE *fp)
fwrite(void *buf, const bit32u count, struct FILE *fp)

These two functions are in the STDIO library which calls the VFS, who in turn calls the file system driver, then will read or write from/to the current file's position. They should return the number of bytes read from or written to.

Since the fseek() function below can specify a position past the end of the file, the fwrite() function must anticipate this, padding the file to this position before the fwrite() takes place. A fread() should return EOF in this case.

fseek(const bit64u pos, const int from, struct FILE *fp)

This function is in the STDIO library and does not call the VFS or the file system driver. It simply changes the FPB's current file position pointer. If for some reason it changes it to be past the current length of the file, it is up to the fwrite() function to pad the file to that position on the next write.

frewind(struct FILE *fp)

This function is in the STDIO library and does not call the VFS or the file system driver. It simply moves the FPB's current file position to the start of the file.

fremove(const char *name)
This function is also in the STDIO library, calls the VFS, which in turn calls the file system driver to remove a file from the media. It too calls the FileFind() function to see if the file exists. If it does not exist, the VFS driver has no need to call the file system driver and simply returns an unsuccessful attempt.

ftell(const struct FILE *fp)
fgetpos(const struct FILE *fp)
These functions are in the STDIO library and do not call the VFS or the file system driver. They simply return the FPB's current file position pointer.

fsetattrb(const char *file, const bit32u attrib)
fgetattrb(const char *file)
These two functions set or get a file's attributes, calling the file system driver to do so. Again, calling the FindFile() function from within the VFS driver before calling the file system driver.

GetVolSerial(const struct DPB *dpb, struct GUID *guid)
This function calls the file system driver to retrieve the volume's serial number. The FYSOS VFS driver always formats this returned number to a GUID formatted number.

> For example, the FAT file systems return a serial number in the form of XXXX–XXXX. The FYSOS VFS driver then adds the necessary zeros to return it in the form of 00000000-0000-0000-0000-0000XXXXXXXX.

FreeSpace(const struct DPB *dpb)
This function calls the file system driver to get the amount of free space on the volume. However, if you will remember, the DPB has a member called freespace. This member should be updated constantly each time the file system modifies the amount of free space on the volume. Then, all this function has to do is return this saved amount. Since the time it would take for a file system to keep the DPB's freespace member up to date, it is assumed that this value is a close representation of the free space on the drive. It is up to the file system driver on when it is necessary to update the DPB's freespace member.

truename(const char *file, char *truename)
This function uses the FileFind()/FindNext() functions to return the full path name for a file name given. Another advantage of this function is that it will take a path name that uses re-direction and get the actual path for it. By re-direction, I mean the double dot '..' parent directory that DOS uses, or any Symbolic Links that the LEANFS might use. This function should also prefix the path name with the correct drive specification.

fnmatch(const char *wild, const char *tame, const bit32u flags)

This function is used within the VFS and is probably one of the most important functions you will need when using path names and searching for file names. This function is used to compare file names when using wild cards. A wild card is a character used to indicate a specific character that could be used in this position. For example, the asterisk is used to indicate that any character or string of characters can occupy this position in the file name, where a question mark indicates the same as the asterisk, except only one character may occupy this position.

In the example below, the string listed contains a set of wild cards.

```
"filena*.t?t"
```

The above indicates that you need to match a file name that must match the first six characters exactly, but may have any string of characters up to a period in the file name. Then the character after the period must match, but the next character can be any single character, while the last character must match the 't'.

To use this function, you pass a string of wildcard characters, as with the example above, and a string of a filename, along with some attributes to match against. This function then returns TRUE if the filename (tame) can be accepted as a match to the string pointed to by the wild parameter.

The function listed below shows a well-known listing that was posted in the September 2008 issue of Doctor Dobbs Journal. I use a very similar function within my VFS code.

Listing 3-2: fnmatch()

```
// =-=-=-=-=-=-=-=-=-=-=-=-=-=-=-=-=-=-=-=-=-=-=-=-=-=
// fnmatch()
bool fnmatch(const char *wild, const char *tame,
                                   const bit32u flags) {

  bool case_sense = (flags & FNM_NOCASE) ? FALSE : TRUE;
  bool match = TRUE;
  char *last_wild = NULL;
  char *last_tame = NULL
  char t, w;

  // Walk the text strings one character at a time.
  while (1) {
    t = *tame;
    w = *wild;

    // How do you match a unique text string?
```

```c
if (!t || (t == '\0')) {
  // Easy: unique up on it!
  if (!w || (w == '\0'))
    break;                    // "x" matches "x"
  else if (w == '*') {
    wild ++;
    continue;                 // "x*" matches "x" or "xy"
  } else if (last_tame) {
    if (!(*last_tame) || (*last_tame == '\0')) {
      match = FALSE;
      break;
    }
    tame = last_tame++;
    wild = last_wild;
    continue;
  }

  match = FALSE;
  break;                      // "x" doesn't match "xy"
} else {
  if (!case_sense) {
    // Lowercase the characters to be compared.
    if (t >= 'A' && t <= 'Z')
      t += ('a' - 'A');

    if (w >= 'A' && w <= 'Z')
      w += ('a' - 'A');
  }

  // How do you match a tame text string?
  if ((t != w) && (w != '?')) {
    // The tame way: unique up on it!
    if (w == '*') {
      last_wild = (char *) ++wild;
      last_tame = (char *) tame;
      w = *wild;

      if (!w || (w == '\0'))
        break;            // "*" matches "x"
      continue;           // "*y" matches "xy"
    } else if (last_wild) {
      if (last_wild != wild) {
        wild = last_wild;
        w = *wild;
        if (!case_sense && (w >= 'A') && (w <= 'Z'))
          w += ('a' - 'A');
```

```
            if ((t == w) || (t == '?'))
                wild++;
        }
        tame++;
        continue;      // "*sip*" matches "mississippi"
    } else {
        match = FALSE;
        break; // "x" doesn't match "y"
    }
  }
 }
}

    tame++;
    wild++;
  }

    return match;
}
```

Wrap Up

There are a few other functions that you will need. A function to check a file name for valid characters, characters that this file system allows, and other functions of this sort.

However, the list in this chapter lists most of the functions that you will need. Once you have the items in Chapter 2 and 3, you should have a working Virtual File System. Within the next few chapters, I will discuss how directories work, how you keep track of them in your DPB, and then describe a few things about simple file systems and a more elaborate file systems and their advantages and disadvantages.

 Please note that I am leaving it up to you, the reader, to write your own file system driver. It is the intent of this book to only show the link between the kernel and your file system driver and how to make it file system independent. Part 2 of this book shows the details you will need to write your driver for the included file systems.

Chapter 4 – Directories

The use of directories, or folders, allow the organization of groups of files on the media. There is the root directory, the first group of files, which then may contain one or more sub-directories. Each directory is capable of including its own sub-directories, for a possibility of unlimited directories, or group of files.

These directories are usually stored just like files, having an indicator in the file's attributes and then using the file's data section to store the directory information.

The user then transverses these directories using their names and a slash character, similar to the following.

```
D:\somedir\another\then\another
```

Some existing operating systems allow only backslashes, as above, or both back and forward slashes. These slashes indicate the end of one directory name and the start of another. Your file system could use any character you desire, though this character then cannot be allowed as part of a file or directory name.

Depending on the file system, there could be unlimited amount of directory entries with unlimited amount of those entries being sub-directory types pointing to an unlimited depth of directories. However, the limit is usually not with the file system but with the operating system hosting that file system. For example, a well-known operating system has a path and filename length limit of 260 bytes. This means that no matter the depth limit of the file system, the operating system will only allow you to type 260 characters of the path, including the filename.

An example of this limit would be if the file system allowed for long file name and directory names, and the user had five directory names deep, using 32 characters each, that would already use up 160 characters, not counting the file name itself, or the back slash delimiters.

Figure 4-1 on the next page shows a typical layout of a set of directories.

Figure 4-1: Typical Directory Structure

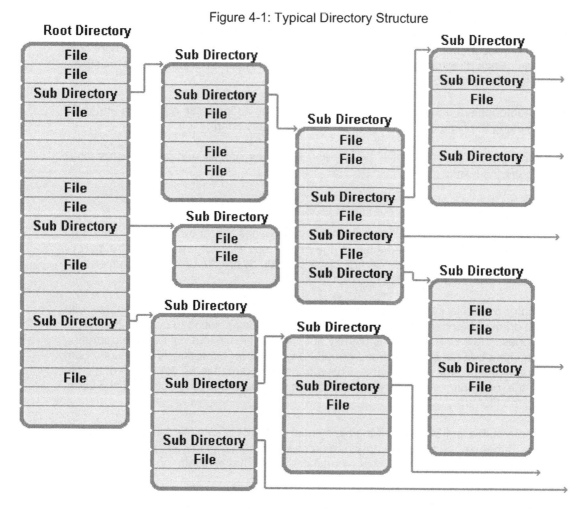

For a more detailed way of storing directories on a file system, see Part 2 of this book and the file systems described there.

Directories and your VFS

Your Virtual File System needs to keep track of what directory is currently being accessed. For example, if the user does not give a path name, they only give a file name, your VFS must use the last accessed directory to search for that file name. By last accessed, I mean, the last directory that was set as the current directory.

When you create the data within your info memory in the DBP, you will need to create a few members to save the current directory information for each file system mounted.

Listing 4-1: Current Directory

```
// =-=-=-=-=-=-=-=-=-=-=-=-=-=-=-=-=-=-=-=-=-=-=-=-=-=-
// Current Directory
struct S_CURDIR_DATA {
  bit64u parent;        // location of parent directory
  bit64u current;       // location of current directory
  char   path[MAX_PATH_LEN]; // saved current path
};
```

The listing above is an example of how to keep track of the current directory. At initialization time or mount time, you would point the `parent` and `current` members to the root directory sector, cluster, or Inode, and set the `path` member to a single slash, or whatever delimiter you choose.

Each mounted DPB would need one of these within its data block pointed to by its `info` member.

When the VFS receives a request to change the directory, it should call the file system to see if that directory name exists within the current directory, or if a full path is given, transverse the path to make sure all these directories exist. If so, make sure to update the members in Listing 4-1 above and continue. The file system itself does nothing but return a success or fail if the directory exists. It is always up to the VFS to keep track of the current directory.

Of course, it will depend on the current file system of what actually needs to be stored to save the current and parent directories. This is why you put it in the `info` member instead of directly in the DPB itself.

Reversing Directory Lookup

As with any file system, at some time the user will want to back up to the parent directory. This is done differently by many file systems. A most common way to back up to the parent directory is to use the following command line.

```
cd..
```

Where `cd` is the `Change Directory` command and the '`..`' is the previous or parent directory indicator.

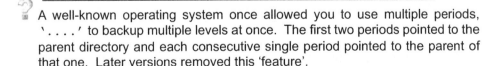

A well-known operating system once allowed you to use multiple periods, '`....`' to backup multiple levels at once. The first two periods pointed to the parent directory and each consecutive single period pointed to the parent of that one. Later versions removed this 'feature'.

The Microsoft® FAT file system stores this as an actual directory name entry in the current directory. It also stores the information for the current directory position as a single period. Listing 4-2 below shows an example of a FAT directory listing.

Listing 4-2: Directory Listing Example

```
D:\temp>dir
 Volume in drive D has no label.
 Volume Serial Number is 07D1-0817

 Directory of D:\temp

06/22/2022  04:03 PM    <DIR>          .
06/22/2022  04:03 PM    <DIR>          ..
06/22/2022  04:16 PM    <DIR>          directory
06/22/2022  04:07 PM    <DIR>          yet
06/22/2022  04:13 PM    <DIR>          another
06/22/2022  04:03 PM    <DIR>          one
06/22/2022  06:19 PM                43 temp0.txt
06/22/2022  01:23 PM                46 temp1.txt
               2 File(s)             89 bytes
               6 Dir(s)   3,457,220,608 bytes free
```

Notice that the FAT file system actually stores the current and parent directory entries on the disk and then displays them as so.

Other file systems use this same technique but may not actually store the '.' and '..' directory entries on the disk. The VFS knows what to do when these two names are found. It is up to the VFS to process the '.' and '..' requests, whether it does it itself, or passes it on to the file system driver.

Wrap Up

Your VFS will also need to parse path names as listed below.

```
cd\temp\another\..\this\.\that\..\..\thisone
```

However, as noted in the previous chapter, the TrueName() function can be called to convert the pathname above to the correct and true path name before you send it to the ChangeDir() function.

Most file systems use a similar technique of storing directories on the media. They use a file name to point to the directory, and store the directory structure within its data area.

However, each file system will store the transverse data differently, i.e.: the way you find the parent directory will be stored differently.

There are other things you should remember, one being that the size of a directory may be limited. The early FAT file system limits the size of the root directory. Others may do the same and even limit the size of sub-directories.

One thing to remember, something that I think most people new to file systems forget, a directory is only a file, with the file's data storing the directory information. Directories, or Folders, are nothing more than files with an additional file attribute set.

Chapter 5 – A Simple File System

Within this chapter I will explain what a simple file system is, a file system with little information about the files and directories that it contains, along with a simple but limited way to store the way you find the blocks that contain the file's data.

The Microsoft® FAT file system is considered a simple file system, especially the 12- and 16-bit versions. I will describe the ways it uses to store information on the disk as an example of this simple but limited file system. See Part 2 of this book for a detailed explanation of this file system.

The FAT file system has a limit on the length of a file name. Therefore, Microsoft created a "hack" to be able to have longer file names. The bad thing is, they patented this hack. Therefore, it isn't against this patent to use this hack as long as you do not write to the file system using this hack. In other words, you can read these long file names, but if you write a long file name to the file system, you have gone against this patent.

The FAT 12- and 16-bit file systems, discussed within this chapter, are identical other than the size of the cluster number, therefore, when I use the term FAT, I am discussing these two versions and will specify a version when there is a difference. The 32-bit version of this file system is detailed in Part 2 of this book.

BIOS Parameter Block

The FAT file system, or any file system, simple or not, needs a little bit of data at a known location on the volume to be able to function properly. The FAT file system uses a BIOS Parameter Block (BPB) in the first block of the volume. This BPB contains a little information about the disk to send to the BIOS disk read service as well as a bit of information about the volume.

Listing 5-1: BIOS Parameter Block

```
// =-=-=-=-=-=-=-=-=-=-=-=-=-=-=-=-=-=-=-=-=-=-=-=-=-=-
// FAT12/16 BIOS Parameter Block
struct S_FAT1216_BPB {
  bit8u  jmp[3];
  char   oem_name[8];
  bit16u bytes_per_sect;
  bit8u  sect_per_clust;
  bit16u sect_reserved;
  bit8u  fats;
  bit16u root_entrys;
  bit16u sectors;
  bit8u  descriptor;
  bit16u sect_per_fat;
```

```
    bit16u sect_per_trk;
    bit16u heads;
    bit32u hidden_sects;
    bit32u sect_extnd;
    bit8u  drive_num;   // not FAT specific
    bit8u  resv;
    bit8u  sig;
    bit32u serial;
    char   label[11];
    char   sys_type[8];
};
```

 FAT actually defines this BPB a little different, mixing two different table names to create the above listing. However, to make it simpler to understand, I just use the term BPB as the whole memory block.

This block of information gives the information needed to parse the file system; Number of FATs, Root Entries, Sector per FAT, etc., along with the Hidden Sectors value, the number of sectors on the disk before this BPB.

For a simple file system, this amount of information is sufficient. However, it lacks other information such as security and other means of data integrity.

Directory Entries

File names, which include directory names, are a big part of a file system. The length of a file name and the characters allowed within this file name determine how a file system stores these file names. Along with a file name, the file system should store information about the file along with where the file's data is located.

Long file names, or Virtual FAT file names, are discussed in Part 2 of this book. I will use the standard FAT file name length here.

The FAT file system uses a 32-byte directory entry and is listed below.

Listing 5-2: FAT's Directory Entry
```
// =-=-=-=-=-=-=-=-=-=-=-=-=-=-=-=-=-=-=-=-=-=-=-=-=-
// FAT12/16 Root Directory Entry
struct S_FAT_ROOT {
    bit8u  name[8];     // name
    bit8u  ext[3];      // ext
    bit8u  attrb;       // attribute
    bit8u  resv[10];    // reserved
```

```
    bit16u time;        // time
    bit16u date;        // date
    bit16u strtclst;    // starting cluster number
    bit32u filesize;    // file size in bytes
};
```

This is definitely a simple file system. The listing above shows the only thing that is listed for a file. The name and ext members only allow for a file name to be 11 bytes in size, 12 if you include the implied period. There is an 8-bit attribute member, allowing only 8 different attributes. The time and date members only allow 16-bit values. The strtclst member only allows 16-bit cluster numbers and the filesize member has a limit of a 4-Gigabyte file size.

The advantage of this file system is that it only requires 32 bytes to store all but the used cluster numbers. It takes very little memory and code to extract information about a file within this file system.

The disadvantage is that the file name can only be 11 characters in length and FAT only allows upper case characters, there are only 6 used attribute bits, the time and date values are only accurate to two seconds, the starting cluster number can only be 32,767 clusters from the start of the volume, and a file length can only be 4 Gigabytes or less.

Clusters

The FAT file system uses 12- and 16-bit cluster numbers to locate the file on the disk. A Cluster is defined as a fixed number of consecutive sectors. This set size is defined in the FAT's BPB. The starting cluster number is stored in the directory entry. The file system then uses this number to index a cluster number within a table of cluster numbers. The number points to the next cluster on the disk and cluster number in the table. Since a cluster number only points to the next cluster number in the table, you must go through the whole list to get to the cluster number you need. Also, if one of these cluster numbers is corrupt, the remaining clusters after this one for this file is lost. Please see Part 2 of this book for more on clusters and the FAT file system.

Wrap Up

Since this is a very simple file system, it is quite portable and is used on a lot of removable media, like floppy disks and smaller USB thumb drives. The file system hasn't changed in years and can store the data on the media in a cheap and easy format for most systems to deal with. If you only need a few characters for the file name, not many attributes, and a simple way to store the chain of clusters, a file system like this one is a good choice. However, where is the fun in creating a small and simple file system? Therefore, let's go to the next chapter and find all the goodies in a more detailed file system.

Chapter 6 – Inodes and File Extents

Within this chapter, I will discuss a more detailed, a more complex file system. A file system that has many more features and much higher limits to the length of a file name, file sizes, date and times, and other items that help a file system be robust.

Within this chapter, I will use the Lean file system as an example. For a detailed and accurate description of this file system, see Part 2 of this book.

 The Lean file system was originally written by Salvatore ISAJA for use with the Freedos-32 project. I had the opportunity to converse with him with this file system in its later versions. Thank you, Salvatore for that opportunity and for letting me detail it in this book.

The Super Block

As with any file system, you have to have enough information in a known place to be able to extract and then read and parse the remaining items within the file system. In the Lean file system, and many others, this is called the Super Block.

The Super Block is used to hold all initial data needed to parse the file system, including data integrity, item location, volume placement and size, along with other essential items to successful parse and transverse the file system.

The following listing is the Super Block from the Lean file system.

Listing 6-1: LeanFS Super Block

```
// =-=-=-=-=-=-=-=-=-=-=-=-=-=-=-=-=-=-=-=-=-=-=-=-=-
// LeanFS Super Block
struct S_LEAN_SUPER {
    bit32u checksum;          // bit32u sum of all fields.
    bit32u magic;             // 0x4E41454C ('LEAN')
    bit16u fs_version;        // 0x0007 = 0.7
    bit8u  pre_alloc_count;   // count -1 of contiguous blocks
    bit8u  log_blocks_per_band; // 1 << log_blocks_per_band
    bit32u state;             // bit 0: unmounted, bit 1: error
    struct S_GUID uuid;       // Universally Unique IDentifier
    bit8u  volume_label[64];
    bit64u block_count;       // Total number of blocks
    bit64u free_block_count;  // Number of free blocks
    bit64u primary_super;     // block of primary super block
    bit64u backup_super;      // block of backup super block
    bit64u bitmap_start;      // first band's bitmap
    bit64u root_inode;        // root directory.
    bit64u bad_inode;         // bad blocks start.
```

```
  bit64u journal_inode;     // if used, journals inode
  bit8u  log_block_size;    // block size used (9 = 512)
  bit8u  reserved[7];       // zeros (used for padding)
  bit8u  reserved[344];     // zeros (padding to end of block)
};
```

Unlike a simple file system, this Super Block contains security and integrity measures to make sure that the data is accurate before it is used. The `checksum` member is the integrity measure, this value is the check sum of all values within this Super Block. If the data does not pass this checksum, it is not to be mounted as a valid file system. The `magic` member is a signature to also verify that this is a valid block of memory.

Another integrity measure is the `backup_super` member. If for some reason the integrity of the primary super block becomes damaged, the backup Super Block's integrity can be checked. If it passes, it can them be copied to the primary and then used to mount the file system. See the chapter in Part 2 about the correct way to find this backup Super Block.

This Super Block also allows for a much longer label, much larger volumes, and a very unique serial number.

In the previous chapter, the simple file system, there was a single field used to indicate where a volume starts relative to the start of the disk. If there is no integrity check, if this value is read incorrectly, this could drastically damage the file system. In the file system in this chapter, numerous checks are made to verify the integrity of the values read.

File Names
This file system has a directory entry as listed below.

Listing 6-2: LeanFS Directory Entry
```
// =-=-=-=-=-=-=-=-=-=-=-=-=-=-=-=-=-=-=-=-=-=-=-=-=-=-=-=-
// LeanFS Directory Entry
struct S_LEAN_DIRENTRY {
  bit64u inode;      // The inode number.
  bit8u  type;       // Entry type.
  bit8u  rec_len;    // total record len in 16 byte units.
  bit16u name_len;   // total length of name.
  bit8u  name[4];    // Start of UTF-8 name
};
```

This entry stores the information needed to find the file's Inode, the type of file, and the file name. The information is stored in records of 16 bytes each. An entry may contain up to

255 records, which will allow a file name as short as a single byte or up to 4,068 bytes. Each record after the first in a directory entry may contain up to 16 bytes for the file name.

Figure 6-1: LeanFS Root Entry

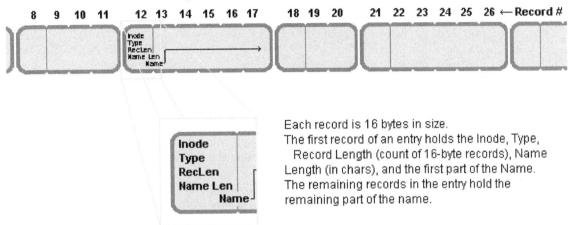

Each record is 16 bytes in size.
The first record of an entry holds the Inode, Type,
     Record Length (count of 16-byte records), Name
Length (in chars), and the first part of the Name.
The remaining records in the entry hold the
remaining part of the name.

No information about the file, other than a generic type, is stored in this record. All file information is stored in the Inode pointed to by this entry.

Inodes

Once you have a valid Super Block, you can then search for the root directory and start parsing the directory entries. In this file system, a directory entry is declared as an Inode. An Inode is a block of memory that has much more information about the file it represents than the Directory Entry in the file system described in the previous chapter.

The Lean file system's Inode is listed below.

Listing 6-3: LeanFS Inode

```
// =-=-=-=-=-=-=-=-=-=-=-=-=-=-=-=-=-=-=-=-=-=-=-=-=-=-==
// LeanFS Inode
struct S_LEAN_INODE {
   bit32u checksum;          // bit32u sum of all fields
   bit32u magic;             // 0x45444F4E  ('NODE')
   bit8u  extent_count;      // count of extents
   bit8u  reserved[3];       // reserved
   bit32u indirect_count;    // indirect blocks owned by file
   bit32u links_count;       // hard links
   bit32u uid;               // currently reserved, set to 0
   bit32u gid;               // currently reserved, set to 0
   bit32u attributes;        // attributes
```

```
    bit64u file_size;          // file size
    bit64u block_count;        // count of blocks used
    bit64s acc_time;           // last accessed
    bit64s sch_time;           // status change
    bit64s mod_time;           // last modified
    bit64s cre_time;           //         created
    bit64u first_indirect;     // first indirect block
    bit64u last_indirect;      // last indirect block
    bit64u fork;
    bit64u extent_start[LEAN_INODE_EXTENT_CNT];
    bit32u extent_size[LEAN_INODE_EXTENT_CNT];
};
```

As with the Super Block, this block of memory also comes with items to check its integrity. It also comes with much larger limits on file sizes and locations.

Another improvement is the time and date stamp. In the file system in the previous chapter, we had only 32 bits to represent the date and time, and its time is only updated on change to the file. With the Inode above, there are four date and time stamps. One is created at file creation time and never changes after that. The other three are updated throughout the life of the file, especially the last time the file was accessed. This time stamp is also accurate to the microsecond, where the other file system is only to two seconds.

An advantage of having a microsecond time stamp compared to an actual date given, is that you can very simply sort a directory listing by a single value. See Appendix G for more on Time Stamps.

File names are stored in the root directory and have a much larger character limit. This file system allows for a file name to be 4,068 bytes in length. This doesn't necessarily mean 4,068 characters, since these bytes are UTF-8 encoded characters allowing for many more character types and languages. See Appendix D for more information on UTF-8 characters.

The Lean file system also has many more attributes and types of attributes. You can give a file a standard attribute like read-only, but now you can also give it an access right and a file type.

Data Blocks

The Lean file system accommodates small files to be stored within the Inode or allows external blocks to accommodate large files, only limited by the 64-bit file size member.

This file system uses Extents to store data blocks for the file. An extent is a pair of values with the first giving a block number and the second giving the count of consecutive blocks starting with the first value. These values are stored in the Inode using no more disk space for small files. If the file is larger and needs more extents than the Inode can give, this file system then allows for additional blocks to be used as indirect blocks. These indirect blocks have a small header to help with integrity and then a number of more extents.

Wrap Up

Compared to the file system described in the previous chapter, this is a much better, much more extendable file system, used on smaller media as well as large media. This file system allows for long file names without wasting space for short file names, allows for small files without wasting block space, but allows for very large files. It also allows for numerous attributes and access rights to each file.

However, this file system requires more overhead space and more processing of blocks and other data. If you need a simple file system, one that doesn't require much security or integrity, but has the advantage of very fast access times, use one like the FAT file system explained previously. However, if you need a file system that is robust, accommodates small and large files and volumes, and long or short file names, you need to use a file system similar to the one explained here.

There are other items that you can add to a file system to give it much more integrity. One of these is a Journal, which is explained in the next chapter.

The Lean file system also allows for Linked files. These are file Inodes that do not have any blocks associated to it. It links to another Inode, which then has blocks and extents. This allows for the same file to be in multiple directory listings but only occupies one file on the disk. This is very valuable when multiple projects use and modify the same source file. When it is modified in one project, the other project sees the change instantly. No need to go find that file and give it the same modification.

For more detailed information on this file system, see the chapter in Part 2 of this book.

Chapter 7 – Journals

A journal, as the word suggests, is a history of what the file system is doing. However, to make this journal valuable to the file system, you send all read and write requests to the journal and let it perform the operations. This way, the journal can keep a history of the operations. On a crash of the file system or a complete system crash, the file system driver can walk through the journal and validate the data.

For example, if the user is updating a file, a file that must be completely overwritten or not written to at all, what happens if there is a system crash half way through the write. An example file could be a backup of the day's proceeds of a grocery store. What if the first part of the file gets updated, but before the rest of the file can be updated, the system crashes? Not only have you lost the first half of last night's backup, but now today's backup has last night's back half.

When the system comes back up, and since the file system has a journal, it can finish the operation it started before the crash. The Journal marks the operation as complete only after it is completely successful. Since the operation was not successful, the Journal can start over and write the whole file.

To do this, the Journal stores the pending writes within its "pages". i.e.: the file system sends the journal a write operation and the journal stores the write within a specific place reserved for pending writes. If the write to this temporary location is successful, the journal returns a success to the caller and adds this file to the queue. If the write is not successful, the requesting file system attempts to write it again. As far as the file system is concerned, there is no journal. It either wrote the file to the disk or it did not.

The journal then walks the queue and attempts to write a pending write to the actual file of the disk. Once that operation completes, it can mark the whole operation complete and empty that operation from its queue. If the write does not complete, the journal may try again on the next rotation through the queue. The operation is never marked complete until the write is physically written to the intended file on the disk.

If the system crashes, at the next start up the Journal checks everything in its queue to see if an operation was successfully written to the journal's "pages". If not, the operation is not valid and advises the user that it was not written. If the operation to the journal's "pages" was successful, but not marked as written to the disk as successful, the Journal will attempt to write the operation to disk. Then and only then will the operation be removed from the queue.

With this in mind, you always have a valid version of the file in question. If one version is invalid, the other version will always be valid. If the pending version becomes corrupt and un-writable, the original version on the disk is untouched. If the original version on the disk becomes corrupt, the version within the journal's pages is still valid and can be written to the disk.

A Farmer and His Hens

To better visualize this, take a small rancher that has a small field enclosed with a fence and also divided in half with another fence. In one half, hens, in the other half, foxes. The farmer notices that the fence dividing the two is starting to fail and must tear it down to rebuild it. During the day, he can watch to see if the fox crosses to the hen house, but at night, he must go home. Therefore, he must tear down this fence and rebuild it complete before the crash of night, or not tear it down at all.

The solution to the farmer's problem is to build another fence 10 feet away from the current fence. Only when the new fence is completely erected can the farmer safely remove the old fence. If crash of nightfall comes, the farmer can safely go home and return in the morning.

The old fence has not been repaired, but there is a copy of it 10 feet away. Finally, when the old fence is completely repaired and operational, the farmer can remove the temporary new fence he placed before.

At any given time, the hens were safe from the fox. There was always at least one valid fence in use. Only when the old fence repair was successful, did the farmer consider the operation a success and allow the temporary fence be removed from the queue.

Other Considerations

To be able to have a journaling file system, your operating system should be multitasking so that you can create a task to run the journal. Also, the journaling occupies a percentage of the disk to store the pending operations. This percentage specifies how many pending operations can be queued. Each pending write must have an entry in the queue and a free area to write it to.

All reads from the system may go straight through the journal and to the file system, since reads are non-destructive. However, please note that a read must not be performed to the same file as a pending write for this file. All reads must check that there is not a pending write operation for this file already on the disk.

If there is a pending write, that write must be completely successful before the read takes place. Don't think that you can just read from the journal's pending queue and return. This will quickly destroy the integrity of the file system if a crash takes place. All pending writes must be successfully physically written to the disk before a read of that same data is returned successful.

Another thing to consider would be to make sure that a successful write to an Inode or an associated item takes place, before a read takes place from that same file. You can do this by saving the Inode number in every operation in the Journal. If a read from an Inode or an area within that Inode's file is requested, make sure all writes to that Inode and file are successful before the read.

> There is not an Inode number in the Inode structure of most file systems. There doesn't need to be. The sector or cluster that the Inode resides in is the Inode number. No Inode can occupy another Inode's sector or cluster number.

The outline shown on the next page is a minimal idea of a journal. Depending on the file system you use, it will need to be more detailed for that file system. However, this one will show you a minimal technique.

An Example

In the above explanation, the journal might have been a per-sector journal. In some cases, this is sufficient. However, in other cases, this is not. For example, in Chapter 11, I discuss the Lean File System, which contains an Inode for each file written to disk. If we only worry about sectors, the Inode could become incoherent to the file it represents. Therefore, you must also journal the Inode.

For example, if you allocate another Extent for the file, yet the actual writing of the blocks contained within that Extent never get written to the disk, the Inode will indicate invalid blocks occupying the file. Therefore, the Inode must always be up to date with the actual contents of the file it represents.

A simple but inefficient example would be to create a whole new file, a copy of that file, within the journal. When the system opens the file for write access, the journal should copy that file to another location on the disk and always use that file for read and write access. Then once the file is closed, simply update the directory entry with the new Inode number and delete the original Inode and file.

The actual journal only needs to contain three values for that opened file, the original Inode number, the new Inode number, and a Flags field.

Listing 7-1: LeanFS Journal Entry Example
```
struct S_LEAN_JOURNAL_ENTRY {
  bit64u new_inode;
  bit64u org_inode;
  bit32u flags;
};
```

Now, all Inode access goes through the journal. When the file system driver requests an Inode, the journal checks for an entry containing this Inode Number. If it contains this number, it returns the new Inode number. The driver doesn't need to do anything else, but call the journal when an Inode number is requested.

Outline 7-1: Minimal Journal

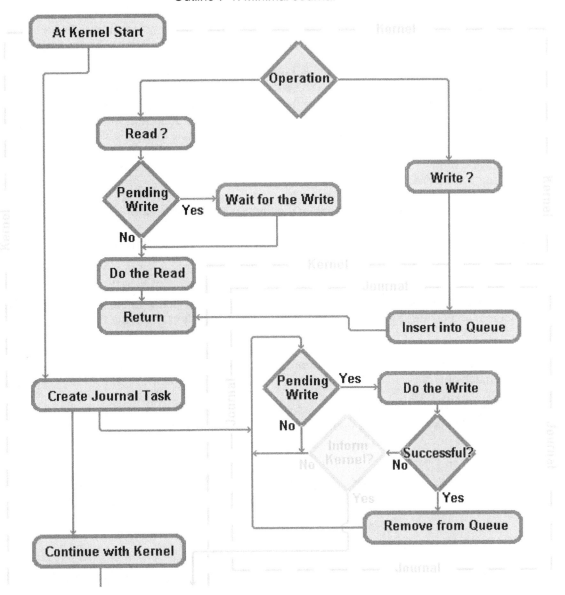

When the file is opened, the driver calls the journal passing the Inode number and a flag. If the flag value indicates that the file is being opened for write access, the journal will add this Inode to the Journal System, only after it creates a new Inode and copies the contents of the original file to this new one, returning the new Inode number. If the file is not opened for write access, the passed Inode number is simply returned.

All access is then done via this Inode number, whether it is the new Inode number or the original. Once the file is closed, the file system passing the Inode number and a flag to the journal, the journal can then update the Inode entry in the Directory Entry, delete the old Inode, and be done.

With this in mind, let's look to see what will happen if a crash happens.

A file is opened for write access. The journal creates a new Inode and copies the complete file from the original Inode to the new Inode. Now the Journal returns this new Inode number to the file system driver, which in turn uses the new Inode for all access. The file system then writes a few blocks to the file, modifying some, adding others, but before the file system driver can update the Inode structure, the computer crashes, destroying the integrity of the file.

The user reboots the system, thinking that the file contents is lost.

However, since the Directory Entry was never updated and the original Inode and file data was never modified, the original data is completely intact. The only thing that was lost was the new modifications.

The journal, at mount time, simply sees that there were some entries remaining in the journal and deletes the new corrupt Inode and its file contents from the disk.

With this in mind, the file system driver should make sure that all journal entries are completely updated before the system un-mounts the volume, in essence, shutting down the machine.

This is one form of a Journal and would work quite well, though inefficient, for file systems that use Inodes such as the Lean File System shown in Chapter 11.

Chapter 8 – File System Creation

When designing a file system, you will need to ask yourself what this file system needs and what features it will need to support. What is the media that this file system will live on? Does it need to support large files, large media, long file names, and other questions of this sort. Here is a list of things that might need to be considered.

> - Does it need large file support (64-bit block numbers and file sizes)?
> - Does it need long file names?
> - Does it need to support extended attributes?
> - Forks and/or Symbolic Links?
> - Encryption?
> - Journaling?
> - Will it have many small files?
> - Will it have mostly large files?
> - Will file fragmentation be an issue?
> - Is speed an issue? Read, Write, or both?
> - Is portability an issue?
> - What about file placement?
> - Fast search and find features?
> - File names as ASCII, UTF, or other forms?
> - Is the media specific to the hardware it will reside in?
> - Is it removable media?

There are many things to consider when designing a file system. The main thing is to remember what this file system will be used for. If the media has space to spare, long file names and extended attributes would be something to consider. If the media is sparse on space and all free space is a valuable asset, meta-data needs to be as little as possible.

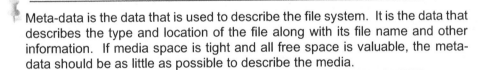

Meta-data is the data that is used to describe the file system. It is the data that describes the type and location of the file along with its file name and other information. If media space is tight and all free space is valuable, the meta-data should be as little as possible to describe the media.

There are many file systems already in use today. Some of them are used by most modern operating systems, some for their portability, some for their robustness.

In theory, you should be able to use one of these file systems with your work. However, where is the fun in that? Why would you be reading this book if you didn't have the slightest idea of designing your own file system? Besides, designing your own file system is a great way to learn what is involved in file systems and what advantages and disadvantages they might have.

Part 2 of this book describes and details a few file systems, a simple popular (commercial) well-used file system, a few file systems designing by various hobbyists like you and I, and the standard file system used on CD-ROMs. I suggest that you read through these and find the features that you like and dislike, then start to think about designing your own.

Above all, enjoy. It isn't about the destination, but the journey you take to get there.

Intentionally Left Blank

Intentionally Left Blank

Part 2

Part 2 of this book describes in detail two well-known and used file systems, along with three hobby file systems, designed by hobbyists like you and I.

Chapter 9 – The FAT File System

The FAT, or File Allocation Table, file system was created back in the early DOS days, and then has roots that go back before that. It has three different versions, each allowing for larger volumes, but each very similar in technique.

It was used by Microsoft for quite a while, even through some of the windowed versions of their operating systems, and is still used on floppies and other removable media. If your operating system will support floppy disks and now the existing USB thumb drives, you will most likely need to support two of the three versions.

Within this chapter, I will detail the FAT file system, the 12- and 16-bit versions and the later 32-bit version. I will also point out the quirks and tweaks that you will need to watch for and implement.

Be sure to read later in this chapter, the note about the patent Microsoft was awarded before you implement this file system.

Overview of a FAT Formatted Volume

The FAT file system is a Cluster based file system. i.e.: It uses a determined number of sectors to create a cluster and each file has a number of these clusters in it. A cluster can be a single sector making the file system use a sector for sector layout. However, the FAT file system has a few limitations on the number of clusters a file can occupy. Therefore, the larger the cluster size the larger a file can be and the larger a volume it will support. However, since the number of sectors per cluster is the same for all files on the volume, large cluster sizes can create a lot of wasted space.

The FAT file system uses separate areas of the volume to hold its contents. The File Allocation area, or FAT Table, is at the first of the volume with the file contents occupying the remainder of the volume.

The FAT file system allows up to and/or has the following limits.

Maximum Volume Size (FAT12)	256 Megabytes (64k clusters)
Maximum Volume Size (FAT16)	4 Gigabytes (64k clusters)
Maximum Volume Size (FAT32)	16 Terabytes (4k sectors and 64k clusters)
Maximum File Size	2^{32} -1 bytes
Number of files (FAT12)	4,068 (8k clusters)
Number of files (FAT16)	65,460 (32k clusters)
Number of files (FAT32)	268,173,300 (32k clusters)
Filename length (Standard)	11 chars, upper case only, ASCII
Filename length (Virtual FAT)	255 chars, case insensitive, UCS-2
Extended Attributes	None
Sector Sizes	Any power of two, usually 512

The reason there is a difference in limits of number of files with different cluster sizes is that the number of available clusters will limit the number of files you can use. A larger cluster size gives a smaller available number of clusters. Also, with FAT32 having 28-bit cluster numbers, with 64k clusters, it would handle a 16 Terabyte volume. However, the BPB's `sector_count` field is 32-bit limiting the count to 4 Gig – 1 sectors. Using 512-byte sectors, you need more than this 32-bit limit of sectors to get to the 16 Terabyte volume size.

 There are a number of specific limits or values for certain items within this file system. They are so rarely used that it isn't worth mentioning here. Within this chapter, I describe a typical, widely used format, not the rarely used items that may or may not be available.

A Typical FAT Formatted Volume

A typical FAT formatted volume will try to use an optimal cluster size for the media it resides on. A few things must be figured when deciding the size of a cluster. The larger the cluster size, the smaller the FAT tables, and the larger the media it can use. However, the larger the cluster size, the more wasted space will be used when small files are used or when a file has just a few bytes in the last cluster. No matter the file size, they all use the same cluster size.

A typical FAT formatted volume will have four regions. The first is the BIOS Parameter Block, aka the BPB, and is in the first sector of the volume. The next region is the cluster map, the root area, and finally the data region.

The figure on the next page shows a typical layout of a FAT 12 formatted volume for a 1.44M Floppy Disk.

The whole disk has 2880 sectors. If we have a cluster size of 1 sector, we will have just less than 2880 clusters available. Since a cluster map entry for this file system is 12 bits, we will need just less than 8 ½ sectors per cluster map.

$$2880 \times 12 \text{ bits} = 4320 \text{ bytes}$$
$$4320 \div 512 = 8.4375 \text{ sectors}$$

A cluster map must start on a new sector which means we will need a total of 9 sectors per cluster map, and have the typical count of 2 maps, one used and one for backup.

A typical root directory for a 1.44 Meg FAT12 disk is 224 entries, each entry occupying 32 bytes. This means that we need 14 sectors for the root directory.

This leaves 2847 clusters remaining for the data region, or 1,457,664 total bytes.

Figure 9-1: Typical FAT12/16 Volume

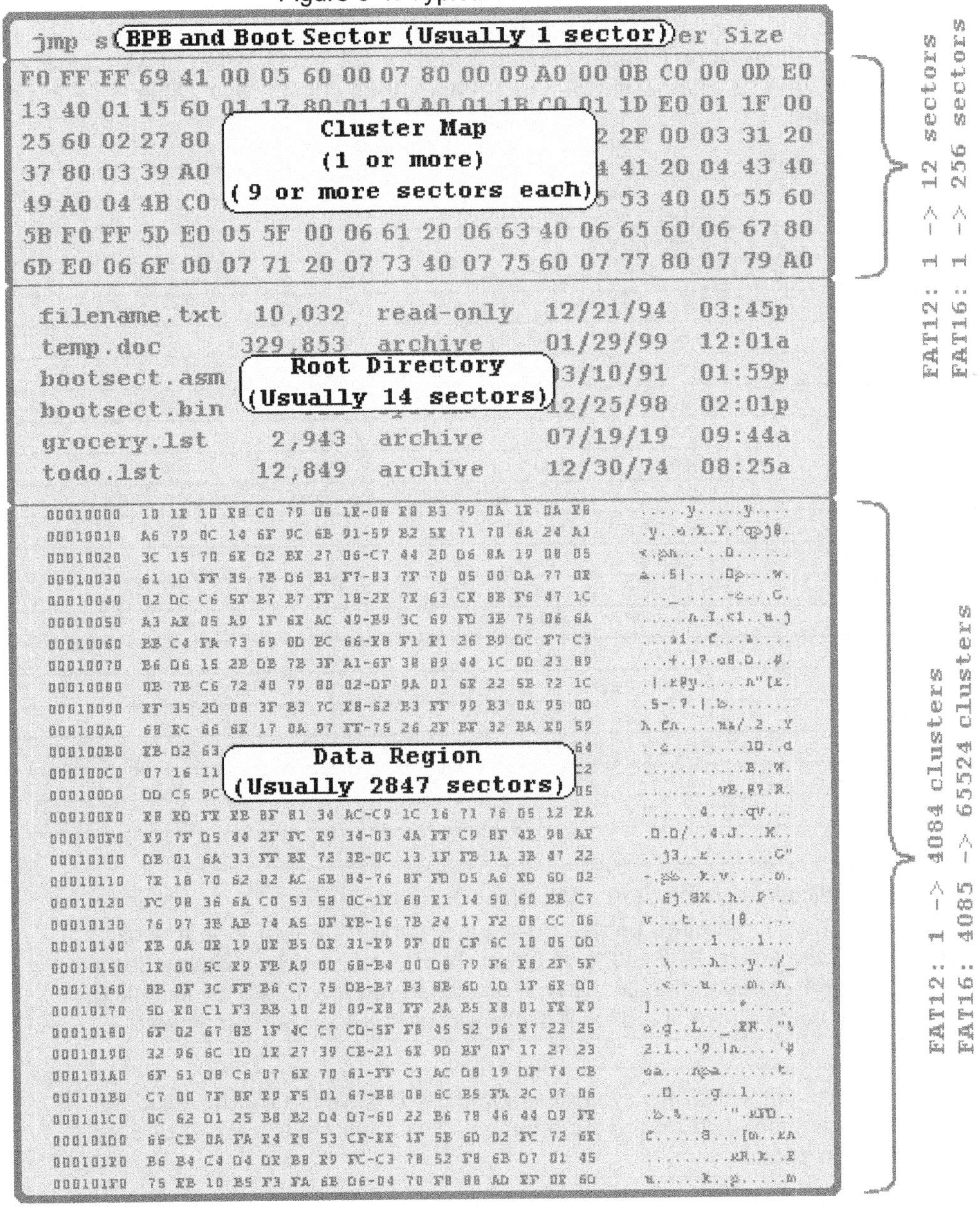

```
jmp s BPB and Boot Sector (Usually 1 sector) er Size

FO FF FF 69 41 00 05 60 00 07 80 00 09 A0 00 0B C0 00 0D E0
13 40 01 15 60 01 17 80 01 19 A0 01 1B C0 01 1D E0 01 1F 00
25 60 02 27 80      Cluster Map          2 2F 00 03 31 20
37 80 03 39 A0      (1 or more)          4 41 20 04 43 40
49 A0 04 4B C0  (9 or more sectors each) 5 53 40 05 55 60
5B FO FF 5D E0 05 5F 00 06 61 20 06 63 40 06 65 60 06 67 80
6D E0 06 6F 00 07 71 20 07 73 40 07 75 60 07 77 80 07 79 A0
```

filename.txt	10,032	read-only	12/21/94	03:45p
temp.doc	329,853	archive	01/29/99	12:01a
bootsect.asm	Root Directory		3/10/91	01:59p
bootsect.bin	(Usually 14 sectors)		2/25/98	02:01p
grocery.lst	2,943	archive	07/19/19	09:44a
todo.lst	12,849	archive	12/30/74	08:25a

```
00010000  1D 1E 10 E8 C0 79 06 1E-08 E8 B3 79 0A 1E 0A E8   ....y.....y....
00010010  A6 79 0C 14 6F 9C 6B 91-59 B2 5E 71 70 6A 24 A1   .y..o.k.Y.^q@j8.
00010020  3C 15 70 6E D2 BE 27 06-C7 44 20 06 8A 19 08 05   <.pn...'..D.....
00010030  61 1D FF 35 7B D6 B1 F7-83 7F 70 05 00 DA 77 0E   a..5{....Dp....w.
00010040  02 0C C6 5F B7 B7 FF 18-2E 7E 63 CE 8B F6 47 1C   ..._......~c...G.
00010050  A3 AE 05 A9 1F 6E AC 49-E9 3C 69 FD 3B 75 06 6A   .....n.I.<i.;u.j
00010060  EB C4 FA 73 69 0D EC 66-E8 F1 E1 26 B9 0C F7 C3   ...si..f...&....
00010070  B6 D6 15 2B DB 7B 3F A1-6F 38 89 44 1C 00 23 89   ...+.{?.o8.D..#.
00010080  0B 7B C6 72 40 79 80 02-0F 9A 01 6E 22 5B 72 1C   .{.r@y.....n"[r.
00010090  EF 35 20 08 3F B3 7C E8-62 B3 FF 99 B3 0A 95 00   .5 .?.|.b.......
000100A0  68 EC 66 6E 17 0A 97 FF-75 26 2F BF 32 BA E0 59   h.fn....u&/.2..Y
000100B0  EB D2 63            64   .c........10..d
000100C0  07 16 11            E2   .......B..W.
000100D0  DD C5 9C            05   .........vB.87.R.
000100E0  E8 E0 FE EB BF 81 34 AC-C9 1C 16 71 76 06 12 EA   ......4...qv..
000100F0  E9 7F 05 44 2F FC E9 34-03 4A FF C9 BF 4B 98 AE   .D/..4.J...K..
00010100  DB 01 6A 33 FF BE 72 3B-0C 13 1F FB 1A 3B 47 22   ..j3..r;.....;G"
00010110  7E 18 70 62 D2 AC 6B 84-76 BF FD D5 A6 E0 6D D2   ~.pb..k.v.....m.
00010120  FC 98 36 6A C0 53 5B 0C-1E 68 E1 14 50 60 EB C7   ..6j.S[..h..P`..
00010130  76 97 3B AB 74 A5 DF EB-16 7B 24 17 F2 08 CC D6   v.;t.....{$.....
00010140  EB 0A 0E 19 0E B5 0E 31-E9 DF 00 CF 6C 10 05 D0   .......1....l...
00010150  1E 00 5C E9 FB A9 00 68-B4 00 D8 79 F6 E8 2F 5F   ..\....h...y../_
00010160  BB 0F 3C FF B6 C7 75 DB-B7 B3 BB 6D 1D 1F 6E 00   ..<...u....m..n.
00010170  5D E0 C1 F3 BB 10 20 09-EB FF 2A B5 E8 01 FE E9   ].... ....*.....
00010180  6F 02 67 BE 1F 4C C7 CD-5F FB 4S 52 96 E7 22 25   o.g..L.._.ER..."%
00010190  32 96 9C 1D 1E 27 39 CB-21 6E 9D BF 0F 17 27 23   2.1..'9.!n....'#
000101A0  6F 61 D8 C6 07 6E 70 61-FF C3 AC D8 19 DF 74 CB   oa..npa.......t.
000101B0  C7 00 7F BF E9 F5 01 67-B8 08 6C B5 FA 2C 97 D6   .D...g.l..,..
000101C0  DC 62 D1 25 B8 B2 D4 07-60 22 B6 78 46 44 D9 FE   .b.%....`".xFD..
000101D0  66 CB 0A FA E4 E8 53 CF-EE 1F 5B 6D D2 FC 72 6E   f....S....[m..rn
000101E0  B6 B4 C4 D4 DE B8 E9 FC-C3 78 52 F8 6B D7 D1 45   .........xR.k..E
000101F0  75 EB 10 B5 F3 FA 6B D6-D4 70 F8 88 AD EF DE 6D   u....k...p.....m
```

Data Region
(Usually 2847 sectors)

FAT12: 1 -> 12 sectors
FAT16: 1 -> 256 sectors

FAT12: 1 -> 4084 clusters
FAT16: 4085 -> 65524 clusters

The BIOS Parameter Block

Each FAT formatted volume will have a BPB in the first sector of the volume. The 12- and 16-bit versions use the same format while the 32-bit format is a bit different with additional sectors added. Table 9-1 below shows the 12- and 16-bit version with Table 9-3 showing the 32-bit version.

Table 9-1: FAT12/16 BPB

Offset	Size	Description
0x00	3	Jump Instruction
0x03	8	OEM Name
0x0B	2	Bytes per Sector
0x0D	1	Sectors per Cluster
0x0E	2	Reserved Sectors
0x10	1	Number of FAT's
0x11	2	Root Entries
0x13	2	Total Sectors
0x15	1	Media Descriptor
0x16	2	Sectors per FAT (Sectors per cluster map)
0x18	2	Sectors per Track
0x1A	2	Heads
0x1C	4	Hidden Sectors (Base LBA)
0x20	4	Extended Sectors
0x24	1	Drive Number
0x25	1	Reserved
0x26	1	Boot Signature
0x27	4	Serial Number
0x2B	11	Label
0x36	8	System Type

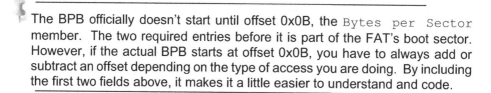

The BPB officially doesn't start until offset 0x0B, the Bytes per Sector member. The two required entries before it is part of the FAT's boot sector. However, if the actual BPB starts at offset 0x0B, you have to always add or subtract an offset depending on the type of access you are doing. By including the first two fields above, it makes it a little easier to understand and code.

Early versions of the FAT file system stopped the BPB with a two-byte Hidden Sectors field, offset 0x1C in the table above. The latter fields were added for DOS 3.x and above.

The Jump Instruction is the first three bytes of the BPB. These three bytes are used to jump over the remaining items in the BPB and any data you might have afterward. The allowed two formats are a 2-byte short jump or a 3-byte long jump. Since a short jump is

only two bytes in size, the third byte should be a NOP instruction. Therefore, the following
two lines show the possible values allowed.

```
    EB xx 90   ; jmp short xx
or
    E9 xx xx   ; jmp xxxx
```

The jump instruction does not have to jump to the byte just after the BPB, it can jump to
anywhere within the first sector.

The OEM Name can be anything you want. Since a lot of older boot sectors expected this
to be a set value, the string of 'MSWIN4.1' should be used. However, if you are not going
to worry about other operating systems, you can put whatever you wish.

The Bytes per Sector, Sectors per Track, and Heads fields are all filled with the values
returned from the disk BIOS services. Since the tool that is writing the BPB to the disk
knows these values and knows that they will not change, it writes them here. The Bytes
per Sector field is usually 512, but you must allow and should implement a size of 128 to
4096.

Sectors per Cluster is used to allow for larger volumes. Since 12-bit sector numbers would
only allow up to 4,096 sectors, this would only allow 2,097,152 byte volumes. A cluster is
a set number of consecutive sectors used as an allocation unit. i.e.: When a cluster
number is given, it is the cluster unit index rather than the sector index. If a cluster size is
two sectors, you now have twice the volume size. A cluster number of 2 would now point
to the 5th sector. The FAT file system allows a cluster size of a count of sectors that is 1 or
a power of 2 up to 128. However, to be compatible with most systems, you should not use
a number that has a cluster size of more than 32,768 bytes. i.e.: If the sector size is 512
bytes, you should not use a cluster size larger than 64.

The Reserved Sectors is the count of sectors starting with the BPB to the first FAT. This
is usually a count of 1 since most existing FAT drivers assume a single sector for the boot
code. However, incrementing this value allows you to have 2 or more sectors for the boot
code. For a 32-bit FAT BPB, this should be a value of 32, using 32 reserved sectors before
the first FAT.

The Number of FATs can be a value greater than zero. Usually there are two. An
advantage of using only one is that this would give you a few more sectors of available
data space, or clusters on the disk.

The Root Entries field indicates the maximum number of entries allowed in the root
directory. This value must be a multiple so that the last sector of the root directory is always
complete. i.e.: If 1024-byte sectors are used, you must have a multiple of 32 total root
entries, 16 for 512-byte sectors. A common value for this field is 224 for FAT12 volumes,
which uses fourteen 512-byte sectors.

The Total Sectors and Extended Sectors fields are used to indicate the total amount of sectors in this volume. The Total Sectors field is only 16-bit, therefore can only handle a value less than 0x10000. Since FAT volumes can be larger than this, the Extended Sectors field was added. If the total sectors on the volume is 0x10000 or more, the Total Sectors field is zero and the Extended Sectors field is used. If the value is less than 0x10000, then the Total Sectors field is used and the Extended Sectors is zero. If one is used, the other must be zero. In a FAT32 volume, the Total Sectors field must be zero and the Extended Sectors field is used.

The Media Descriptor was used to indicate what kind of media the volume is on. Back in the DOS 1.0 days, this field was important. It is no longer used for that purpose. However, it is important to note that this byte must match the value of the first byte in the FAT. See later in this chapter for more on this requirement. The following table shows all IDs that are known to be used.

Table 9-2: Media Descriptor Byte

Media Descriptor Byte values used in early DOS versions	
0xE5	8" single sided, 26 spt, 77 tracks, 128-byte sectors
0xED	5.25" double sided, 9 spt, 80 tracks
0xEE	Reserved for DR-DOS
0xEF	Reserved for DR-DOS
0xF0	1.44M and 2.88M Floppies. (DOS 3.3+)
0xF4	Double density (Altos MS-DOS 2.11 only)
0xF5	Fixed Media (Altos MS-DOS 2.11 only)
0xF8	Fixed Media (DOS 2.0+)
0xF9	1.20M (DOS 3.00) and (DOS 3.20) 720K Floppies.
0xFA	320K and Ram Disks
0xFB	640K
0xFC	5.25" 180K floppies
0xFD	5.25" 360K (DOS 2.0) and 8" floppies
0xFE	5.25" 180K (DOS 1.0) and 8" floppies
0xFF	5.25" 320K (DOS 1.1)

The Sectors per FAT field indicated how many sectors that are needed to hold a single FAT.

The Hidden Sectors field indicates how many sectors there are before this volume. i.e.: This is the Base LBA of the volume. On a floppy disk, this should be zero. On a hard drive this could be any number.

The Drive Number field holds the drive number of the DL register from the BIOS POST. i.e.: It is the DL value used to access the drive this volume resides on. However, note that this can change depending on the disk that gets booted first. Therefore, the value that is written to this field at format time is usually 0x80 for hard drives and 0x00 for floppies. Your boot code should update this field (in memory, not on disk) as one of the first things it does.

The Boot Signature field should be 0x29 and indicates that the next three fields are present. If this field is not 0x28 (WinNT only) or 0x29, you should not rely on the Volume ID, Label, and Type field.

The Serial Number is written to the BPB at format time. It should be unique as possible and used to identify a volume. The commonly used formula to calculate this number is listed below.

Listing 9-1: Serial Number Calculation

```
// =-=-=-=-=-=-=-=-=-=-=-=-=-=-=-=-=-=-=-=-=-=-=-=-=-=-=-=-=-
// Calculate serial number from current time and date
//    AA = Second
//    BB = Hundred / 2
//    CC = Month
//    DD = Day
//    EE = Hour (24 hour clock)
//    FF = Min
// GGGG = Year
//
// Serial = ((0xAABB + 0xCCDD) << 16) | (0xEEFF + 0xGGGG))
```

The Label field is also used to identify the volume. If there is a root directory entry with the Volume Label attribute set, its file name should match this field. If no volume name is given, this field should read 'NO NAME   '. This field is not valid if the Boot Signature field is not 0x29.

The System Type should be 'FAT12   ' or 'FAT16   '. This field should not be used to indicate which type of FAT is used for this volume. Appendix F shows the proper process to find the type of FAT used. This field is not valid if the Boot Signature field is not 0x29.

The 32-bit BIOS Parameter Block

The previous section described the 12- and 16-bit BPB. The 32-bit BPB has the same format up to offset 0x24. Starting at this offset, the structure has changed to the table below.

Table 9-3: FAT32 BPB Additions

Offset	Size	Description
0->0x23	36	Same as FAT12/16
0x24	4	Sectors per FAT (Sectors per cluster map)
0x28	2	Extended Flags
0x2A	2	File System Version
0x2C	4	Root Cluster Number
0x30	2	FSInfo Sector Number
0x32	2	Boot Sector Backup Sector Number
0x34	12	Reserved

0x40	1	Drive Number
0x41	1	Reserved
0x42	1	Boot Signature
0x43	4	Serial Number
0x47	11	Label
0x52	8	System Type

Again, the bytes up to offset 0x24 are the same as in Table 9-1. Starting with offset 0x24, there are a few more fields.

The Sectors per FAT is now a 32-bit number and the field at offset 0x16 in Table 9-1 should now be zero.

The Extended Flags shows the number of the active FAT, 0 to 15, in bits 3:0, but only if bit 7 is set, meaning mirroring is active. The other bits are reserved and should be zero.

The current File System version is defined as 0.00 (go figure), with the major version in the high byte (offset 0x2B) and the minor in the low byte (offset 0x2A). Your driver should check this field before mounting.

The Root Cluster Number is the cluster number of the first cluster of the Root directory. Note that it is the cluster number, not the sector number. This means that the Root Directory can be anywhere within the data section, whereas the 12- and 16-bit FAT versions must be just after the last FAT used.

The 32-bit FAT version also contains an additional sector of information. The value in offset 0x30 gives this sector number relative to the start of the volume. This value is usually 1, but can be any sector in the reserved area that is not already occupied. See the next section for more on this Info Sector.

The reserved area also contains a backup of the 32-bit FAT boot sector. Offset 0x32 gives this sector number, which is usually a value of 6. See later in this chapter for a description of this field and what it points to.

Starting with offset 0x40, the remaining fields are identical to the fields starting at offset 0x24 in Table 9-1. The only difference is that the File Type field is now to be 'FAT32   '.

The 32-bit Information Sector

At this point, we have a boot sector, the first sector of the volume, with a valid BPB, whether it be the 12- or 16-bit version or it be the 32-bit version. If we have a non-32-bit version, we don't need the next few items and can skip the next three sections. However, if we do have a 32-bit version, we now also need another sector, usually the second sector, to hold an Information Sector. The figure on the next page shows a typical FAT32 volume.

Figure 9-2: Typical FAT32 Volume

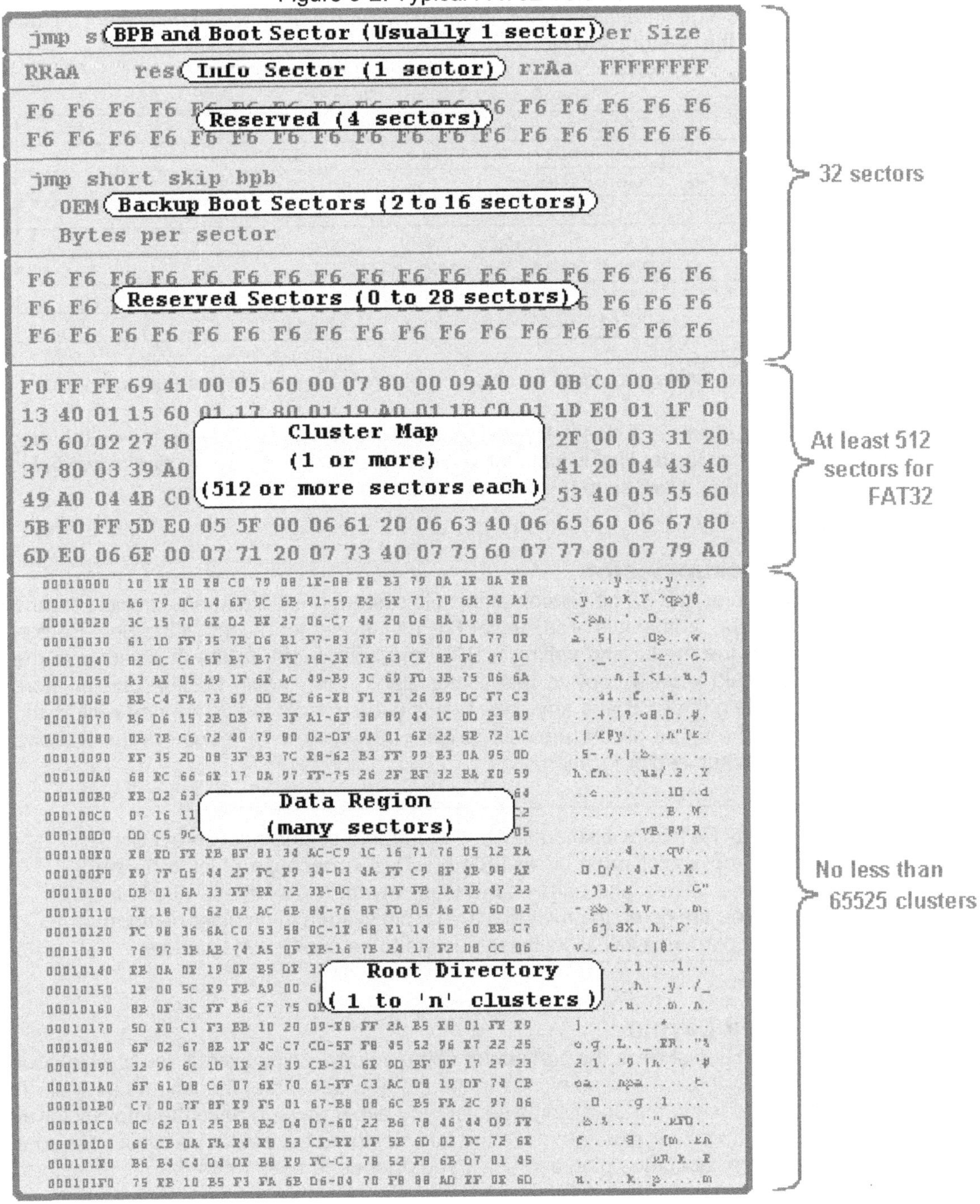

The Info Sector is used by the file system driver during execution of the file system. Currently, besides signature fields, there are only two items used within this sector. Table 9-4 below shows this sector's format.

Table 9-4: FAT32 Info Sector

Offset	Size	Description
0x000	4	Signature (0x41615252) ('RRaA')
0x004	480	Reserved
0x1E4	4	Signature (0x61417272) ('rrAa')
0x1E8	4	Free Cluster Count
0x1EC	4	Next Free Cluster Hint
0x1F0	12	Reserved
0x1FC	4	Trailing Signature (0xAA550000)

The three signature fields should all be checked before you assume this sector is valid.

The Free Cluster Count is a close representation of the amount of free space on the disk while the Next Free Cluster Hint is just that, a hint to the next free cluster. These two fields should be updated and written to the disk as you unmount the file system.

The 32-bit Backup Sector

As mentioned earlier, the 32-bit version of this file system has 32 reserved sectors for the boot code and data. Within this area, sector 6 is usually set for a copy of the Boot Sector. When formatting the media and writing a BPB and boot sector to the first sector of the volume, you should write a copy to this sector also. You should backup one or more sectors that contain the BPB and any code that is used to boot the volume as well as the Info Sector. In the figure on the previous page, you would write a copy of the first two sectors to this backup sector location.

The Microsoft® FAT Specification states that the Info sector must be at LSN 1 and the Backup sector must be at LSN 6. This is because older software assumed these values and hard coded their drivers to use these numbers. However, if you are going to never place your file system in an older platform, most modern platforms will allow these sectors to be in different locations.

Example 32-bit Layout

Of course the BPB must be in the first sector of the volume. However, if you plan to boot this volume, you will place bootable code in the first few sectors of the volume as well. If this bootable code is more than a single sector, you either have to have the Info Sector at LSN 1 and jump over it, or you can move the Info Sector to the sector just past your boot code and not worry about jumping over it. If you boot code uses more than five sectors, you will have to place your Backup Sector at a location after LSN 6. Just remember that the Info Sector should be before the Backup Sector and the sectors starting at the Backup Sector needs to contain a copy of all of the boot code as well as the Info Sector. Therefore, your boot code cannot be more than 15 sectors in length.

The File Allocation Tables (Cluster Map)

Whether we are working with a 12-, 16-, or 32-bit file system, the File Allocation Tables, Cluster Map, or FATs, follow the reserved section. The FATs occupy enough sectors to have a single entry for every cluster of the volume's data region.

A FAT contains the chains of clusters for a file. The file's directory entry contains the starting cluster for the file. To find the next cluster, you read the cluster number at that index in the FAT. For example, if the starting cluster number is 16, retrieved from the directory entry for this file, you read the 16th FAT entry. This value, say 32 for example, is the second cluster number of the file. To find the next, you read the 32nd FAT entry. You continue doing this until you read the last cluster value.

There are two reserved cluster entries at the first of the FAT, each marked used. The first cluster of the Data Region is actually the third cluster entry in the FAT. The first entry uses the BPB's Media Descriptor byte for the lower 8 bits of the entry, with the high order bits all set to 1. The second FAT cluster entry is always the End of Cluster Chain marker. In a 16- and 32-bit FAT, the top most bits are used for Dirty FAT flags. Top most bit is the Volume Clean bit, second top most bit indicates if there were any errors reading or writing to the disk.

Please remember that the top most bit for a 32-bit FAT is 27, not 31. A 32-bit FAT has the top most nibble reserved and set to zeros, and must be ignored.

A cluster entry will always point to the next cluster in the file except for the following values. FAT12 only uses the bottom 12 bits while FAT16 uses the bottom 16 bits and FAT32 uses the bottom 28 bits.

Table 9-5: Valid Cluster Numbers

Valid Cluster Numbers	
0x00000000 to 0x00000001	This is an illegal value. Cluster zero and one each point to sectors before the data cluster area.
0x00000002 to 0x0FFFFFF6	Valid Cluster number.
0x0FFFFFF7	Bad Cluster Number.
0x0FFFFFF8 to 0x0FFFFFFE	Reserved.
0x0FFFFFFF	End of Cluster Chain marker.

Figure 9-3 below shows an example of the first ten cluster entries in a 12-bit FAT using the example at the end of this chapter. Normally, the first two entries would point to the next two entries respectively, and each having the value of 001 and 002 respectively. However, since these two are the reserved entries, they have FF0 and FFF. In this example, since the first file written to the disk was less than or equal to the size of a cluster, it only needs one cluster entry. The Starting Cluster in the Directory Entry is 002, or the third cluster entry in the FAT. If the file needed more than a single cluster, the third entry would contain 003, however it does not, so it contains the End of Cluster Chain value of FFF. The next file on the disk uses at least seven entries and has a Starting Cluster number of 003. Once the first cluster is read, the cluster entry number 003 is read, which has a value of 004. Therefore, it will read cluster four, and then will continue until the next cluster number is FFF.

Cluster values are stored on the media in little-endian format. In FAT16 and FAT32 maps, this is easy to represent. The lowest byte is stored first, then then next byte, etc. In FAT12 maps, it is a little more difficult to see.

Figure 9-3: FAT Chain Example #1

Example first 10 cluster entries in a 12-bit FAT.
FF0 FFF FFF 004 005 006 007 008 009 00A

Same cluster entries read directly from the disk.
F0 FF FF FF 4F 00 05 60 00 07 80 00 09 A0 00

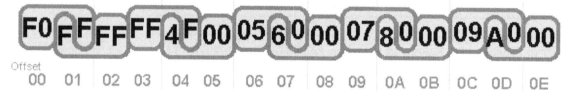

To retrieve a 12-bit FAT entry, you multiply the entry number by 1½ and read the 16-bit word at that offset. Then if the original number was odd, you take the top 12 bits. If it was even, you take the bottom 12 bits.

Listing 9-2: Get 12-bit FAT Entry

```
offset = Starting + (Starting >> 1)
word = 16-bit word at [offset]
if Starting is odd
  entry = word >> 4
else
  entry = word & 0FFF
```

The first cluster in the data region has a cluster number of two. To get the next cluster number for this file, you read the 16-bit word at byte offset $(2 + 2 \div 2) = 3$ to get a value of 0x4FFF. Since the original offset is even, we mask off the top 4 bits to get 0x0FFF. This value indicating that there are no more clusters in this chain.

Notice that a 16-bit read from byte offset 5 would return an invalid FAT entry. However, using the formula in Listing 9-2, there is no way to get a value of 5 as the offset.

A 16- or 32-bit FAT is much easier to read. You simply read in the little-endian 16- or 32-bit value at the Starting Cluster's index of that same size.

Please note that if you have enough room on the media to have a cluster numbered 0xFF7 (FAT-12), 0xFFF7 (FAT-16) or 0x0FFFFFF7 (FAT-32), you may not use that cluster number or any cluster after it. All clusters numbered xxxxFF7 and later are considered unused. For example, in a 16-bit FAT system, if you have a volume with 131,062 sectors in the data area, using a cluster size of 2, the last 10 sectors must not be used. With a FAT-16 formatted volume, cluster number 0xFFF6 is that last available cluster number.

```
(131062 / 2) = 65531 = 0xFFFB.   (0xFFF6 * 2) = 131052.
```

The figure on the next page is another example of a FAT12 formatted disk's FAT chain, containing thirteen small files.

The first two entries are the 0xFF0 and 0xFFF entries. Then starting with cluster number 2, the first file has two entries, 0x003 and 0xFFF. This means that the file's data begins at cluster number 0x002 and occupies two clusters, 0x002 and 0x003.

The next file's cluster starts at offset 0x06 and uses bytes 0x06, 0x07, and 0x08. The next file occupies three clusters, clusters 0x006 through 0x008.

This example shows all files consecutively following one another without any fragmentation. What happens if we delete the third file occupying clusters 0x006 through 0x008, and copy another file to the disk larger than the one we just deleted?

Figure 9-4: FAT Chain Example #2

	00	01	02	03	04	05	06	07	08	09	0A	0B	0C	0D	0E	0F
00	F0	FF	FF	03	F0	FF	05	F0	FF	07	80	00	FF	AF	00	0B
10	C0	00	0D	E0	00	0F	00	01	11	20	01	13	F0	FF	15	F0
20	FF	17	80	01	19	A0	01	1B	C0	01	1D	E0	01	1F	00	02
30	21	20	02	23	40	02	25	60	02	27	80	02	29	A0	02	2B
40	C0	02	FF	EF	02	2F	00	03	31	F0	FF	33	40	03	35	60
50	03	37	80	03	39	A0	03	3B	C0	03	3D	E0	03	3F	00	04
60	41	20	04	43	40	04	45	60	04	47	F0	FF	49	A0	04	4B
70	C0	04	4D	E0	04	4F	00	05	51	20	05	FF	4F	05	55	60
80	05	FF	8F	05	59	A0	05	5B	C0	05	5D	E0	05	5F	00	06
90	61	20	06	63	40	06	65	60	06	FF	8F	06	69	A0	06	6B
A0	C0	06	6D	E0	06	6F	00	07	71	20	07	73	40	07	75	60
B0	07	77	80	07	79	A0	07	7B	C0	07	7D	E0	07	7F	00	08
C0	81	20	08	83	40	08	FF	6F	08	87	80	08	89	A0	08	8B
D0	C0	08	8D	E0	08	8F	00	09	91	20	09	93	F0	FF	00	00
E0	00	00	00	00	00	00	00	00	00	00	00	00	00	00	00	00
F0	00	00	00	00	00	00	00	00	00	00	00	00	00	00	00	00

The figure on the next page shows this result. The contents of bytes 0x07, 0x08 and 0x09 are still the same since the new file still occupies those clusters, with the exception of the FAT entry at offset 0x0C is no longer the *end of file* marker, but now points to cluster 0x094. Then starting at byte offset 0xDE, the file's FAT chain continues.

Just a note of interest, the application I was using for this example to erase the first file, then copy the new larger file to the disk found that the now unoccupied space starting at cluster 0x007 was no longer large enough to hold the whole file. Therefore, it found the next available cluster chain that would be consecutively written, in this case, starting at cluster 0x094. In other words, it was optimizing the read and write operations by finding a place on the disk that all clusters could be written one after another. I had the opportunity to code the change in Figure 9-5 by hand. :-)

Figure 9-5: FAT Chain Example #3

	00	01	02	03	04	05	06	07	08	09	0A	0B	0C	0D	0E	0F
00	F0	FF	FF	03	F0	FF	05	F0	FF	07	80	00	94	A0	00	0B
10	C0	00	0D	E0	00	0F	00	01	11	20	01	13	F0	FF	15	F0
20	FF	17	80	01	19	A0	01	1B	C0	01	1D	E0	01	1F	00	02
30	21	20	02	23	40	02	25	60	02	27	80	02	29	A0	02	2B
40	C0	02	FF	EF	02	2F	00	03	31	F0	FF	33	40	03	35	60
50	03	37	80	03	39	A0	03	3B	C0	03	3D	E0	03	3F	00	04
60	41	20	04	43	40	04	45	60	04	47	F0	FF	49	A0	04	4B
70	C0	04	4D	E0	04	4F	00	05	51	20	05	FF	4F	05	55	60
80	05	FF	8F	05	59	A0	05	5B	C0	05	5D	E0	05	5F	00	06
90	61	20	06	63	40	06	65	60	06	FF	8F	06	69	A0	06	6B
A0	C0	06	6D	E0	06	6F	00	07	71	20	07	73	40	07	75	60
B0	07	77	80	07	79	A0	07	7B	C0	07	7D	E0	07	7F	00	08
C0	81	20	08	83	40	08	FF	6F	08	87	80	08	89	A0	08	8B
D0	C0	08	8D	E0	08	8F	00	09	91	20	09	93	F0	FF	95	60
E0	09	FF	0F	00	00	00	00	00	00	00	00	00	00	00	00	00
F0	00	00	00	00	00	00	00	00	00	00	00	00	00	00	00	00

Root Directory Entries

In the 12- and 16-bit versions, the root directory follows the last sector of the last FAT and has a size calculated from the Root Directory Entries field from the BPB and is a fixed size. In the 32-bit version, the cluster number of this root directory is in the BPB and the size is calculated just like a normal file would be from the FAT chain, and can be resized just like a regular file.

A directory entry is 32 bytes and uses the two formats listed starting below and on the next page.

Table 9-6: FAT12/16 Directory Entry

Offset	Size	Description
0x00	8	File Name
0x08	3	File Extension
0x0B	1	Attribute
0x0C	10	Reserved
0x16	2	Time
0x18	2	Date
0x1A	2	Starting Cluster
0x1C	4	File Size

Table 9-7: FAT32 Directory Entry

Offset	Size	Description
0x00	8	File Name
0x08	3	File Extension
0x0B	1	Attribute
0x0C	1	Reserved
0x0D	1	Tenths of a Second
0x0E	2	Creation Time
0x10	2	Creation Date
0x12	2	Date Last Accessed
0x14	2	High order word of starting cluster
0x16	2	Time
0x18	2	Date
0x1A	2	Low order word of starting cluster
0x1C	4	File Size

The Name field contains eight characters, the first part of the name, the part before the implied period. The File Extension is the three-byte extension after the implied period. The Name and Extension allow uppercase characters, numbers, and a few other characters listed below. The period is not saved in the entry.

The first byte in the Name field is also used for Directory Entry identification.

First byte of Name field only:
    0x00   This is an entry that is free for use. At format time, all entries will have this value. **This value also means that there are no more used entries after this one.**
    0xE5   This is an entry that has been used before, but is now free for use. File has been deleted.
    0x05   This is used as the same as 0xE5 above. 0xE5 is a valid char for a Japan file name, so 0x05 was used instead.

SFN: The following characters are legal*:
                    A to Z and 0 to 9
            $ % ' - _ @ ~ ` ! ( ) { } ^ # &
                  ascii(128)->ascii(255)

LFN: The following characters are legal*:
        Same as SFN above with the following additions:
                        a to z
                    . + , ; = [ ]

*Assuming the ASCII character set

Both Short File Name (SFN) and Long File Name (LFN) entries allow a space character. However, a value of 0x20 is not allowed as the first character, and if the SFN entry name or extension does not occupy all bytes of the field, you must right pad the field with space characters. LFN entries will ignore leading and trailing space characters.

A LFN will allow multiple period characters in the name, using the last one, if found, as the name and extension separator.

SFN path names limits are set to 80 characters. This includes the drive and root specifier (3), the path name, the current filename (12) and the NULL ending byte (ASCIIZ strings). A LFN path name limits are set to 260 total bytes in the ASCIIZ string, with the file name itself limited to 255 characters. See the section on Long File Names later in this chapter for this limit.

The 8-bit Attribute has the following bit representations.

Table 9-8: File Attributes

Bits	Description
7:6	Reserved and unused
5	Archive
4	Directory
3	Volume ID
2	System
1	Hidden
0	Read Only

The Tenths of a Second is a count of tenths of a second at creation time. It is to be used with the Seconds part of the Time field, and has a value of 0 to 199.

The Time and Date fields are stored in two 16-bit values with the following formats.

Table 9-9: Date

Bits	Description
15:9	Count of years since 1980. Value + 1980 = year.
8:5	One based Month. 1 = January.
4:0	One base Day. 1 to 31

Table 9-10: Time

Bits	Description
15:11	Zero based hours. 0 - 23.
10:5	Zero based minutes. 0 - 59.
4:0	Two seconds. 0 - 29 times 2 = 0, 2, 4, 6, ..., 58

With the addition Cluster Number field in the 32-bit FAT entry, cluster numbers are 28 bits in size, therefore combine the two Starting Cluster fields. For the other two versions, use the Starting Cluster number Low Word only.

The File Size is 32-bits allowing for a file size to be up to 4 Gig – 1 in size.

The Root Directory

A directory, root or sub, will contain as many of these 32-byte entries consecutively, to the byte size of the directory block. In a newly created Root Directory, you should have a single entry with the Volume ID attribute set and the file name set to the volume's label, same name as in the same field in the BPB. The Starting Cluster field will be zero. This entry does not point to a file, does not have any FAT entries, and does not occupy anything but this directory entry.

In any sub-directory, two entries are required and are to be the first two entries. The first is the 'dot' entry. This one is to have a Name of '.   ' and an Extension of '   '. It's Starting Cluster field points to the cluster of this sub directory. This is called the Self Pointer. The next entry is the 'dotdot' entry, or the Parent Pointer. It is identical to the first entry except that it contains two dots, '..   ' and its Starting Cluster number points to the parent directory's cluster or zero for the root directory.

Long File Names

The FAT file system has a small limit on the length of a file name, eight plus three. Therefore, Microsoft created a "hack" to be able to have longer file names. The bad thing is, they patented this hack. However, it isn't against this patent to use this hack as long as you do not write to the file system using this hack. In other words, you can read these long file names, but if you write a long file name to the file system, you have gone against this patent.

The hack uses the fact that a combination of the Read Only, Hidden, System, and Volume ID attributes would give an illegal directory entry. Therefore, if this combination is found, the system will check to see if it is a Long File Name entry, or LFN. If this entry, an entry with this illegal combination, was found by a non-LFN compatible system, it would be considered illegal and free for use. If that system now used one of these illegal entries, an LFN aware system would check the CRC field of all included entries, before it assumed a correct LFN chain.

The way the system stores LFNs is fairly easy. The LFN uses as many consecutive 32-byte entries as it needs, plus one more for the Short File Name, or SFN. The first entry is actually the last entry of the LFN, counting down to the first entry of the LFN, then the SFN entry. For an example, if the LFN needed 4 + 1 entries, it would look something like the list shown on the next page.

Long File Name part:
    4th   Last part of LFN. Ordinal – 0x44
    3rd   Middle part of LFN. Ordinal – 0x03
    2nd   Middle part of LFN. Ordinal – 0x02
    1st   First part of LFN. Ordinal – 0x01
Short File Name part:
            Standard Short File Name Entry

An LFN entry has the following format.

Table 9-11: LFN Directory Entry

Offset	Size	Description
0x00	1	Ordinal. Index in LFN entries.
0x01	10	Characters 1 - 5 in this LFN entry.
0x0B	1	Attribute: 0x0F
0x0C	1	Type: 0x00
0x0D	1	Check Sum.
0x0E	12	Characters 6 - 11 in this LFN entry.
0x1A	2	Must be zero.
0x1C	4	Characters 12 - 13 in this LFN entry.

Each entry can hold up to thirteen 16-bit Unicode characters. An LFN is limited to 255 characters, so an LFN can occupy at most 20 LFN entries plus one SFN entry.

 See Appendix D for Unicode encoded characters.

The SFN entry's name now uses the '~' character to truncate the LFN. You take the first six characters of the LFN, append a '~' character and a number to create the file name. You need to make sure that that new file name is not currently being used in the current directory. If you need two digits for the number, you then only use the first five characters of the LFN name. If there are any spaces in this first part of the name, the SFN is truncated at the space location.

For example, the SFN for the example LFN discussed below would be "THE~1.BUS".

Each LFN entry is numbered from highest entry to lowest entry using 1 as the lowest entry. The highest entry will have bit 6 set, indicating that it is the last entry when looking backward. Bit 7 set indicates that the file this chain points to has been deleted.

The figure on the next page shows an example of an LFN chain of entries with the SFN entry following, for the file name 'The Universal Serial.Bus'.

Figure 9-6: LFN Example

LFN[0]						
0x42	Seri		0Fh	00h	CRC	
	al.Bus		0000h			
LFN[1]						
0x01	The U		0Fh	00h	CRC	al
	nivers		0000h			
SFN						
	THEUNI~1	USB	20h			
			Cluster	File Size		

The CRC field in each LFN entry is a check sum of the eleven name characters in the SFN entry. All LFN entries will have this same CRC value. If any of the LFN entries are found to not match this value, the whole LFN chain is to be considered invalid.

Listing 9-3: Calculate the SFN CRC

```
crc = i = 0
do
  crc = crc rotated to the right 1 bit position
  crc = crc + character at index i
  i = i + 1
while i < 11
return crc
```

To rotate an 8-bit value to the right, you shift all bits to the right one bit position. The value of bit 0 before the shift is now placed into bit 7 after the shift. If I were to use the C language to rotate an 8-bit value to the right one bit position, I would use the following code.

```
crc = ((crc & 1) ? 0x80 : 0x00) + (crc >> 1);
```

The FAT specification states when storing a long filename to the media, if there is room in the entry, a filename should be null terminated and any character space after the name should be stored as 0xFFFF. i.e.: unless the filename uses all 13 characters in the last slot, any remaining characters after the end of the file name should be set to a NULL, then 0xFFFF values.

Building a Volume

Now that we know, in a 12-bit FAT system for example, that there is a boot sector with a BPB, at least one FAT table following that, the root directory following that, and then the data region of the volume, let's build a 1.44M floppy disk image.

We know we need a BPB, two FATs, a Root, and the data sectors. With 2880 sectors on a 1.44M floppy, with one sector per cluster, we need at most 2880 12-bit FAT entries.

```
(2880 * 12 bits) / 512 bytes per sector = 9 sectors per FAT
```

We will also have 224 directory entries in the root, each being 32 bytes, we know we need fourteen 512-byte sectors.

Therefore, 1 for the boot and BPB, 9 per FAT times 2, and 14 for the Root.

Now, create the BPB with these known values and write it to the first sector of the disk/image. Don't worry about the boot code for now, we are only interested in the file system on it.

Now create a nine-sector buffer, clearing it to zeros. Remember that the first two FAT entries are considered reserved and should be set to the Media Descriptor Byte and End of Cluster Chain marker respectively. You might mark all unused, extra FAT entries in the last sector as 0xFFF so to not 'accidentally' count them as free sectors.

 The count of unused entries would be calculated as:

```
Remaining = SectorsReserved + (NumFATs * SectorsPerFAT)
   If FAT Type == 12- or 16-bit
      Remaining = Remaining + RootSectors


Unused Entry Count =

   (SectorsPerFat * BytesPerSector)   _
        BytesPerFATEntry


             TotalSectors     _  Remaining
             SectorsPerCluster
```

So, in the case of the example shown on the previous page,

```
(((9 * 512) / 1.5) - ((2880 / 1) - 1 - (2 * 9) - 14))
```

The FAT specification states to mark all unused cluster entries at the end of the last FAT sector as zero. However, this can be confusing when looking at a FAT table. If you mark them to xxxxFFF, they will not get used, in case your FAT code doesn't calculate the last entry position correctly.

Now create a fourteen-sector buffer, clearing all to zeros and write it to the disk/image. You may write the Volume ID entry to the buffer before you write it to the disk, if you so desire.

Then it is up to you if you clear the data sectors of the disk/image. Please note that most format utilities will write a value of 0xFE to all bytes within a sector when it formats that sector.

Wrap Up

In the remaining section of this book, I will show a few memory dumps of a FAT12 formatted hard drive image with a partition, to show how a BPB, FAT, and Root Directory might look, along with a few directory entries. This is so that you can compare your work. I have included the image in the FYSOS\MAIN\FILESYS\IMAGES directory as FAT12.IMG.

With four sectors per cluster, the example image has two FATs at 8 sectors each and a root directory with 128 entries using 8 sectors.

Listing 9-4: Example: BPB

```
00007E00   EB 3C 90 4D 4B 44 4F 53-46 53 20 00 02 04 01 00
00007E10   02 80 00 21 27 F8 08 00-3F 00 10 00 3F 00 00 00
00007E20   00 00 00 00 00 00 29 F2-17 05 17 54 68 69 73 20
00007E30   69 73 20 61 20 64 46 41-54 31 32 20 20 20 00 00


      Fat12/16 BIOS Parameter Block (0x00007E00)
                    Jump: EB 3C 90
                OEM Name: MKDOSFS
        Bytes per Sector: 512
      Sectors per Cluster: 4
        Sectors reserved: 1
                    Fats: 2
            Root Entries: 128
                 Sectors: 10017
              Descriptor: 0xF8
         Sectors per FAT: 8
       Sectors per Track: 63
                   Heads: 16
          Hidden Sectors: 63
         Sectors Extended: 0
               Drive Num: 0
                reserved: 00
                     Sig: 29
                  Serial: 170517F2
                   Label: This is a d
               sys type: FAT12
```

The first FAT has the default first two entries and three 'runs' for the three files on the disk.

Listing 9-5: Example: FAT
```
00008000  F8 FF FF 03 F0 FF 05 F0-FF 07 F0 FF 00 00 00 00
00008010  00 00 00 00 00 00 00 00-00 00 00 00 00 00 00 00
00008020  00 00 00 00 00 00 00 00-00 00 00 00 00 00 00 00
```

The first three entries in the root directory are the Volume ID label entries. The first two are the Long File Name entries while the third is the Short File Name entry. In this instance, we chose to create a FatGen103 (patent violating) SFN entry.

Listing 9-6: Example: SFN: Volume ID
```
0000A000  42 61 00 75 00 6C 00 74-00 20 00 0F 00 A6 6C 00
0000A010  61 00 62 00 65 00 6C 00-00 00 00 00 FF FF FF FF
0000A020  01 54 00 68 00 69 00 73-00 20 00 0F 00 A6 69 00
0000A030  73 00 20 00 61 00 20 00-64 00 00 00 65 00 66 00
0000A040  54 48 49 53 49 53 7E 31-20 20 20 08 00 00 00 00
0000A050  00 00 00 00 00 00 96 81-45 54 00 00 00 00 00 00
```

```
FAT Root Entry (LFN) (0x0000A000)
             Sequ_flags: 42  (deleted = N last = Y number = 2)
                   Name: ault
              Attribute: 0x0F
               Reserved: 00
                    crc: 0xA6
                   Name: label·
                   Zero: 0x0000
                   Name:  ··

FAT Root Entry (LFN) (0x0000A020)
             Sequ_flags: 01  (deleted = N last = N number = 1)
                   Name: This
              Attribute: 0x0F
               Reserved: 00
                    crc: 0xA6
                   Name: is a d
                   Zero: 0x0000
                   Name: ef

FAT Root Entry (non LFN) (0x0000A040)
                   Name: THISIS~1
              Extension:
              Attribute: 0x08  Volume Label
         FAT12:reserved: 00 00 00 00 00 00 00 00 00 00
         FAT32:reserved: 00
    FAT32:creation 10th: 0x00
    FAT32:creation time: 0x0000
```

```
      FAT32:creation date: 0x0000
      FAT32:last accessed: 0x0000
   FAT32:hi word start cluster: 0x0000
                   Time: 0x8196  (16:12:44)
                   Date: 0x5445  (2022/02/05)
       Starting Cluster: 0x0000 (0x00000000)
              File Size: 0
```

The next two entries contain a single LFN entry with a trailing SFN entry for the file name "fat12.txt", also creating a correct SFN.

Listing 9-7: Example: LFN Chain: "fat12.txt"

```
0000A060   41 66 00 61 00 74 00 31-00 32 00 0F 00 0D 2E 00
0000A070   74 00 78 00 74 00 00 00-FF FF 00 00 FF FF FF FF
0000A080   46 41 54 31 32 20 20 20-54 58 54 20 00 00 00 00
0000A090   00 00 00 00 00 00 96 81-45 54 02 00 15 0A 00 00
```

```
FAT Root Entry (LFN) (0x0000A060)
            Sequ_flags: 41  (deleted = N last = Y number = 1)
                  Name: fat12
             Attribute: 0x0F
              Reserved: 00
                   crc: 0x0D
                  Name: .txt
                  Zero: 0x0000
                  Name:


FAT Root Entry (non LFN) (0x0000A080)
                  Name: FAT12
             Extension: TXT
             Attribute: 0x20  Archive
        FAT12:reserved: 00 00 00 00 00 00 00 00 00 00
        FAT32:reserved: 00
    FAT32:creation 10th: 0x00
   FAT32:creation time: 0x0000
   FAT32:creation date: 0x0000
   FAT32:last accessed: 0x0000
   FAT32:hi word start cluster: 0x0000
                   Time: 0x8196  (16:12:44)
                   Date: 0x5445  (2022/02/05)
       Starting Cluster: 0x0002 (0x00000002)
              File Size: 2581
```

The next two entries contain a single LFN entry with a trailing SFN entry for the file name "fat16.txt".

Listing 9-8: Example: LFN Chain: "fat16.txt"

```
0000A0A0   41 66 00 61 00 74 00 31-00 36 00 0F 00 14 2E 00
0000A0B0   74 00 78 00 74 00 00 00-FF FF 00 00 FF FF FF FF
0000A0C0   20 00 1E 05 06 00 00 00-2F 00 00 20 00 00 00 00
0000A0D0   00 00 00 00 00 00 96 81-45 54 04 00 15 0A 00 00
```

```
FAT Root Entry (LFN) (0x0000A0A0)
              Sequ_flags: 41  (deleted = N last = Y number = 1)
                    Name: fat16
               Attribute: 0x0F
                Reserved: 00
                     crc: 0x14
                    Name: .txt
                    Zero: 0x0000
                    Name:

FAT Root Entry (non LFN) (0x0000A0C0)
                    Name:   · · · · · · ·
               Extension: / · ·
               Attribute: 0x20   Archive
         FAT12:reserved: 00 00 00 00 00 00 00 00 00 00
         FAT32:reserved: 00
    FAT32:creation 10th: 0x00
    FAT32:creation time: 0x0000
    FAT32:creation date: 0x0000
    FAT32:last accessed: 0x0000
FAT32:hi word start cluster: 0x0000
                    Time: 0x8196   (16:12:44)
                    Date: 0x5445   (2022/02/05)
        Starting Cluster: 0x0004 (0x00000004)
               File Size: 2581
```

Notice that there is no name in the SFN entry. This is the hack to still use long file names, but not violate the patent.

The last two entries in the root directory are the "fat32.txt" entries. They are identical to Listing 9-8 other than the name change.

Please remember that the image has a MBR and the FAT partition doesn't start until LBA 63.

A commonly used format command creates a volume where there is a Label entry in the root directory, but the BPB still has 'NO NAME   '. This format utility asks for a label, creates the root directory entry, but did not update the BPB. I am guessing the reason is that the utility already wrote the BPB, the two FAT's, and now is ready to create the Root Directory, when asking for the label. The programmer should have asked at BPB time, not Root Directory time. Just my opinion though.

Within the source code repository for this book, see Appendix B, there is a utility to make a FAT image file called `mkdosfs`. It is a command line utility that takes a text file as input describing the image to make.

Also, within this repo, is a Windows GUI based utility called `Ultimate` that will create, view, and edit disk image files. See Appendix B for more information.

Chapter 10 – The FYSFS File System

The FYSFS file system allows for almost unlimited volume sizes, file sizes, and file name lengths, contains a Super Block, and is fairly easy to implement. It contains many forms of redundancy and compensates for different volume types.

The FYSFS file system was created at the same time I was creating my Virtual File system for the FYSOS operating system. Its purpose was to have more than one file system supported to make sure that there was no file system dependent code within the Virtual File System (VFS). I also created it for the enjoyment of doing so.

On the other side, the FYSFS isn't going to break any records or replace any existing file systems. It was simply designed for the enjoyment of doing so and to verify my work.

Within this chapter, I will detail the FYSFS file system. This way you can see different options that you can do to create your own file system, showing advantages and disadvantages. In fact, this file system does have a flaw in it when it comes to directories and the allocation of sub directories. But more on this later.

The next chapter shows a much better file system, the default file system for FYSOS.

 Please see http://www.fysnet.net/fysfs.htm for the latest news and updates.

A Typical FYSFS Formatted Volume

A typical FYSFS formatted volume contains sixteen sectors reserved for the boot, a Super Block, at least one bitmap, and the Root Directory.

The figure on the next page shows a typical layout of an FYSFS formatted volume for a 1.44M Floppy Disk.

 This file system is one of the first things I made when I first started this hobby so many, many years ago. At the time, I thought that it was going to work out to be a pretty good file system. I had high hopes. :-)

Throughout the years I learned what makes a good file system and this file system no longer looked so good. I include it here to show what can be done, some good things, and then to show what should not have been done. It was a good learning experience that I hope to pass on to you.

Figure 10-1: Typical FYSFS Volume

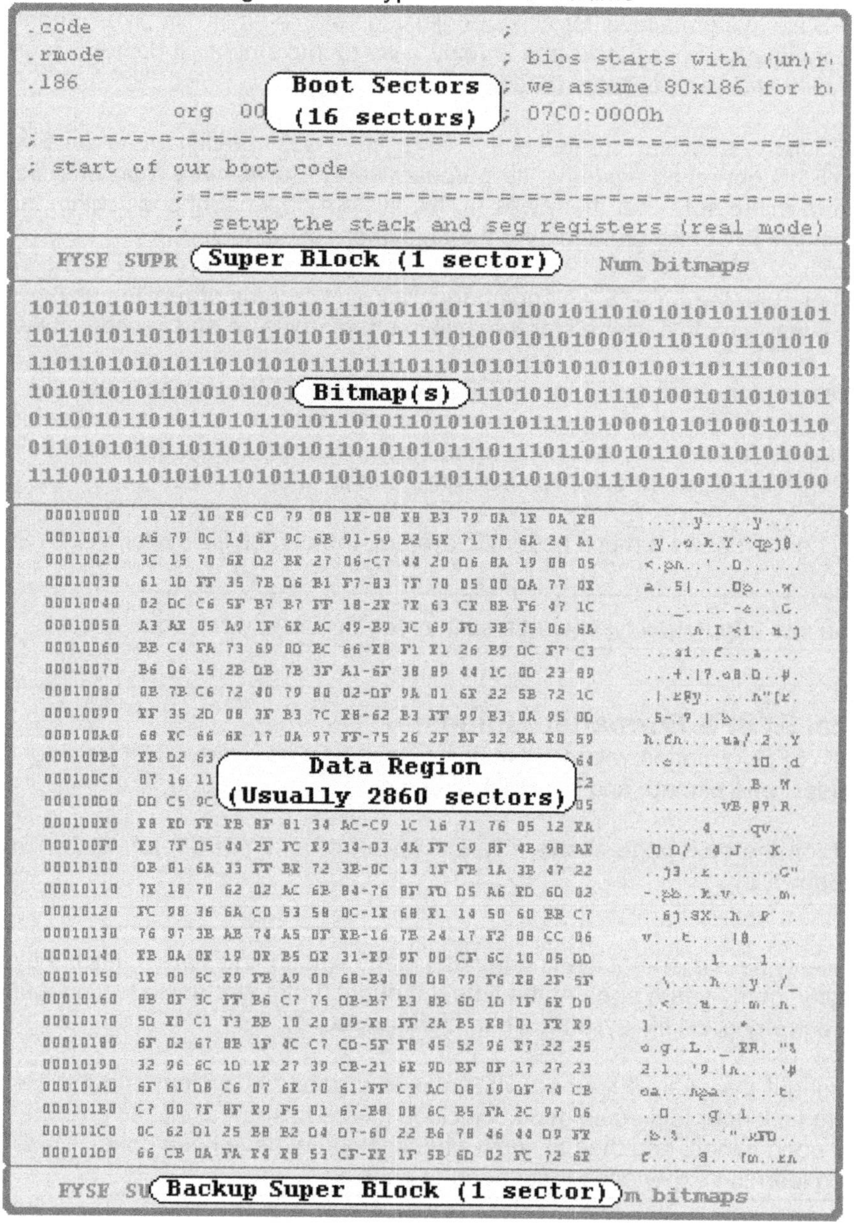

The Boot Sector

The Boot Sector is always at Linear Sector Number zero, or LSN 0, the first sector of the volume. The FYSFS leaves the first 16 sectors free for the boot. These 16 sectors are reserved for the boot code, if needed, and should contain all of the necessary code and data needed to load the operating system, or at least a loader file to do so.

Unlike the FAT file system explained in the last chapter, there is very little information about the file system in the boot sector. This file system stores the information needed in the Super Block at LSN 16, explained later in this chapter. Therefore, you load this Super Block to obtain this information.

However, we have a chicken-and-the-egg situation here. We don't know the Base LBA where our volume is located until we read the Super Block. The Master Boot Record (MBR) knew where to read the boot sector, since it read from the base it has stored in the Partition Table. However, there is no documented standard way to pass this base LBA to the volume's boot sectors. We need to know the base LBA to read the Super Block, but need to read the Super Block to know the base LBA. Therefore, we need to have the Base LBA in the first sector of the boot code, since the BIOS has already read that sector for us. To do this, the last 16 bytes of the first sector of the Boot Sector must have the format listed in Table 10-1 below.

 Remember that this is at offset (512 - 14) no matter the sector size.

Table 10-1: Boot Sector Info Block

Offset	Size	Description
0x1F2	4	Signature: random serial number for this volume
0x1F6	8	64-bit Base Address of this volume
0x1FE	2	Boot Signature 0xAA55 (0x55 0xAA)

The Signature field is a random 32-bit serial number to help identify this volume. The Base Address field will be located here and in the Super Block so that the boot code knows where the Super Block is relative to the start of the disk. The last two bytes of this block is the normal boot sector signature of 0xAA55.

The remaining 15 sectors of the first 16 are used for any remaining code and data that is needed to load the operating system. If they are not used, they should be cleared to zeros.

 Remember that you cannot use any code or data within LSN 1 through LSN 15 before you load them into memory. The BIOS only loaded the first sector.

The Super Block

The Super Block is used to store the information needed to load and use the file system contained on this volume. This Super Block is at LSN 16, occupies the whole sector no matter the sector size, and has the format shown below. Any space after this Super Block and to the end of the sector is reserved for future expansion and should be preserved when written to.

Table 10-2: FYSFS Super Block

Offset	Size	Description
0x000	8	Signature 'FYSF' 'SUPR' (0x46595346 0x53555052)
0x008	2	Version in BCD (0x0161 = 1.61)
0x00A	2	Sectors per Cluster (1 or a power of 2 <= 512)
0x00C	1	Encryption type
0x00D	1	Number of Bitmaps (1 or 2)
0x00E	2	Flags describing the bitmap(s)
0x010	4	Count of 'slots' in the root directory
0x014	8	Base LBA where the volume starts
0x01C	8	Root LSN relative to volume start
0x024	8	Data Block LSN relative to volume start
0x02C	8	Count of sectors in Data Block
0x034	8	Total Sectors in volume
0x03C	8	Bitmap LSN relative to volume start
0x044	8	Bitmap Spare LSN relative to volume start
0x04C	4	Last Chkdisk. Seconds since 0:00 1-1-1980
0x050	4	Last Optimize. Seconds since 0:00 1-1-1980
0x054	4	Volume Flags
0x058	4	CRC of Super Block(s)
0x05C	16	GUID serial number of Volume
0x06C	64	Asciiz Volume Label
0x0AC	250	Reserved and Preserved
0x1A6	90	Encryption Check

All LSN pointers in the Super Block are zero based from the start of the volume. All LSN pointers within the data block are zero based from the start of the data block. i.e.: all starting sectors and fat entries for any file within the data block are zero based within that data block, not the start of the volume. Typically, the data block occupies all remaining sectors, except for the bitmaps, explained later.

The Signature field is used to verify that this is actually the start of the Super Block. You need to verify this signature and the CRC field to verify that the data in this Super Block is valid before you mount the volume. The CRC is explained on the next page.

The Version field is to verify that your driver supports this volume. Verify this value before you mount the volume.

Like the FAT file system, this file system uses clusters to store data in the data area. The Sectors per Cluster field must be a 1 or a power of 2 up to 512.

The Encryption Type field is to specify the type of encryption used on this volume. A value of zero indicates no encryption used. See later in this chapter about encryption.

See the section on Bitmaps later in this chapter for the bitmap fields used in the Super Block.

The Flags field in the Super Block only has bits 1:0 used while the remaining 30 bits must remain reserved and preserved. Bit 0 is use to indicate if the volume's file names are case sensitive. If set, they are case sensitive. This flag should only be modified at format time. It can be set to use case sensitivity at any time during the life of the volume, however it must not be cleared after a volume has been used unless only after a complete check of the volume to make sure there are no conflicts with case sensitivity, can it be cleared.

Bit 1 in the Flags field indicates if there is a copy of this Super Block at the end of the volume. If there is, this copy must be in the first sector of the last cluster of the data block. Note that it is in the last cluster, not last sector. This cluster must also be marked as 'system' in the bitmap(s). To verify that this copy is a valid copy, you must perform a CRC check on the copy. Only if it passes can you copy it to LSN 16. If the primary Super Block ever goes bad, you can always check the last cluster of the volume for the copy. If it passes the CRC check and has the correct signature, it is safe to assume that it is a valid copy.

Since the Super Block may be corrupt and this file system only supports up to 512 sectors per cluster, you can check the last 512 sectors of the volume for this Backup Super Block. However, you only need to check a sector that is a power of 2. For example, check only sectors 512, 256, 128, down to 2, then 1 sector before the end of the volume.

The use of a bit in the Super Block to indicate if there is a backup Super Block is redundant in itself. Since a single bit can only show two options, it is very easy for a faulty Super Block to indicate a backup Super Block is present. If your file system references a backup Super Block, it should always be present.

The CRC check follows that of the official CRC-32 standard and is described in the included specification for this file system. See Appendix A for more information on this specification.

The GUID serial number follows the rules also explained in the included specification. The calculation algorithm used for this serial number is not specified. Any values may be used.

From this point on, the rest of the items on the volume are not located in fixed locations, each item is pointed to by the Super Block.

The Bitmaps

On a typical FYSFS partition, the bitmap(s) would be next. These bitmaps are double-bit representations of the use of each cluster in the volume. This two-bit field must be one of the four values shown below.

Table 10-3: Bitmap Bit Pair Values

Value	Description
00	Unoccupied - Is free and can be used for cluster allocation
01	Occupied - Is an occupied cluster, and should be left as so
10	Deleted - Was occupied, now is free for use
11	System - Used to mark bad and/or system non-movable clusters

Since files can be undeleted, you can mark a cluster as free for use, using 10b, marking them as deleted. Then when checking for a free cluster, you may skip any cluster that is marked as deleted. Therefore, you can undelete a file later. However, when unoccupied clusters are becoming scarce, an optimizer should be used to change some/all deleted entries to unoccupied entries, including any deleted slots in the corresponding directories.

The high two bits (bits 7:6) in the first byte of the bitmap represents Cluster 0, while the low two bits (bits 1:0) represents Cluster 3. The high two bits in the second byte of the bitmap represent Cluster 4, and so on. There are typically two bitmaps, though the Super Block contains a field stating how many there are. There can be 1 or 2, no more, no less. Bits 1:0 in the Bitmap Flag field in the Super Block denote which bitmap is to be used and if the inactive bitmap is to be updated as the active bitmap is updated.

Within the Super Block, if bit 0 of the Bitmap Flag field is clear, then the first bitmap is the active bitmap. If it is set, the second, if present, is active. If this bit is set and the Bitmaps field is 1, then the OS should return an error at time of mount.

If bit 1 is clear, the active bitmap is used, while the inactive bitmap is not touched. If this bit is set, the inactive bitmap needs to be updated to match the active bitmap at a time when the system is in a stable state. The time and state to update the inactive bitmap is to be determined by the host. However, no more than 128 modifications should be made to the active bitmap before the inactive bitmap is updated. A modification in this sense is a single write to the bitmap. If multiple bits will be modified, but there is only one read/write sequence, this is considered a single modification. No more than 128 of these modifications should be made before the second bitmap is updated to match the active bitmap.

The Data Area

On a typical FYSFS partition, the Data Area follows the bitmap(s) and contains the Root Directory within that Data Area. The Root Directory block can be anywhere within this Data Area. The Root Entrys field in the Super Block determines the size of the Root Directory. The Root Directory must be continuous and not fragmented. The Root Directory can be resized as long as it remains continuous on the disk and this field is updated. Each entry, or slot, is 128 bytes fixed and there are six (6) types of data blocks that can occupy each slot. The bitmap(s) must be marked 'used' for the clusters that occupy any data in the data block, which includes directory blocks.

In a good file system, the space the Root Directory occupies should not have to be continuous. It should be treated just like a regular file, allocated, written to, and resized just like a regular file. Unfortunately, the way this file system is used, the Root Directory must be continuous.

The way this file system stores files on the media is by using at least one directory entry with possible extra entries to continue the name or location on the disk. For example, a small file with a short file name will take only one entry in its directory block, where a small file with a long file name may take two or more entries, and where a large file with a long file name may take three or more entries. These entries are called 'slots' and they reside in the current directory block.

The first type of slot is the actual directory entry of a file and is shown in Table 10-4 below.

Table 10-4: FYSFS Root Directory: Slot

Offset	Size	Description
0x00	4	Signature 'SLOT' (0x534C4F54)
0x04	4	File's attributes
0x08	5	Reserved and preserved
0x0D	1	FAT entries in this slot
0x0E	1	CRC
0x0F	1	Scratch Byte
0x10	4	Created time stamp
0x14	4	Last accessed time stamp
0x18	8	File Size
0x20	4	FAT continue
0x24	4	Name continue
0x28	2	Flags
0x2A	1	Name length (in this slot only)
0x2B	5	Reserved and preserved
0x30	80	Name and/or FAT

The Signature indicates that this is a 'SLOT' and will hold the first part of the name and possibly the FAT entries. Every file must have one of these entries.

The valid attributes of a file are:
```
#define FYSFAT_ATTR_ARCHIVE   0x00000001
#define FYSFAT_ATTR_SUB_DIR   0x00000002
#define FYSFAT_ATTR_SYSTEM    0x00000008
#define FYSFAT_ATTR_HIDDEN    0x00000010
#define FYSFAT_ATTR_READ_ONLY 0x00000020
```

At this time, there are no other attribute types. However, if you read the value with any unused bits set, you must preserve these bits and write them back as they were read.

The FAT Entries count is the number of cluster entries that are in this slot. This count may be zero due to a zero-length file or there is a FAT Continuation slot associated with this slot.

 Please note that the FAT Entries and Name Length fields in this or other slots are the count of this item within this slot only. There may be more characters in the name within another slot entry.

A directory entry (slot) may contain both the name and the FAT for a specified file. Since the FYSFS allows a filename to be many chars in length, a slot must contain a link to the next slot that contains the remainder of the name if the name will not fit in the current slot. The same goes for the FAT.

The name and the FAT entries are located in the last field of the slot. The name must be first and must have at least 1 character included in the first slot. The name must also be end padded with nulls to the next 32-bit alignment. However, the name does not have to end in a null if the last char is the byte before a 32-bit aligned byte. The name length field does not include any null padding in its length.

If the name occupies the whole name/fat field and needs more room, the host must allocate another unused slot, place this zero-based slot number in the Name Continue field and then continue placing the name in the new slot (not allowing slot 0 to be a continuation slot). See later for the format of this new slot. The 32-bit FAT entries follow the same format as the name does. The only difference is that there cannot be any FAT entries before any file name chars in the same slot. All FAT entries must proceed file name characters. To know where the first FAT entry is located in the name/fat field, you simply skip 'name length' bytes and start on the next dword aligned byte. If the 'name length' field contains a value of 77 or greater, then the FAT entries start at the slot pointed to by the Fat Continue field.

Please note that when calculating the offset of the first FAT entry, you cannot assume that the name/fat field will be dword aligned in memory. When you calculate using

$$dword\_offset - ((x + 3) \ \& \ \sim0x03)$$

make sure that the offset of name/fat field is not included in the calculation above. If I were going to use the C language for my driver, my source would be similar to

```
ptr = (bit32u *) (root[i].name_fat + ((root[i].namelen + 3) & ~0x03));
```

Notice that the offset of the name/fat field was not included in the rounding calculation.

The first FAT entry in the slot chain is the starting cluster number of the file. With this in mind, there must always be at least one FAT entry, whether in this slot or a FAT continue slot, unless this is a zero sized file. The cluster number is zero based from the start of the data block given in the Super Block.

The starting slot does not have to contain any FAT entries as long as there is at least one FAT Continue slot.

Since the starting slot (a slot with a signature of 'SLOT') must use only 32-bit fat entries, this slot may only contain fat entries if the file's clusters are 2^32 from the start of the volume's Data Block. However, this sets a limit on the volume size used. If you use a cluster size of 128 sectors, this still gives you a volume size of 128 * 512 * 2^32 bytes, or a 256-terabyte volume. However, when drives start to exceed this size, and/or with smaller cluster sizes, you may want to have a volume larger than this limit. To do so, simply place all FAT entries in a FAT Continue slot, set the Large flag, and use 64-bit FAT entries. This has a max volume size limit of 512 * 512 * 2^64, or 2^82, or a 4.8 yottabyte volume size. A yotta is a 1 with 24 digits after it, or a terabyte of terabytes.

There is a Catch22 when it comes to using 64-bit FAT entries in a continuation slot. When creating a continuation slot, you must check all of the entries to make sure that they are 32-bit entries, or you must use the large flag. Therefore, you must check 28 cluster entries to see if they will fit in the given space in this slot. Now, let's say the 15th entry is the first 64-bit entry, you would now need to use the large flag to store the entries. Since this will now require another continuation slot, and by doing so, you only have enough room to store the first 14 entries as 64-bit entries, all entries in this continuation slot are now only 32-bit entries and no longer need the large flag. Yet, when you clear the large flag, you now include the 15th entry again. Since either method, in this situation, would use the same number of slots, it is up to your driver what to do in this situation.

However, please note that if one FAT entry is 64-bit, then every other one will most likely be that way too.

The Created field contains the seconds since 00:00:00 1-1-1980 to the time this file was created. The Last Access field contains the seconds since 00:00:00 1-1-1980 when the file was last read or written to. When a file is first created, these two fields should be identical. If this entry points to a sub-directory, the Last Access field must be ignored, though not assumed zero.

A good time stamp should use a fraction of a second rather than seconds since a given time. A compiler could build many files within a second, yet each file would have the same timestamp if a second iteration was used. Milliseconds or even microseconds are recommended.

The File Size field is the size of the file in bytes. If this entry points to a sub-directory, this field must be ignored, though not assumed zero.

The Scratch field may be used by the driver as a scratch byte and it should be written to the disk as zeros, though it is not mandatory. However, due to multiple hosts using this partition, this field, if read from the disk as non-zero, should not be assumed valid. FYSOS uses bit 0 in this field to indicate if this slot has been modified before the commit to disk has taken place. The Continuation Slots defined below also have this field. This field must remain at offset 15 in all types of slots.

The valid flags of a file are defined in Table 10-5 below.

Table 10-5: File Flags

Bits	Description
15:3	Reserved and Preserved
2:0	Format of file name
	000 – Ascii
	001 – UTF-8
	010 – UTF-16
	011 -> 111 – reserved and preserved

The file name can be stored using one of the types specified above. All characters in the first slot and any continuation slot for this file name, and this file name only, use this type of character storage. If type 000b is used, please remember that it is not stored as ASCIIZ, meaning it might not have a terminating null character. It is recommended that once the encoding type is chosen for a filename, that it remains this type. A host may change the encoding type of a file name, though it is not recommended.

The CRC field contains the lower 8 bits of the 32-bit CRC check (explained in the specification included) in this 128-byte slot not counting this field. i.e.: zero this byte, then do a 32-bit CRC of all 128 bytes, then store the lower 8-bits of this CRC value to this byte. This field must remain at offset 14 in all types of slots.

Continuation Slots

The second and third types of slots are Continuation Slots. The format of the Name Continue and FAT Continue slot is shown in Table 10-6 below.

Table 10-6: FYSFS Root Directory: Continuation Slot

Offset	Size	Description
0x00	4	Sig: 'NAME' (0x4E414D45) or 'FAT ' (0x46415420)
0x04	4	Previous
0x08	4	Continue
0x0C	1	Count: Name Length or count of FAT Entries
0x0D	1	Flags
0x0E	1	CRC
0x0F	1	Scratch Byte
0x10	112	Name and/or FAT

A Continuation slot must have a Previous value to point to a parent Continuation Slot or the initial Slot. A Continuation slot is a part of a chain of slots to either allow a long file name or multiple FAT entries.

Other Slot Types

The fourth type of a 128-byte slot is the empty slot. It simply contains zeros in all fields if a truly empty slot. The signature field will be filled with zeros.

The fifth type contains 'DLTD' (0x444C5444) in the signature field denoting that this slot chain has been deleted. When deleting slot chains, you must mark all slots in that slot chain with this id, making sure to not update the CRC. No other field, besides the signature, in this slot should be modified. This is so that if the user decides to undelete the file, you can check the chain. To determine what type of slot was deleted, change the signature to 'SLOT' and check the CRC. If not valid, try the next type of slot signature until the CRC is valid. If you have tried all of the slots and the CRC field is not valid, then this is an invalid slot and you must mark it with all zeros.

The last type is the sub-directory type and contains 'SUB ' (0x53554220). See the section on Directories for more information on this type.

If the signature field contains anything other than one of these five types, or the sub-directory type explained later, it is considered a used slot. With this version of the file system, this is a bad slot and will be deleted with the next "Check Disk" or "Optimize" performed. Since a later version of this file system may contain other valid slot signature values, you should not modify any slot that does not have the six defined values already mentioned. Typically, all empty slots should have a value of zero in the signature field.

Modifying Slot Chains

The list below shows what rules apply when deleting or adding slots to a slot chain:

- ✓ You may move the current FAT entries further down the slot to make room for a longer name as long as there is room in this slot to do so. If there is not room to move all FAT entries down, you can do one of two things:
  - a) You may create a new slot for the remaining chars in the name
  - b) you may "scroll" the existing FAT entries through to the next FAT Continue slot(s), creating a new slot if necessary.
- ✓ You may make room in this slot by moving all or some of the FAT entries to another new (or occupied by this slot chain) slot. You may use multiple partial slots, but this would fragment the slot chain and use unnecessary space. Typically, you would never have more than two partial slots in each slot chain, one partial for the name and one for the FAT. If the host operating system supports the optional optimization of FYSFS systems, the user can optimize all fragmented/partial slots to have at most two partials.
- ✓ A slot may not contain FAT entries that do not start directly on the next dword-aligned location after the filename.
- ✓ When the OS calls to rename the file name and the new name is shorter than the current name, you must move the FAT entries in this slot to align after the new shorter name. You can leave "blanks" at the end of the slot if desired. I.e.: you do not have to append the newly moved FAT entries with FAT entries from an existing fat continue slot.
- ✓ The first slot in the slot chain is the only slot in this slot chain that can have both Name and FAT entries. Every other slot in the slot chain must contain a valid NAME or FAT slot header and contain only that type of item.
- ✓ When deleting a file, marking all associated slots with 'DLTD', you must not change any other part of the slot, especially the CRC. This way, when you go to undelete the slot, you change the signature to 'SLOT' and check the CRC. If it matches, you have correctly undeleted this slot. If the CRC does not match, you continue to change the signature to one of the remaining slot types until the CRC matches. This is the only way to tell what type of slot it was before the deletion.

When allocating a new slot for a new file, you must mark the signature entry as 'SLOT' (0x534C4F54). This denotes the first slot of this slot chain. When allocating a new slot to continue the name and/or FAT, you must mark the signature entry as 'NAME' (0x4E414D45) for continuing the name, and 'FAT ' (0x46415420} for continuing the FAT. Be sure to never allocate the first slot in the directory block as a continuation slot.

Remember that the Name Length field contains the length of the name in the current slot only, not the total length of the name used by the whole slot chain. Same for the FAT Entries field, it contains the count of FAT entries in this slot only.

Directories

FYSFS directories are implemented similar to the FAT File System. A directory entry (slot) simply points to a data block containing another set of directory entries (slots). A sub-directory can grow just like a file does. It is up to the host to decide on how many clusters to allocation on sub-directory creation, however at least one (1) must be allocated at creation time. When the host requests a new slot to be created in this sub-directory and there is no more room, at least one more cluster must be allocated and added to the FAT entry list of the SUB slot. In other words, the sub-directory can grow to use as much of the volume as desired. See the note below on the size limit of a directory.

The first slot in the Directory Block must be a starting slot, a signature value of 'SLOT'. This must be so, since zero is used to denote that there are no more Continue slots in slot chain. When implementing this file system, a "find empty slot" routine should ignore the first slot in any directory block when looking for an empty slot when creating a Continue slot for a slot chain.

When a SLOT entry has the attribute of FYSFAT_ATTR_SUB_DIR, meaning that this slot points to a sub-directory, this slot must contain only 1 fat entry and this fat entry must point to the starting cluster of the sub-directory's directory block. This slot does not contain the fat entries for the sub-directory. The 'SUB ' slot type in the sub-directory's first slot contains the fat entries (see below). As with normal file slot entries, the parent slot may contain as many Name Continuation slots as needed, but may contain only one FAT Continuation slot if one is needed due to the name being longer than 77 chars, and/or the cluster number is a 64-bit cluster number.

 This is where I failed with this file system. The method explained to store sub-directories is nowhere efficient, nor is it easy to code. See later for more comments on this failed method.

When a sub-directory is created, the first slot must be filled with a sub-directory slot entry. This entry has the format displayed below.

Table 10-7: Sub-directory Slot

Offset	Size	Description
0x00	4	Signature: 'SUB ' (0x53554220)
0x04	8	Starting Cluster of the Parent Directory
0x0C	1	Reserved and Preserved
0x0D	1	Count of FAT Entries

0x0E	1	CRC
0x0F	1	Scratch Byte
0x10	4	Created Time Stamp
0x14	4	Reserved and Preserved
0x18	8	File Size
0x20	4	FAT Continuation
0x24	4	Slot Index in Parent
0x28	2	Reserved and Preserved
0x2A	1	Zero
0x2B	5	Reserved and Preserved
0x30	80	FAT Entries

This slot type indicates to the system, how many and where the remaining clusters are for this sub-directory. It also gives the starting cluster for the parent directory block. If more than 20 clusters are needed, or 64-bit cluster numbers are needed, you may use a standard Continuation slot as you would with a regular Slot entry. This Continuation slot is not required to be directly after the 'SUB ' slot entry. It can be anywhere within this sub-directory's slot entries.

Please remember that this 'SUB ' slot must be the first slot in the directory block.

A sub-directory block cannot grow beyond 2^32 * 128 bytes and can only have 2^32 slots. However, this allows a sub-directory to occupy one gigabyte of the drive, and have four billion directory entries. Please note that this limit is only the limit for the slots, not the files themselves.

The Root Directory may grow, as long as it does not exceed this limit and it uses consecutive clusters. To grow the Root Directory, you may use unused consecutive clusters at the end of the current Root Directory or you may copy the current Root Directory to another location in the volume, then marking the old location as free. You may also move clusters at the end of the Root Directory to other locations updating the corresponding slot chains to make room for a larger Root Directory. If you move the Root Directory to a larger consecutive block of clusters, remember to update the Super Block (and Backup Super Block) on the volume.

With this type of sub-directory allocation, I could change the way the Root Directory is stored. It could be exactly as detailed above with sub-directories. However, this would give more work to the boot code. I may change it later, though I believe I will leave it as is to not add more work for the boot code. See the note below for a problem that may occur if not managed well.

Note that all slots in a directory must remain within that directory block. You cannot have a continuation slot chain span directory blocks. Any continuation slot chain must remain within the directory block allocated to that directory.

 Please note that if the directory block uses FAT Continuation slots to store the clusters of the directory block, you must be careful with their placement in the directory block. For example, if you use only 64-bit cluster numbers, requiring a FAT Continuation slot, this continuation slot must be within the first cluster of the directory block since you have not read any other clusters yet. Also, if you use more continuation slots for the sub-directory block that can fit in the first cluster, you must have one of the entries in the first few slots point to the remaining clusters. Do not put a continuation slot in a position where you have not made access to that cluster yet.

For an example of a sub-directory, let's say you have a slot in the Root Directory block that has the name 'test_dir' and the FYSFAT_ATTR_SUB_DIR attribute set. This slot must only have 1 FAT entry, no matter the size of the sub-directory it points to, and must be the cluster number of the first cluster of the sub-directory's directory block.

Then, the first slot in the sub-directory's directory block must be the 'SUB ' slot type explained earlier. It will contain all of the cluster numbers that occupy the directory block including the first cluster, which was in the root directory's slot above. The 'SUB ' slot type here may use a standard FAT Continuation slot, if needed, to allocate all of the clusters used. This slot also contains the cluster number of the first cluster of the parent's directory block, along with the slot offset of the 'test_dir' entry above. This is so that a sub-directory can find its parent if needed.

 Usually, as in other file systems, the directory entry that points to the directory block contains all the information about the directory block. However, then you have to have some form of entry to point to the parent directory. FAT does this with the dotdot directory entry. By using a single SUB type slot entry in the directory block itself, the FYSFS file system does the same task, though using the information in the SLOT instead of the dotdot technique.

Notes on optimizing/defragmenting the volume

A typical optimized volume would have as much of the name in the first slot ('SLOT') as possible, with any needed Name Continue slots ('NAME') following this slot, and with any FAT Continue slots ('FAT ') following the Name Continue slots. Since a decent host, on opening the file, will load and cache the whole FAT chain in memory, the FAT chain will be read and then written only once per opening/closing of the file, file sharing aside. However, the name of the file may be needed multiple times when looking for file names, due to many FileFind()/FindNext() function calls.

Defragmentation of the volume is typical of most volume types. Simply place all file clusters in consecutive placement on the volume.

When the bitmap(s) get scarce of unoccupied entries (00b), you may change deleted entries to unoccupied entries to free up disk space. However, please remember to also change any corresponding deleted slots to free slots. The best way to do this is to find deleted slots in a directory, change them to free slots, then change all corresponding bitmap entries for this slot chain, moving to the next slot chain as needed.

Sector sizes

Since each slot is 128 bytes, as long as the sector size is evenly divisible by 128, it doesn't matter what the sector size is. Usually it is 512, but this may change in the future to 1024, 4096, or even more. If there ever is a sector size found that is not evenly divisible by 128, the slots occupy the first bytes of the sector up to the point where another 128-byte slot will not fit. This lost space is just that, lost. A 128-byte slot must not cross a sector boundary. However, it is very unlikely that a sector size will not be evenly divisible by 128.

Encryption

Encryption on a FYSFS volume is done on the cluster level. Encryption is used on a volume if the Encryption field in the Super Block is non-zero. The non-zero value indicates what type of encryption is used. At this time, only the value of 0x01 is allowed and indicates RC4 encryption explained at http://www.fysnet.net/cypher.htm and http://en.wikipedia.org/wiki/RC4.

Since it would be very destructive to use an invalid key on a volume that first didn't verify the encryption key, the Super Block contains a field at the end of the Super Block for verification. The volume does not store the key used for encryption, this would defeat the purpose, however the volume does store the 10-byte suffix for the key.

When the volume is mounted, the user should be asked for the encryption key. Once received, the system should verify the key is valid by using the 10-byte suffix, stored in the Super Block, and the given key to decipher the Encryption Check field in the Super Block. This field is at offset 0x01A6 in the Super Block and is defined below.

Table 10-8: Super Block: Encryption Test

Offset	Size	Description
0x00	10	The 10-byte suffix used to encrypt the data
0x0A	16	Copy of the volume's GUID serial number
0x1A	64	Copy of the volume's 64-byte label

To verify the given key is correct, use the Suffix field appended to the given key to decipher the GUID and Volume Label fields above. If they correctly match the corresponding fields in the Super Block, then you have a valid key.

Please note that all encryption is at the cluster level and is only encrypted or decrypted a cluster at a time. Only clusters in the Data Area are encrypted. The bitmaps, boot block, and Super Block are not to be encrypted. The encryption/decryption should be done as the cluster is read or written.

Since encryption can and may be restrictive in most countries, please verify all laws before passing encryption files across country lines.

Please note that the CRC field in the Super Block is calculated on the encrypted data in the Encryption Check field as it was read from the disk. Do not calculate the CRC from the unencrypted data in this field when writing back to disk.

Please note that if Encryption is used and the Serial Number or Label is changed in the Super Block, you must also change the fields in the Encryption Check field in the Super Block.

Wrap Up

The remaining section of this book, I will show a few memory dumps of a FYSFS formatted hard drive image with one partition, to show what a Super Block and a Root Directory may look like, along with a few directory entries. This is so that you can compare your work. I have included the image in the \MAIN\FILESYS\IMAGES directory as FYSFS.IMG.

The first of the image, skipping the first 63 sectors, has 16 sectors reserved for the boot code with the Super Block at LSN 16, the 17th sector.

Listing 10-1: Example: Super Block

```
00009E00   46 53 59 46 52 50 55 53-62 01 08 00 00 02 02 00
00009E10   80 00 00 00 3F 00 00 00-00 00 00 1B 00 00 00
00009E20   00 00 00 00 1B 00 00 00-00 00 00 05 27 00 00
00009E30   00 00 00 00 20 27 00 00-00 00 00 11 00 00 00
00009E40   00 00 00 00 16 00 00 00-00 00 00 00 00 00 00
00009E50   00 00 00 00 02 00 00 00-37 62 E6 44 A3 07 FF 61
00009E60   00 00 00 00 29 00 23 48-00 00 BE 18 54 68 69 73
00009E70   20 69 73 20 61 20 76 6F-6C 75 6D 65 20 6C 61 62
00009E80   65 6C 20 66 6F 72 20 74-68 69 73 20 46 59 53 46
00009E90   53 20 76 6F 6C 75 6D 65-2E 00 00 00 00 00 00 00
```

```
FYSFS Super Block (0x00009E00)
              sig[0]: 0x46595346   ('FYSF') [1]
```

```
              sig[1]: 0x53555052  ('SUPR') [1]
             Version: 1.62
  Sectors per Cluster: 8
     Encryption Type: 0
   Number of Bitmaps: 2
         Bitmap Flag: 0x00000002
        Root Entries: 128
            Base LBA: 63
            Root LSN: 27
            Data LSN: 27
Sectors in Data Block: 9989
   Sectors in Volume: 10016
    First Bitmap LSN: 17
   Second Bitmap LSN: 22
 Seconds since ChkDisk: 0
 Seconds since LostOpt: 0
    Volume Flags: 0x00000002  (Not Case Sensitive) (Has Copy)
                 CRC: 0x44E66237 (correct)
                guid: 61FF07A3-0000-0000-0029-23480000BE18
   Label: This is a volume label for this FYSFS volume.
```

The two bitmaps are next, the first at LSN 17 (0x0000A000) and the second at LSN 22 (0x0000AA00). Since 55 50 is 01010101b 01010000b, this means that the first six entries are occupied, four for the root directory, and one each for the two files.

Listing 10-2: Example: Bitmap(s)

```
0000A000   55 50 00 00 00 00 00 00-00 00 00 00 00 00 00 00
  . . .
0000AA00   55 50 00 00 00 00 00 00-00 00 00 00 00 00 00 00
```

The first entry in the root directory is the first file on the volume. Its Name and FAT entries fit within the first slot. The second file's name is a long file name and therefore occupies three slots.

Listing 10-3: Example: Root Directory

```
0000B400   54 4F 4C 53 01 00 00 00-00 00 00 00 00 01 E3 00
0000B410   33 FF 2F 4F 33 FF 2F 4F-7F 0A 00 00 00 00 00 00
0000B420   00 00 00 00 00 00 00 00-00 00 09 00 00 00 00 00
0000B430   66 69 6C 65 73 2E 74 78-74 00 00 00 04 00 00 00
0000B440   00 00 00 00 00 00 00 00-00 00 00 00 00 00 00 00
0000B450   00 00 00 00 00 00 00 00-00 00 00 00 00 00 00 00
0000B460   00 00 00 00 00 00 00 00-00 00 00 00 00 00 00 00
0000B470   00 00 00 00 00 00 00 00-00 00 00 00 00 00 00 00
```

```
FYSFS Slot (0x0000B400)
                sig: 0x534C4F54  ('SLOT')
```

```
            Attribute: 0x00000001  Archive
                 resv: 00 00 00 00 00
          Fat Entries: 1
                  CRC: 0xE3
              scratch: 0x00
              Created: 0x4F2FFF33
        Last accessed: 0x4F2FFF33
            File Size: 2687
         Fat Continue: 0
        Name Continue: 0
                Flags: 0x0000
          Name Length: 9
                resv1: 00 00 00 00 00
                 name: files.txt
                 fats: 0x00000004,


0000B480   54 4F 4C 53 01 00 00 00-00 00 00 00 00 00 25 00
0000B490   33 FF 2F 4F 33 FF 2F 4F-E0 09 00 00 00 00 00 00
0000B4A0   00 00 00 00 02 00 00 00-00 00 50 00 00 00 00 00
0000B4B0   61 5F 66 69 6C 65 5F 6E-61 6D 65 5F 74 68 61 74
0000B4C0   5F 68 61 73 5F 61 5F 6C-6F 6E 67 5F 66 69 6C 65
0000B4D0   5F 6E 61 6D 65 5F 74 6F-5F 75 73 65 5F 6D 75 6C
0000B4E0   74 69 70 6C 65 5F 64 69-72 65 63 74 6F 72 79 5F
0000B4F0   73 6C 6F 74 73 5F 74 6F-5F 73 68 6F 77 5F 68 6F
```

FYSFS Slot (0x0000B480)
```
                  sig: 0x534C4F54   ('SLOT')
            Attribute: 0x00000001  Archive
                 resv: 00 00 00 00 00
          Fat Entries: 0
                  CRC: 0x25
              scratch: 0x00
              Created: 0x4F2FFF33
        Last accessed: 0x4F2FFF33
            File Size: 2528
         Fat Continue: 0
        Name Continue: 2
                Flags: 0x0000
          Name Length: 80
                resv1: 00 00 00 00 00
name: a_file_name_that_has_a_long_file_name_to_use_
                      multiple_directory_slots_to_show_ho


0000B500   45 4D 41 4E 01 00 00 00-03 00 00 00 20 00 44 00
0000B510   77 5F 74 6F 5F 75 73 65-5F 61 5F 63 6F 6E 74 69
0000B520   6E 75 61 74 69 6F 6E 5F-73 6C 6F 74 2E 74 78 74
```

```
0000B530   00 00 00 00 00 00 00 00-00 00 00 00 00 00 00 00
0000B540   00 00 00 00 00 00 00 00-00 00 00 00 00 00 00 00
0000B550   00 00 00 00 00 00 00 00-00 00 00 00 00 00 00 00
0000B560   00 00 00 00 00 00 00 00-00 00 00 00 00 00 00 00
0000B570   00 00 00 00 00 00 00 00-00 00 00 00 00 00 00 00
```

```
FYSFS Continue Slot (0x0000B500)
              sig: 0x4E414D45   ('NAME')
         Previous: 1
             Next: 3
          Entries: 32
            Flags: 0x0000   (Using 32-bit fats)
              CRC: 0x44
          scratch: 0x00
             name: w_to_use_a_continuation_slot.txt
```

```
0000B580   20 54 41 46 02 00 00 00-00 00 00 00 01 00 66 00
0000B590   05 00 00 00 00 00 00 00-00 00 00 00 00 00 00 00
0000B5A0   00 00 00 00 00 00 00 00-00 00 00 00 00 00 00 00
0000B5B0   00 00 00 00 00 00 00 00-00 00 00 00 00 00 00 00
0000B5C0   00 00 00 00 00 00 00 00-00 00 00 00 00 00 00 00
0000B5D0   00 00 00 00 00 00 00 00-00 00 00 00 00 00 00 00
0000B5E0   00 00 00 00 00 00 00 00-00 00 00 00 00 00 00 00
0000B5F0   00 00 00 00 00 00 00 00-00 00 00 00 00 00 00 00
```

```
FYSFS Continue Slot (0x0000B580)
              sig: 0x46415420   ('FAT ')
         Previous: 2
             Next: 0
          Entries: 1
            Flags: 0x0000   (Using 32-bit fats)
              CRC: 0x66
          scratch: 0x00
             fats: 0x00000005,
```

The first slot contains all of the file name characters and the FAT entries needed for the first file. However, the second file requires three slots in the root directory, the first is the standard SLOT style, containing most of the file name and the other information needed for the file, the second and third slots are the continuation slots, the first a NAME and the second, the FAT continuation slot containing the FAT entry(s).

Please remember that the image has a MBR and the FYSFS partition doesn't start until LBA 63.

As you might see, there are a few items that can be greatly improved upon. However, I created this file system when I was first starting Operating System development for the purpose of testing my code. You might do the same with yours and then move on to another, more efficient file system. The LeanFS for example. :-)

One of the flaws, I may call it, is that the cluster numbers for a subdirectory are located within the subdirectory, mainly the "SUB " slot. As the note stated in that section, this can create a problem if a cluster list within a CONT slot is not first identified with another slot. The reason I did it this way was to simplify reading subdirectories via a boot process. However, in general use, this makes it quite difficult and possibly problematic. Something you will want to avoid if you ever make your own file system.

Chapter 11 – The Lean File System

The Lean File System was written by Salvatore ISAJA for use with his Freedos-32 project. He named it, "Lean yet Effective Allocation and Naming", as a bacronym of the current FAT file system that was being used, FAT being the File Allocation Table file system and also used as the excess form of meat, compared to the heart of the meat, also called the Lean.

The term bacronym is uses as an opposite to the term acronym and is defined as a "reverse acronym". Salvatore took an acronym, LEAN, and created a name using the four letters of LEAN. An acronym is taking the first letters of an existing multiword name, just the opposite.

As most readers may know, I am very fond of file systems and have studied many. When I saw the Lean file system, it caught my eye more than other file systems and I have been hooked ever since.

I have had a bit of communication with Salvatore and he has added a few of my suggestions, which I am grateful for. Just recently he has allowed me to take this file system, add upon it, and release the next version.

I want to thank Salvatore for his work and allowing me to take it and include it within this book. To see more information and our work, please go to:
http://www.fysnet.net/leanfs/index.php

I have added to and extended the specification to version 0.7. Anything after version 0.6 is of my own doing and has no bearing on Salvatore or his work. I hold him free of any liability of my additions.

A Typical Lean Formatted Volume

Unlike the FAT or FYSFS file systems explained earlier in this book, which use lists of cluster numbers to store the block allocation information, the Lean file system uses Extents which are lists of consecutive blocks.

This file system also stores very little information about the file in the directory entries. All of this information is stored in Inodes stored in the first block of the file. Therefore, every file occupies at least one block on the disk, but allows for detailed information about the file.

Since very little information is stored in the directory entry, it makes for fast directory searches and allows for long file names.

The Lean file system uses bands to store the files on the volume. A band is a small number of sectors used as a bitmap for this band, followed by a larger set of blocks. Bands are then consecutively placed after each other. Imagine a flag similar to the United States of America flag, with 13 red and white stripes. Each of these stripes, starting at the beginning of the disk, would be considered a band, with the 13th stripe occupying the last blocks of the disk.

Each band's bitmap only represents the blocks within its own band. Therefore, if that bitmap becomes corrupt, it only corrupts that band of blocks. This also allows for disk access to be within certain parts of the disk for both file access and metadata access.

For example, comparing this and the FAT file system, if a file's data is stored at the end of the disk, for the FAT file system, the disk hardware would have to access metadata from the start of the disk and file data at the end of the disk for each access. For the Lean file system, it only has to access this one band for all disk access.

The Lean file system also allows for very large volumes and files and tries to optimize for very small files. This file system also allows for security access, mutli-user access, and other items such as symbolic links and file forks.

A typical Lean formatted volume will have multiple bands, each band having a bitmap representing the blocks within its own band. The first band will have at least two and up to 33 initial blocks reserved for the boot code and a Super Block. Except for the first band, all bands have their respected bitmaps occupy the first few blocks. Since the BIOS assumes the first sector of the first band is boot code, the first band must allocate its bitmap after this boot code and Super Block area.

For even better redundancy, this file system could use a journal. Therefore, with version 0.7 of this specification, a journal is introduced. See chapter 7 for an example.

This system allows up to and/or has the following limits.

Maximum Volume Size	2^{63} -1 blocks
Maximum File Size	2^{64} -1 bytes
Number of files	Arbitrary
Files per directory	Arbitrary
Filename length	4068 bytes, case sensitive, UTF-8
Extended Attributes	Arbitrary
Blocks Sizes	Any power of two, at least 256

Volume Block Size

Starting with version 0.7 of this specification, a Lean volume may have a block size larger than 512 bytes. For example, with newer media devices, a sector size of 4096 bytes may be common in the newer future. Therefore, a member in the Super Block specifies the block size this volume expects.

A Lean volume may support any block size of at least 256 bytes and larger as long as the size is a power of two. For example, a block size of 256, 512, 1024, 2048, and 4096 bytes are all valid block sizes.

Block size should not affect the function of any part of this specification. However, there are places that block sizes will affect certain structures. For example, currently we only use 168 bytes for the Super Block and on a typical 512-byte block, the remaining 344 bytes are reserved. However, on a 4096-byte block, this reserved space is now 3,928 bytes. The CRC check must be done on all bytes within the block, no matter the block size.

Another structure affected by the block size is the Indirect Block structure. The first part of the block is used for describing the Indirect Block with the remaining portion of the block used for Extents. With a 512-byte block, this leaves room for 38 Extents. However, with a 4096-byte block size, this extends this count to 336 Extents.

Another location would be the area after the Inode Structure. This area is used for either Extended Attributes or the start of the file's data.

No matter the size of the block, a single entry in the bitmap represents a single block.

See each subject noted above for more about the effects on block sizes for that subject.

The Boot Blocks and Super Block

Each Lean formatted volume may reserve up to the first 32 blocks for the boot code and data. These blocks are used to load and boot the volume, or at least find and load a loader file to do it.

Unlike the FAT file system and more like the FYSFS file system, this file system has a Super Block to describe the items within this volume. This Super Block does not have a set location, however. It may reside anywhere within the first 33 blocks of the disk. It is up to the code to find this Super Block and verify its contents.

I don't remember if I ever asked Salvatore why the location of the Super Block was not fixed. Obviously, it cannot be in the first block. His specification comments a little on why, but I think the main reason is to have the Super Block information directly after the boot code, while saving a few extra blocks.

The Lean specification states that all blocks before the Super Block, must be used only for the purpose of the boot process. No other information may be stored within this space. The first band's bitmap then follows the Super Block.

The figure below shows a typical layout of a Lean formatted volume.

Figure 11-1: Typical Lean Volume

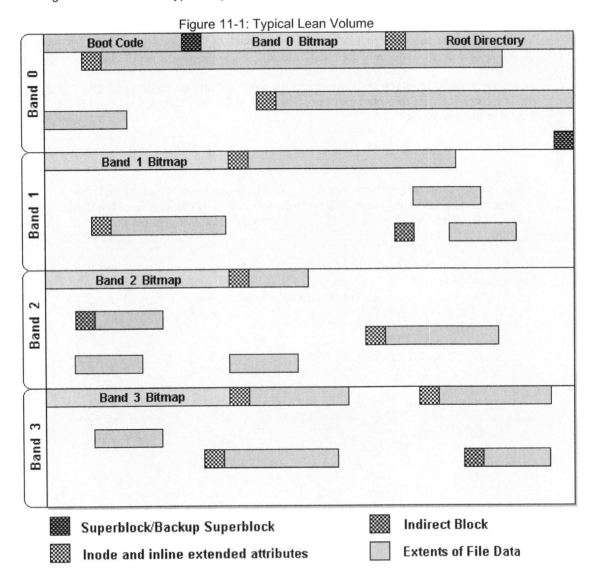

If the volume was used on a Legacy BIOS system, the first few blocks would be needed for the boot code, which could use up to 32 blocks, the Super Block would follow at the 33rd block, and then the first band's bitmap would follow that. This may use up to the first 33 blocks of the disk for the boot code and Super Block.

However, on newer machines that boot using EFI, this boot code is no longer needed since the system will boot using the installed firmware. Since no boot code is needed, in theory, the Super Block could now be placed in the first block of the disk, with the bitmap starting at the second block. This would save 32 blocks.

However, to be safe, since the drive could be removed and placed in a Legacy machine, the first block must be reserved for boot code only. With this in mind, the Super Block must not be in the first block.

Therefore, the Super Block must be one of the blocks from LBA 1 to LBA 32 inclusively.

 If no boot code is used, whether it be a EFI based system, or a non-bootable volume on a Legacy system, it is recommended that the first block of the disk have a minimal amount of 16-bit code to simply show an error message and halt.

The Super Block contains all the information needed to mount the volume and has the format listed below.

Listing 11-1: LeanFS Super Block

```
// =-=-=-=-=-=-=-=-=-=-=-=-=-=-=-=-=-=-=-=-=-=-=-=-=-=-=-=-
// LeanFS Super Block
struct S_LEAN_SUPER {
  bit32u checksum;          // bit32u sum of all fields.
  bit32u magic;             // 0x4E41454C ('LEAN')
  bit16u fs_version;        // 0x0007 = 0.7
  bit8u  pre_alloc_count;   // count -1 of contiguous blocks
  bit8u  log_blocks_per_band; // 1 << log_blocks_per_band
  bit32u state;             // bit 0: unmounted, bit 1: error
  struct S_GUID guid;       // Universally Unique IDentifier
  bit8u  volume_label[64];  // UTF-8 volume label
  bit64u block_count;       // Total number of blocks
  bit64u free_block_count;  // Number of free blocks
  bit64u primary_super;     // block of primary Super Block
  bit64u backup_super;      // block of backup Super Block
  bit64u bitmap_start;      // first bands bitmap
  bit64u root_inode;        // root directory Inode
  bit64u bad_inode;         // bad blocks Inode
  bit64u journal_inode;     // journal Inode
  bit8u  log_block_size;    // 1 << n = size of a block
```

```
    bit8u   reserved0[7];      // padding
    bit8u   reserved[344];     // zeros (remainder of block)
};
```

The Super Block contains security and integrity measures to make sure that the data is accurate before it is used. The Checksum field is calculated on all bytes of the whole block. This calculation is shown below.

Listing 11-2: LeanFS CRC Calculation
```
/* Always skip the first dword since it is the crc field.
 *   The CRC is calculated as:
 *        crc = 0;
 *        loop (n times)
 *           crc = ror(crc, 1) + dword[x]
 */
bit32u lean_calc_crc(const void *ptr, unsigned int size) {
    bit32u crc = 0;
    const bit32u *p = (const bit32u *) ptr;

    size /= 4;
    for (unsigned int i=1; i<size; i++)
       crc = (crc << 31) + (crc >> 1) + p[i];

    return crc;
}
```

The Magic field is used to verify that this data block is actually what you are expecting.

The Version field should also be checked. As of this writing, only version 0.7 is allowed.

This file system will try to allocate consecutive blocks and pre-allocate blocks as allocation takes place. The number of blocks to pre-allocate is in the Pre-Allocate Count field of the Super Block. For example, when creating a file and allocating a block for the Inode, your driver should allocate Pre-Allocate Count blocks. This will give one for the Inode, and already have the others allocated when the file grows.

The Log Blocks per Band field indicates the count of blocks per band. The count of blocks must be a power of 2. Except for the last bitmap (which could also be the first and only), a bitmap must be fully occupied. Therefore, a band must have a minimum size associated with the block size. For 512-byte blocks, a band must be no less than 4096 blocks, since 4096 blocks will occupy 512 bytes of bitmap. For 4096-byte blocks, a band must be no less than 32768 blocks since 32768 blocks will occupy 4096 bytes of bitmap.

The list on the next page shows the first five allowed sizes for the Log Blocks per Band field.

✓   256-byte blocks: 11 (2048 blocks = 256 bytes of bitmap)
✓   512-byte blocks: 12 (4096 blocks = 512 bytes of bitmap)
✓ 1024-byte blocks: 13 (8192 blocks = 1024 bytes of bitmap)
✓ 2048-byte blocks: 14 (16384 blocks = 2048 bytes of bitmap)
✓ 4096-byte blocks: 15 (32768 blocks = 4096 bytes of bitmap)

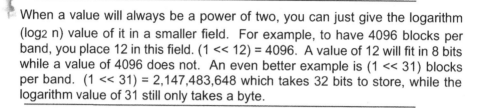

When a value will always be a power of two, you can just give the logarithm ($\log_2 n$) value of it in a smaller field. For example, to have 4096 blocks per band, you place 12 in this field. (1 << 12) = 4096. A value of 12 will fit in 8 bits while a value of 4096 does not. An even better example is (1 << 31) blocks per band. (1 << 31) = 2,147,483,648 which takes 32 bits to store, while the logarithm value of 31 still only takes a byte.

The State field uses bits 1:0 to indicate the state of the volume. Bit 0, when set, indicates that this volume is currently unmounted. When your system shuts down and unmounts this volume, you should set this bit. Bit 1 is used to indicate if there was an error found on this volume the last time a check was done. The remaining bits in this field should be preserved.

The Universally Unique Identifier field is set at format time. This is to uniquely identify this volume. There are numerous ways to create this field. This file system does not specify how, as long as you make it as unique as possible.

The Volume Label field is the volume's label. It is up to 64 bytes of UTF-8 encoded characters and is NULL terminated.

The Block Count field is the count of blocks in the volume. This is all of the blocks from Logical Block Number (LBN) zero to the last block in the volume.

The Free Block Count field is used as a hint to the system of how many free blocks there are. It should be kept up to date and accurate on every read of the Super Block. It doesn't have to be written to the Super Block each time you allocate or free a block, you just need to make sure that when the Super Block is ever read, it is accurate. One way to do this is to keep track of the free block count using a static variable in your driver. Then if the Super Block is ever read, update the data by either first writing to the Super Block, or simply updating the data read from the Super Block, not forgetting to update the CRC field either way.

The Primary Super and Backup Super fields indicate which zero-based block the Primary Super Block and Backup Super Block exist, respectively. The Backup Super field is important when trying to find and verify that there is a valid backup Super Block. The Primary Super field is important when verifying the current Super Block. If you didn't read the Super Block from the block indicated in this field, this Super Block may not be valid.

Since the first band's bitmap does not start at the base of the first band, the Bitmap Start field in the Super Block indicates where it starts and is a zero-based value from the start of the volume.

The Root Inode field indicates the first block of the Root Directory. It is usually the first data block in the first band. However, this is not mandatory, though if the volume is ever corrupt, it is easier to find the root if it is in this position.

The Bad Inode field is the block of the Bad Inode file. This is a normal file which happens to have all of its extents point to bad blocks on the media. i.e.: There is an extent for every bad block on the media. For example, if blocks 12345 through 12347 are bad, this Inode has an extent with a base of 12345 and a count of 3. If this field is zero, there are no known bad blocks on the disk.

The Journal field, when non-zero, points to an Inode containing the Journal information. See later in this chapter for more information on a Journal.

The Log Block Size field is the size of the block when this volume was created. It is a value from 8 to n, with 9 representing a block size of 512 bytes, 10 being 1024 bytes, and so on. i.e.: the block size is calculated as $1<< n$. Please see the note in the previous section about using this field.

The Backup Super Block
This file system requires a backup of the Super Block to be stored in the last block of the first band. This backup should be written to any time the primary Super Block is written to. It is suggested that the Primary be written to first, and only after a successful write, the backup to be written.

The Bitmap
The bitmap within each band holds a single bit representation of the corresponding block in that band. If the bit is set, the block is used. If it is clear, the block is free for use. The first block of the band is represented in bit 0 of the first byte of the bitmap, block 1 by bit 1, etc.

Note that bit 0 is the least significant bit of the byte which is actually the 8th bit from the left. Therefore, when looking from left to right, LBA 7 is represented, then LBA 6, down to LBA 0, followed by LBA 15, then LBA 14, etc.

Except for the first band, each band's bitmap starts at the first block of that band and has the bitmap marked as used for those blocks. Since bands use a power of 2-count of blocks, all bits in all but maybe the last bitmap are used. The last bitmap may contain bits that would point to blocks past the end of the volume. These bits that would point to blocks past the end of the volume are considered undefined.

Root Directory Entries

The Lean file system contains a count of blocks, stored as files, containing directory entries for the root directory and any sub-directories. These blocks contain just enough information to hold the file name, minimal type, and Inode block number of the files on the disk.

A directory entry contains a number of 16-byte records to hold this information, the first record to hold the Inode, type, number of records in this entry, length of the filename, and the start of the file name. Then there is a number of remaining needed 16-byte records holding the remaining part of the file name.

The first record of the entry contains the format listed below with Figure 11-2 showing an example.

Listing 11-3: LeanFS Directory Entry

```
// =-=-=-=-=-=-=-=-=-=-=-=-=-=-=-=-=-=-=-=-=-=-=-=-=-=-=-=-
// LeanFS Directory Entry
struct S_LEAN_DIRENTRY {
  bit64u inode;       // The inode number.
  bit8u  type;        // Entry type.
  bit8u  rec_len;     // total record len in 16 byte units.
  bit16u name_len;    // total length of name.
  bit8u  name[4];     // Start of UTF-8 name
};
```

Figure 11-2: LeanFS Root Entry

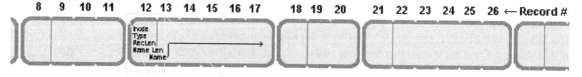

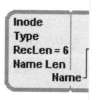

Inode
Type
RecLen = 6
Name Len
        Name

- Each record is 16 bytes in size.
- The first record of an entry holds the Inode, Type, Record Length (count of 16-byte records), Name Length (in chars), and the first part of the Name.
- The remaining records in the entry hold the remaining part of the name.

The Inode field is the Inode number of the file, the starting block of the file. This is the zero-based block of the file and contains the detailed information about this file. Inodes are discussed later in this chapter.

The Type field contains a brief type of the file. It may contain one of the following five values. These values are extracted from the Inode's Attribute field.

Table 11-1: Lean Directory Record: Type

Value	Description
0	No file type (Empty)
1	Regular File
2	Directory
3	Symbolic Link

 The reason the directory entry contains this field is so that when the system searches for files, it does not have to read the Inode of each file each time it does a search. This makes for much faster searching.

The Record Length field is the count of 16-byte records in this entry. Every entry will contain at least 1 and depending on the length of the file name, may contain up to 254 more.

 If an entry can contain a total of 255 records and the first record contains 12 bytes of metadata, a file name has a length limit of (254 * 16) + 4 bytes, giving a max name length of 4,068 bytes of UTF-8 chars.

The Name Length field contains the count of bytes used to store the file name. The name may or may not be null terminated, though this length field only indicates the number of bytes used, not counting the optional null terminator.

The remaining four bytes of the first record and any remaining 16-byte records contain the bytes used to store the file name. The name is stored in UTF-8 encoding. All remaining records in the entry must be consecutively one after another.

 See Appendix D for Unicode encoded characters.

Each directory block will contain these records. If a record is not used, it contains all zeros, except for the rec_len field. A directory block must have each record allocated. i.e.: the last record in the block must occupy all of the remaining records in the block, or if there are too many to fit in one record entry, multiple entries must be used to occupy all remaining records. However, there only needs to be enough records to fill the Inode's FileSize field. i.e.: If the Inode of this directory's file size is 1,000 bytes, only the first 1,000 bytes must have valid directory entries. Any remaining space within the last block or pre-allocated blocks can be ignored.

In any directory, two entries are required and are to be the first two entries. The first is the 'dot' entry. This one is to have a name of '.', a single period. This entry must be a hard link to this directory's Inode. This is called the Self Pointer. The next entry is the 'dotdot' entry, or the Parent Pointer. It is identical to the first entry except that it contains two dots, '..'. It is a hard link to the parent's directory Inode. If this is the root directory, it is a hard link to the root directory, itself. A driver may choose to not show these two entries for the Root Directory.

Note that all directories, including the Root Directory, is actually a file with an Inode, which is described in the next section.

Inodes

Files are stored on the disk using Inodes. A file contains an Inode structure in the first block of the file. Each file must contain an Inode. An Inode number is the zero-based block number of the block that contains the Inode. Therefore, every file will have a unique Inode number.

This Inode stores all the information about the file including the count and location of blocks allocated, directly or indirectly, to store the file. This Inode has the format listed below.

Listing 11-4: LeanFS Inode

```
// =-=-=-=-=-=-=-=-=-=-=-=-=-=-=-=-=-=-=-=-=-=-=-=-=-=-=-==
// LeanFS Inode
struct S_LEAN_INODE {
  bit32u checksum;         // bit32u sum of all fields
  bit32u magic;            // 0x45444F4E  ('NODE')
  bit8u  extent_count;     // count of extents
  bit8u  reserved[3];      // reserved
  bit32u indirect_count;   // indirect blocks owned by file
  bit32u links_count;      // hard links
  bit32u uid;              // currently reserved, set to 0
  bit32u gid;              // currently reserved, set to 0
  bit32u attributes;       // attributes
  bit64u file_size;        // file size
  bit64u block_count;      // count of blocks used
  bit64s acc_time;         // last accessed
  bit64s sch_time;         // status change
  bit64s mod_time;         // last modified
  bit64s cre_time;         //         created
  bit64u first_indirect;   // first indirect block
  bit64u last_indirect;    // last indirect block
```

```
    bit64u fork;
    bit64u extent_start[LEAN_INODE_EXTENT_CNT];
    bit32u extent_size[LEAN_INODE_EXTENT_CNT];
};
```

As with the Super Block, the Inode also has a Checksum field. This field is calculated the same way and calculated on only the size of the Inode. This size is always 176 bytes.

The Magic field is used to verify the information in this block. If it does not contain the value specified, you should not trust this block as a valid Inode.

The Extent Count field is the count of extents used within this Inode. See later in this chapter for information on Extents.

The Indirect Count field is used to indicate how many indirect blocks are used within this file. Indirect blocks allow for more extents, and is discussed later in this chapter.

The Links Count field is used to indicate how many hard links reference this Inode. When a call to delete a file is found, the system should decrement this value. Only when this value is zero should the system delete this Inode. If this value is still greater than zero, there are other hard links pointing to this Inode. A hard link is considered an Inode that is linked to another Inode. For example, all sub-directories will have a parent directory and these sub-directories may contain sub-directories themselves. Therefore, a sub-directory may have a count of 3 hard links. The parent pointing to this Inode, the self-pointer, and a child sub-directory's parent pointer. If this is a forked Inode, described later, this is the count of Inodes pointing to this forked Inode, including itself. The figure below shows and example.

Figure 11-3: Hard Links

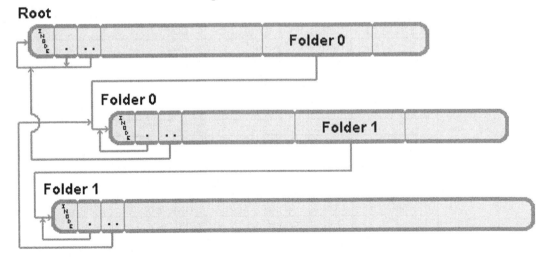

This mechanism is used so that you can't delete a (sub)directory when it contains child sub-directories. For example, a sub-directory that has an Inode Hard Link count of 3 or more, contains links to it, most likely child sub-directories. However, if the link count is 2, you can safely remove the sub-directory, since the two links are the self-pointer and the parent's directory entry.

Link counts are also used with Forks. An arbitrary amount of Inodes can link to a single Fork Inode, described later in this chapter. Only when the Hard Link count is one for regular files and two for sub-directories, can you safely remove the fork or sub-directory.

In the example on the previous page, the Root Directory Inode has a Hard Link count of 3, two self-pointers and one sub-directory pointing to it. The 'Folder 0' sub-directory also has 3 hard links, a self-pointer, a pointer from the Root Directory, and a child sub-directory called 'Folder 1'. The 'Folder 1' sub-directory only has 2 hard links, the self-pointer and the pointer from the parent folder, 'Folder 1'.

Back to the Inode. The UID and GID fields are currently defined as unused and should be reserved and preserved. However, these fields may be designed to be used to identify what user is, local or global, or may currently be accessing this file.

The Attributes field is now the more detailed attribute of the file. The following table shows these values.

Table 11-2: Lean Inode: Attribute

Value	Description
(1 << 0)	Other: Execute permission
(1 << 1)	Other: Write permission
(1 << 2)	Other: Read permission
(1 << 3)	Group: Execute permission
(1 << 4)	Group: Write permission
(1 << 5)	Group: Read permission
(1 << 6)	Owner: Execute permission
(1 << 7)	Owner: Write permission
(1 << 8)	Owner: Read permission
(1 << 9)	Reserved
(1 << 10)	Other: Execute as User ID
(1 << 11)	Other: Execute as Group ID
(1 << 12)	Hidden File
(1 << 13)	System File
(1 << 14)	Archive
(1 << 15)	Synchronous Updates
(1 << 16)	Don't update last access time
(1 << 17)	Don't move file blocks
(1 << 18)	Keep pre-allocated blocks on close
(1 << 19)	End of Inode contains Extended Attr.

(1 << 20)	Reserved
...	
(1 << 28)	Reserved
(1 << 29)	File Type: Regular
(2 << 29)	File Type: Directory
(3 << 29)	File Type: Symbolic Link
(4 << 29)	File Type: Fork

 Please note that if you update the File Type bits in this field, you must also update the directory entry Type field for this Inode, though that won't happen very often.

The File Size field simply shows the size of the file in bytes. It is a 64-bit value allowing for very large files.

The Block Count field is the count of blocks allocated for the file by the Inode. This includes all blocks in all extents including pre-allocated blocks and includes the Inode itself.

The Last Access, Status Change, Last Modified, and Created time fields are the signed count of microseconds from 1970-01-01 0:00:00.0 UTC for their respective functions. The Last Access field is updated every time the file is accessed. The Status Change field is updated every time the Inode is changed. The Last Modified field is updated every time the file data is changed, and the Created field is set at file creation.

The First and Last Indirect fields contain the blocks of the first indirect and last indirect used by this Inode. If there is only one Indirect used, they both point to the same block. If no Indirect is used, they both contain zero.

The Fork field contains a block value used for Extended Attributes. See later in this chapter on Extended Attributes and the use of Forks.

The next two fields contain the array of Direct Extents contained within this Inode for the file. See the next section on how to use Direct and Indirect Extents. Note that the Inode block is included in the extents described below.

Extents
The Inode contains an array of Direct Extents and then allows Indirect Extents if the file block count exceeds these Direct Extents.

An extent is a two-field array of a starting block field and a count of consecutive blocks field, and is shown on the next page.

Listing 11-5: LeanFS Extent

```
bit64u extent_start[ ];
bit32u extent_size[ ];
```

For example, the following list of blocks might be used to store a file's data, listed vertically in three columns.

0x00003425	0x00004539	0x00004542
0x00003426	0x0000453A	0x000062A9
0x00003427	0x0000453B	0x000062AA
0x00003428	0x0000453C	0x000062AB
0x00003466	0x0000453D	0x000062AC
0x00003467	0x0000453E	0x000062AD
0x00004536	0x0000453F	0x000062AE
0x00004537	0x00004540	0x000062AF
0x00004538	0x00004541	0x000062B0

This would create a count of four extents.

```
extent_start[0] = 0x00003425;
  extent_size[0] = 4;
extent_start[1] = 0x00003466;
  extent_size[1] = 2;
extent_start[2] = 0x00004536;
  extent_size[2] = 13;
extent_start[3] = 0x000062A9;
  extent_size[3] = 8;
```

The Inode allows for six (LEAN_INODE_EXTENT_CNT) of these extents to reside within the Inode. Therefore, once you have read the Inode, you have the four extents listed above.

What happens when there are more than six extents? This is where Indirect Extents come into play. An Indirect Extent is a block full of extents and has the format listed below.

Listing 11-6: LeanFS Indirect Extent

```
// =-=-=-=-=-=-=-=-=-=-=-=-=-=-=-=-=-=-=-=-=-=-=-=-=-=--
// Lean Indirect Block
struct S_LEAN_INDIRECT {
   bit32u checksum;          // bit32u sum of all fields
   bit32u magic;             // 0x58444E49 ('INDX')
   bit64u block_count;       // blocks in this indirect
   bit64u inode;             // inode this belongs to
   bit64u this_block;        // block this indirect occupies
   bit64u prev_indirect;     // block of previous indirect
   bit64u next_indirect;     // block of next indirect
```

```
    bit16u extent_count;      // extents used in this indirect
    bit8u  reserved0[2];      // reserved
    bit32u reserved1;         // reserved
    bit64u extent_start[LEAN_INDIRECT_EXTENT_CNT];
    bit32u extent_size[LEAN_INDIRECT_EXTENT_CNT];
    //bit8u  reserved2[];      // reserved (field may not exist)
};
```

This extends the Extent count by 38 (LEAN_INDIRECT_EXTENT_CNT) extents for each Indirect Extent used, when a 512-byte block is used.

Since an Indirect Extent block uses all of the block, if a block size is larger than 512 bytes, more extents are allowed. For example, if the block size is 4096 bytes, there is enough room for 336 extents in each Indirect Extent block, leaving 8 unused bytes at the end of the block (as the reserved2 field above).

As with other structures in the Lean file system, the Check Sum and Magic fields are used to identify the block along with integrity checks. The This Block field is also used for integrity to make sure that this Indirect actually does reside in this block.

The Block Count field identifies how many blocks are addressed using this Indirect.

The Inode field stores the Inode number that owns this Indirect.

The Previous and Next Indirect fields point to the previous and next Indirect blocks respectively. If either are zero, there are no more in that direction.

The Extent Count field indicates the count of valid extents used in this Indirect block, up to LEAN_INDIRECT_EXTENT_CNT, depending on the block size used.

The figure on the next page shows an example of an Inode and three Indirects.

An addition to this file system would be a double indirect system. A double indirect block would be a list of block numbers with those corresponding blocks holding Indirect blocks. However, since this file system allows unlimited Indirects, this isn't really needed. The double indirect technique is somewhat similar to Unix file systems.

A well-written system will try to keep all Indirect blocks together and close to the Inode. When possible, all blocks used for a file, Inode, Indirects, and any data blocks, should all be within the same Band using the same bitmap.

Figure 11-4: Extent/Indirect Example

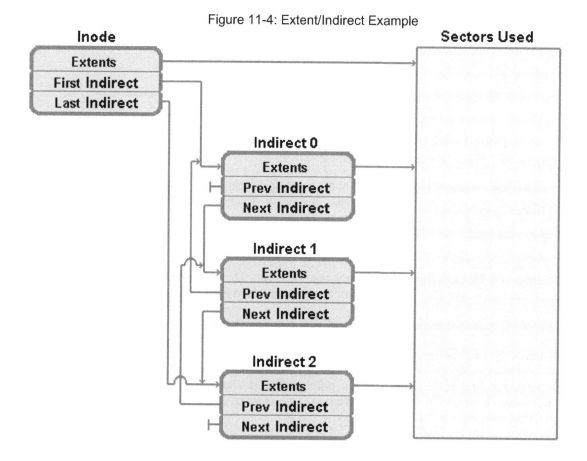

Symbolic Links

A Symbolic Link is a file containing only a path and file name to another file, either local or external, or relative or direct. This Symbolic Link file's attribute must be marked with a file type of LEAN_ATTR_IFLNK. The path and file name are stored using UTF-8 encoding and is not NULL terminated. The File Size field in the Inode indicates the length of the name in bytes.

 Clearing the LEAN_ATTR_EAS_IN_INODE file attribute flag (bit 19), and the technique described in the next section, it is possible to use only the single block of the Inode to store this Symbolic Link.

Storing Small Files

As with Symbolic Link files and other small files, the system can save space by not pre-allocating any extra blocks and storing the file data just after the Inode in the first and only block of the file. The advantage of this is that there is only one block allocated for the whole file, and there is no need to run through the extents. The disadvantage is that this is where the Extended Attributes may reside. You may either store the small file's contents in this area or store Extended Attributes. Either/or, not both.

To store the file's data after the Inode, start from the end of the Inode Structure and use all remaining bytes of that block. Please note that you can only store up to the block size minus the size of the Inode Structure in this area. Once the file's data size exceeds this limit, you must continue to store the data in the next block allocated in the extents.

To use this technique, make sure you clear the LEAN_ATTR_EAS_IN_INODE flag in the Inode's attributes.

Extended Attributes

This file system allows Extended Attributes, EAs, to be (optionally) stored in the unused part of the first block just after the Inode. EAs are attributes that are not defined globally and are only specific to the system using the attribute. EAs are not particularly portable and may or may not be understood by other systems. However, any system compatible with this file system must know and understand the way they are stored, even if it does not understand the content of the attribute.

Each attribute is stored with a 32-bit header to describe the length of the attribute and has a format of 0xNNVVVVVV. The high order byte, the NN part is the length of the attribute name, which starts right after the header. The lower 24-bits, the VVVVVV part is the length of the attribute's data and starts just after the name.

If the NN part is zero, this means an empty attribute and the VVVVVV part is used to find the next attribute. You can only use the space available after the Inode to the end of the block. If you need to store more Extended Attributes, you may use a Fork and place any remaining EAs in that Fork. See later on what a Fork is and how to use it.

If the LEAN_ATTR_EAS_IN_INODE is used, you must have at least one Extended Attribute, even if it is empty, and all of the space must be used. If this bit is clear, and Extended Attributes are present, a Fork must be used.

The Name part of the EA must be in UTF-8 encoding, however the data part has any format specific to the type of attribute it is. The listing on the next page shows an example of a simple Extended Attribute. Remember that the last entry must occupy the remaining area allocated, though not shown in this example.

Listing 11-7: Extended Attribute Example

```
00000000   0D 00 00 0C 45 6C 65 6D-65 6E 74 20 54 79 70 65
00000010   45 4C 4D 4E 54 32 33 38-32 33 34 41 43

   NNVVVVVV = 0x0C00000D

       Name = 'Element Type'
      Value = 'ELMNT238234AC'
```

Forks

When you don't have enough room after the Inode to store the desired Extended Attributes, you may use a Fork. A Fork is another system object with an Inode just like a file. However, this new Inode must have the LEAN_ATTR_IFFRK file type and attribute. Then you store the Extended Attributes in its file area just like a file. Be sure to store the new Inode's block number in the original Inode's Fork field.

Any Extended Attributes in a Fork must occupy all bytes of the file. I.e.: The length of all EAs combined, within this file, must be equal to the Inode's file size.

The new Inode must not have the LEAN_ATTR_EAS_IN_INODE flag set nor can it Fork itself. If a Fork is used, you may place some of the EAs in the area after the Inode of the original (parent) Inode, and the remaining EAs in the Forked Inode's file area.

So that you can have EAs and store the small file after the Inode in the original Inode, clear the LEAN_ATTR_EAS_IN_INODE flag in the original Inode, use that data area to store the file's data, then assign a new block and Inode in the Fork field. When a driver finds a non-zero value in the Fork field, it must assume that there are Extended Attributes within this fork. However, if the LEAN_ATTR_EAS_IN_INODE flag in the original Inode is not set, there are no EAs in this original Inode. If the LEAN_ATTR_EAS_IN_INODE flag is set and the Fork field is zero, there are only EAs stored in this Inode. If the LEAN_ATTR_EAS_IN_INODE flag is set and the Fork field is non-zero, there are EAs in this Inode just after the Inode Structure and there are EAs in the data area of the new Inode, the fork.

The Journal and an example implementation

As the term suggests, a journal is a record of something that takes place. We use a journal here for the purpose of keeping track of writes to the file system. Then using that journal, only committing to the file system when we know a commit will fully write.

An example journaling system would be when we open a file with write access, using the journal, we copy the complete file to a new place on the media and then use that Inode and file data throughout the period of the file being open. Then when we close the file we then, and only then, update the directory entry to point to this new Inode and delete the original Inode, freeing the original space.

By doing this, if the system was to crash during any write to the file, on system restore, the original Inode and file data will be intact since the directory entry points to it, instead of the new Inode. This means that the whole file system will be intact after a crash up to the point of an opened file. i.e.: Any file that was not currently open for write access at the time of the crash will be fully intact, only missing the new writes to that opened file.

When the system boots, the Lean file system driver could then search through the Journal and if any entries remain, do one of two things. It can either simply delete all data associated to any new Inode that was open during time of the crash, erasing any residue of the journaled file, or it can try to update the original file with the new file data. However, by doing the latter, there is a chance that the new data doesn't match the Inode data and file inconsistency can take place.

To keep track of which files are currently being journaled, we could use a standard Inode file containing journal entries, one for each opened file. The format of this file is shown in the figure on the next page and described next.

The data is stored as normal data in a normal Inode file, just like any other file and has the following format.

Listing 11-8: LeanFS Journal File

```
// =-=-=-=-=-=-=-=-=-=-=-=-=-=-=-=-=-=-=-=-=-=-=-=-
// Lean Journal File Header
struct S_LEAN_JOURNAL {
   bit32u checksum;      // sum of all fields in structure
   bit32u magic;         // 0x4C4E524A   ('JRNL')
   bit32u entry_cnt;     // count of journal entries
   bit32u padding;       // reserved and preserved
   bit8u  reserved[16];  // reserved and preserved
};

// Lean Journal Entry
struct S_LEAN_JOURNAL_ENTRY {
   bit64u new_inode;     // LBA (Inode Num) of new Inode
   bit64u org_inode;     // LBA (Inode Num) of orignal Inode
   bit32u flags;         // Flags: valid entry, etc.
   bit32u resv[3];       // for future expansion
};
```

Figure 11-5: Journal File

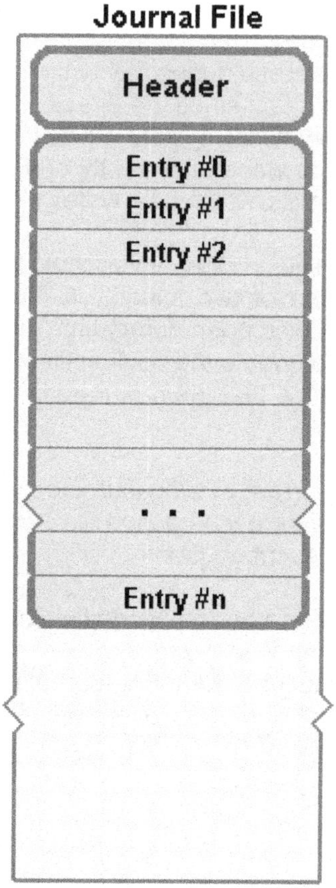

Journal File

Header
Entry #0
Entry #1
Entry #2
. . .
Entry #n

The header contains a little information to verify that this is what it is as well as how many entries are currently in the journal.

The checksum field is calculated on the header itself as well as all of the entries within the file, specified by the entry count field.

The magic field is simply a magic number to make sure we are actually the Journal header.

The entry_cnt field is the count of entries after the header. This count may include used and unused entries.

Note that the Journal Inode may indicate and allocate a file size of much more than the allotted Journal entry count. For example, the Inode might allocate and indicate that there are 4096 bytes available for this Journal though the

entry count may only use a small portion of it. The Journal file may grow or
shrink as needed with any space after the last entry ignored.

The padding and reserved fields are used for future expansion and must be preserved
when written to.

A Journal Entry describes a current entry, a file that has been opened for write-access. It
contains the original Inode number, the new Inode number, and a few flags about the entry.

The new_inode field is the number of the current opened inode, the inode that contains the
new data. It is just like any other inode file.

The org_inode field is the number of the original, unmodified inode this entry is replacing.

The flags field holds a few flags about the entry. At this time, only bit 0 is used and set to
indicate that this is a valid entry. If this bit is clear, this entry is not used. All other bits in
this field should be zero and preserved when written to.

The resv field should be preserved when written to.

Remember that this is just an example implementation, you must also consider a few things
when implementing a Journal. As far as the Virtual File System of your OS is concerned,
it has no idea that there is a Journal. It simply contains a file pointer and passes this
information along to your Lean system driver. The Lean system driver must catch all Inode
access and direct access through the Journal before it loads any Inodes.

For example, when reading from an Inode, if the Inode is currently in the Journal, the
Journal must change the Inode number to the new Inode number and then pass it back to
the read function. The same must be done for any other access to an Inode. If the Inode
number is found in the Journal, as an org_inode vaue, the Journal must change it to the
new_inode value then pass it back. If the inode is not found in the Journal, simply pass
back the same Inode number.

This example makes for a very simple Journalling system. Also, if your Lean system driver
does not support Journalling, there is no difference to the file system if not used. A Lean
Journalling volume may be accessed as a non-Journalling volume without any problems.

There are other things that could be added to make it a more reliable system. For example,
if a certain amount of time has passed since the Journal entry was created, the system
could update the Directory Entry to the new Inode, creating a new Entry as needed.
However, this can cause other issues as well. If there was a crash while updating the
Directory Entry, you now have two unusable Inodes. To get around this, you would have
to add a lot more functionality to your Journalling system.

Remember that the implementation shown in this section is just an example, a way that a journal could be implemented. The Lean File System Specification does not specify an implementation. A journaling implementation is specific to the driver that implemented it.

Bad Blocks

If the Bad Inode field in the Super Block is non-zero, it will point to a normal system file, in which the extents, both direct and indirect (if any), encompass any bad blocks on the media from block 0 to blockCount - 1.

This is considered a pseudo file, in that all bad blocks are allocated for the file's contents, including marking the bitmap accordingly, yet the actual contents of the file are undefined. By doing so, this pseudo file's extents will allocate and occupy all bad blocks in the file system.

The function and structure of this file is identical to all other files, except for the fact that only the book-keeping part of the file is stored on the disk. This being the Inode structure and its direct extents, and any optional indirect blocks as needed. As with any other Inode, this Inode may contain extended attributes, both inline and via a fork.

As for the file system, the use and function of this Inode is identical to any other Inode on the system, except that the actual file data is considered undefined, therefore not read or written.

Wrap Up

This file system is a very interesting file system, and I have it as the default file system of my operating system, FYSOS.

This file system allows for a general set of features. It allows very efficient storage of both very small and very large files. It is also very efficient in file name storage allowing short and long file names. It has numerous checks to make sure the system's objects hold their integrity.

In the remaining section of this book, I will show a few memory dumps of a 20 Meg sized volume, to show how a Super Block, bitmap(s), and Root Directory may look like, along with a few directory entries. This is so that you can compare your work. I have included the image in the \MAIN\FILESYS\IMAGES directory as LEANFS.IMG. The image has 16 blocks reserved for the boot code with the Super Block at LBN 16.

Listing 11-9: Example: Super Block

```
00009E00   DA B6 E4 2D 4C 45 41 4E-07 00 07 0C 01 00 00 00
00009E10   E8 01 FF 61 00 00 00 00-A5 56 E5 69 00 00 B2 57
00009E20   41 20 4C 61 62 65 6C 20-66 6F 72 20 61 20 4C 65
00009E30   61 6E 20 46 53 20 76 6F-6C 75 6D 65 2E 00 00 00
00009E40   00 00 00 00 00 00 00 00-00 00 00 00 00 00 00 00
00009E50   00 00 00 00 00 00 00 00-00 00 00 00 00 00 00 00
00009E60   60 27 00 00 00 00 00 00-10 1E 00 00 00 00 00 00
00009E70   10 00 00 00 00 00 00 00-FF 0F 00 00 00 00 00 00
00009E80   11 00 00 00 00 00 00 00-12 00 00 00 00 00 00 00
00009E90   00 00 00 00 00 00 00 00-00 00 00 00 00 00 00 00
00009EA0   09 00 00 00 00 00 00 00
```

```
LEAN FS Super Block (0x00009E00)
              Checksum: 0x2DE4B6DA
                 Magic: 0x4E41454C   (LEAN)
               Version:     0x0007   (0.07)
    Pre Allocate Count: 7
 Blocks per Band (log): 4096 (12)
                 State: 0x01 (errors = 0) (clean unmount = 1)
                  UUID: 61FF01E8-0000-0000-56A5-E5690000B257
                 Label: A Label for a Lean FS volume.
          Total blocks: 0x0000000000002760   (10080)
           Free blocks: 0x0000000000001E10   (7696)
     Primary Super LBA: 0x0000000000000010   (16)
      Backup Super LBA: 0x0000000000000FFF   (4095)
      Bitmap Start LBA: 0x0000000000000011   (17)
        Root Start LBA: 0x0000000000000012   (18)
         Bad Start LBA: 0x0000000000000000   (0)
     Journal Start LBA: 0x0000000000000000   (0)
      Block size (log): 512 (9)
             reserved0: 00 00 00 00 00 00 00
```

The bitmap in the first band will show all of the blocks marked used; boot, super, bitmap, root, and five files. Notice that the last bit in the bitmap, bit 7 in the last byte in the last row, is set. This is to mark that the Backup Super Block is present.

Listing 11-10: Example: Bitmap

```
0000A000   FF FF FF FF FF FF FF FF-FF FF FF FF FF FF FF FF
0000A010   FF FF FF FF FF FF FF FF-FF FF FF FF FF FF FF FF
           ... repeated ...
0000A100   FF FF FF FF FF FF FF FF-FF FF FF FF FF FF FF FF
0000A110   FF FF FF FF FF FF FF FF-FF FF FF FF FF FF FF FF
0000A120   FF FF FF FF FF FF FF FF-FF 1F 00 00 00 00 00 00
0000A130   00 00 00 00 00 00 00 00-00 00 00 00 00 00 00 00
```

```
0000A140  00 00 00 00 00 00 00 00-00 00 00 00 00 00 00 00
          ... repeated ...
0000A1E0  00 00 00 00 00 00 00 00-00 00 00 00 00 00 00 00
0000A1F0  00 00 00 00 00 00 00 00-00 00 00 00 00 00 00 80
```

Next is the Root Directory Inode.

Listing 11-11: Example: Root Directory

```
0000A200  CD 47 DD 43 4E 4F 44 45-01 00 00 00 00 00 00 00
0000A210  02 00 00 00 00 00 00 00-00 00 00 00 C0 01 04 40
0000A220  C0 00 00 00 00 00 00 00-10 00 00 00 00 00 00 00
0000A230  00 CE CC 7C 47 D7 05 00-00 CE CC 7C 47 D7 05 00
0000A240  00 CE CC 7C 47 D7 05 00-00 CE CC 7C 47 D7 05 00
0000A250  00 00 00 00 00 00 00 00-00 00 00 00 00 00 00 00
0000A260  00 00 00 00 00 00 00 00-12 00 00 00 00 00 00 00
0000A270  00 00 00 00 00 00 00 00-00 00 00 00 00 00 00 00
0000A280  00 00 00 00 00 00 00 00-00 00 00 00 00 00 00 00
0000A290  00 00 00 00 00 00 00 00-10 00 00 00 00 00 00 00
0000A2A0  00 00 00 00 00 00 00 00-00 00 00 00 00 00 00 00
```

```
LEAN FS Inode (0x0000A200)
                Checksum: 0x43DD47CD
                   Magic: 0x45444F4E   (NODE)
       Number of Extents: 1
                Reserved: 00 00 00
          Indirect Count: 0
             Links Count: 2
                     UID: 0x00000000 (0)
                     GID: 0x00000000 (0)
              Attributes: 0x400401C0
                 + Owner: read permission
                 + Owner: write permission
                 + Owner: execute permission
                 + Don't truncate file on close
                 + File Data starts after INODE
                 + File type: directory
               File Size: 0x00000000000000C0   (192)
             Block Count: 0x0000000000000010   (16)
             Last Access: (Saturday 05 February 2022   09:02:00)
      Status Change Time: (Saturday 05 February 2022   09:02:00)
       Last Modification: (Saturday 05 February 2022   09:02:00)
           File Creation: (Saturday 05 February 2022   09:02:00)
     First Indirect block: 0x0000000000000000 (0)
      Last Indirect block: 0x0000000000000000 (0)
                    Fork: 0x0000000000000000 (0)
        Extent 0:  start 0x00000012 (18), size 0x00000010 (16)
```

```
Extent 1:   start 0x00000000 (0), size 0x00000000 (0)
Extent 2:   start 0x00000000 (0), size 0x00000000 (0)
Extent 3:   start 0x00000000 (0), size 0x00000000 (0)
Extent 4:   start 0x00000000 (0), size 0x00000000 (0)
Extent 5:   start 0x00000000 (0), size 0x00000000 (0)
```

And the seven entries in the root directory.

Listing 11-12: Example: Entries

```
0000A2B0   12 00 00 00 00 00 00 00-02 01 01 00 2E 00 00 00
```

```
LEAN FS Directory Entry (0x0000A2B0)
              Inode: 0x0000000000000012   (18)
               Type: 0x02: Directory
         Record Len: 0x01: (16 bytes)
           Name Len: 0x01: (1)
               Name: .
```

```
0000A2C0   12 00 00 00 00 00 00 00-02 01 02 00 2E 2E 00 00
```

```
LEAN FS Directory Entry (0x0000A2C0)
              Inode: 0x0000000000000012   (18)
               Type: 0x02: Directory
         Record Len: 0x01: (16 bytes)
           Name Len: 0x02: (2)
               Name: ..
```

```
0000A2D0   22 00 00 00 00 00 00 00-01 02 08 00 62 73 6F 64
0000A2E0   2E 73 79 73 00 00 00 00-00 00 00 00 00 00 00 00
```

```
LEAN FS Directory Entry (0x0000A2D0)
              Inode: 0x0000000000000022   (34)
               Type: 0x01: Regular
         Record Len: 0x02: (32 bytes)
           Name Len: 0x08: (8)
               Name: bsod.sys
```

```
0000A2F0   29 00 00 00 00 00 00 00-01 02 0C 00 6B 65 72 6E
0000A300   65 6C 33 32 2E 73 79 73-00 00 00 00 00 00 00 00
```

```
LEAN FS Directory Entry (0x0000A2F0)
              Inode: 0x0000000000000029   (41)
               Type: 0x01: Regular
         Record Len: 0x02: (32 bytes)
           Name Len: 0x0C: (12)
               Name: kernel32.sys
```

```
0000A310  F9 03 00 00 00 00 00 00-01 02 0C 00 6B 65 72 6E
0000A320  65 6C 36 34 2E 73 79 73-00 00 00 00 00 00 00 00
```

LEAN FS Directory Entry (0x0000A310)
                Inode: 0x00000000000003F9   (1017)
                Type: 0x01: Regular
          Record Len: 0x02: (32 bytes)
          Name Len: 0x0C: (12)
                Name: kernel64.sys


```
0000A330  71 08 00 00 00 00 00 00-01 02 0A 00 6C 6F 61 64
0000A340  65 72 2E 73 79 73 00 00-00 00 00 00 00 00 00 00
```

LEAN FS Directory Entry (0x0000A330)
                Inode: 0x0000000000000871   (2161)
                Type: 0x01: Regular
          Record Len: 0x02: (32 bytes)
          Name Len: 0x0A: (10)
                Name: loader.sys


```
0000A350  2C 09 00 00 00 00 00 00-01 02 0A 00 73 79 73 74
0000A360  65 6D 2E 73 79 73 00 00-00 00 00 00 00 00 00 00
```

LEAN FS Directory Entry (0x0000A350)
                Inode: 0x000000000000092C   (2348)
                Type: 0x01: Regular
          Record Len: 0x02: (32 bytes)
          Name Len: 0x0A: (10)
                Name: system.sys

This image has a minimal installation of FYSOS with the necessary boot files.

The Inode for the first file, bsod.sys.

Listing 11-13: Example: Inode: bsod.sys
```
0000C200  58 0D E5 D7 4E 4F 44 45-01 00 00 00 00 00 00 00
0000C210  01 00 00 00 00 00 00 00-00 00 00 00 C0 41 00 20
0000C220  83 0C 00 00 00 00 00 00-07 00 00 00 00 00 00 00
0000C230  00 CE CC 7C 47 D7 05 00-00 CE CC 7C 47 D7 05 00
0000C240  00 CE CC 7C 47 D7 05 00-00 CE CC 7C 47 D7 05 00
0000C250  00 00 00 00 00 00 00 00-00 00 00 00 00 00 00 00
0000C260  00 00 00 00 00 00 00 00-22 00 00 00 00 00 00 00
0000C270  00 00 00 00 00 00 00 00-00 00 00 00 00 00 00 00
0000C280  00 00 00 00 00 00 00 00-00 00 00 00 00 00 00 00
0000C290  00 00 00 00 00 00 00 00-07 00 00 00 00 00 00 00
```

```
0000C2A0   00 00 00 00 00 00 00 00-00 00 00 00 00 00 00 00
```

LEAN FS Inode (0x0000C200)
                Checksum: 0xD7E50D58
                   Magic: 0x45444F4E   (NODE)
      Number of Extents: 1
                Reserved: 00 00 00
         Indirect Count: 0
            Links Count: 1
                     UID: 0x00000000 (0)
                     GID: 0x00000000 (0)
              Attributes: 0x200041C0
                + Owner: read permission
                + Owner: write permission
                + Owner: execute permission
                + Archive
                + File Data starts after INODE
                + File type: regular file
              File Size: 0x0000000000000C83 (3203)
            Block Count: 0x0000000000000007 (7)
            Last Access: (Saturday 05 February 2022   09:02:00)
    Status Change Time: (Saturday 05 February 2022   09:02:00)
     Last Modification: (Saturday 05 February 2022   09:02:00)
         File Creation: (Saturday 05 February 2022   09:02:00)
   First Indirect block: 0x0000000000000000 (0)
    Last Indirect block: 0x0000000000000000 (0)
                    Fork: 0x0000000000000000 (0)
        Extent 0:   start 0x00000022 (34), size 0x00000007 (7)
        Extent 1:   start 0x00000000 (0), size 0x00000000 (0)
        Extent 2:   start 0x00000000 (0), size 0x00000000 (0)
        Extent 3:   start 0x00000000 (0), size 0x00000000 (0)
        Extent 4:   start 0x00000000 (0), size 0x00000000 (0)
        Extent 5:   start 0x00000000 (0), size 0x00000000 (0)
```

The image has a MBR and the Lean partition starts at LBA 63.
```

Chapter 12 – The SFS File System

The Simple File System, or SFS, is another hobby file system created by a fellow hobbyist, Brendan Trotter. It is considered a *write-once* file system used for transferring files quite quickly. By write-once, it is assumed that you have an empty non-formatted partition or other removable media device where you can quickly write a number of files to it, then take that media to another system. Once written, it is assumed you will not write to it again, unless you completely erase the media and re-write all files, as the same modified files, or a new batch of files.

Even though this file system is assumed a write-once style file system, a properly written driver can modify files, add to, and even remove files from the media.

As the name implies, it is a very simple file system. There is a small Super Block, a Data Area, and an Index Area. There is no allocation scheme like the previous two file systems, having a cluster table or a bitmap. The Data Area is continuous from the beginning of the volume, then there are zero or more blocks before the Index Area which then occupies the remaining space of the volume.

Credit for the original design goes to Brendan Trotter and his original specification can be found at the following URL:

https://web.archive.org/web/20170315134201/https://www.d-rift.nl/combuster/vdisk/sfs.html

With Brendan's permission, I have added a few details and made a few changes. This chapter explains this new version of his file system, noting that it is no longer 100% compatible with his original design.

> The URL above uses the "way-back-machine" to display a page from a few years ago. I tried to go to the www.d-rift.nl address and for some reason, my browser flagged it as harmful.

The remaining information within this chapter, closely resembles the actual specification for this file system. This specification is in the `docs/` directory of the source code repository for this book. Please see Appendix A for more information on where to get this specification. Though this chapter covers most every aspect of this file system, please have a look at the specification for more details.

A Brief Summary

The Simple File System (SFS) contains a Super Block, a Reserved Area, a Data Block Area, a Free Space Area, and a Metadata area called the Index Data Area. Files are stored in sequential blocks leaving no fragmentation, allowing 64-bit addresses and sizes, and allows more than 16,320 bytes for path and file names. However, the SFS does not have features like permissions, symbolic information, or attributes like other files systems. The

SFS is intended to be mostly a write-once file system, though a properly written driver could easily and successfully use it as a read and write file system.

An Overlook of a Typical SFS Partition

There are a few items in a SFS volume that must be set to fixed values. The boot sector and location, size and location of the Super Block, and size and location of the Index Data Area.

The Boot Sector is always at Logical Block Number (LBN) 0. Also residing in LBN 0 is a Super Block that contains information about the volume. At the end of the volume resides the Index Data Area. This Index Data Area holds information about the files stored on the volume. Somewhere in-between the Super Block and this Index Data Area is the Data Block Area as well as the Free Block Area.

A typical SFS formatted volume will look something like what is shown in the figure below.

Figure 12-1: Typical SFS Volume

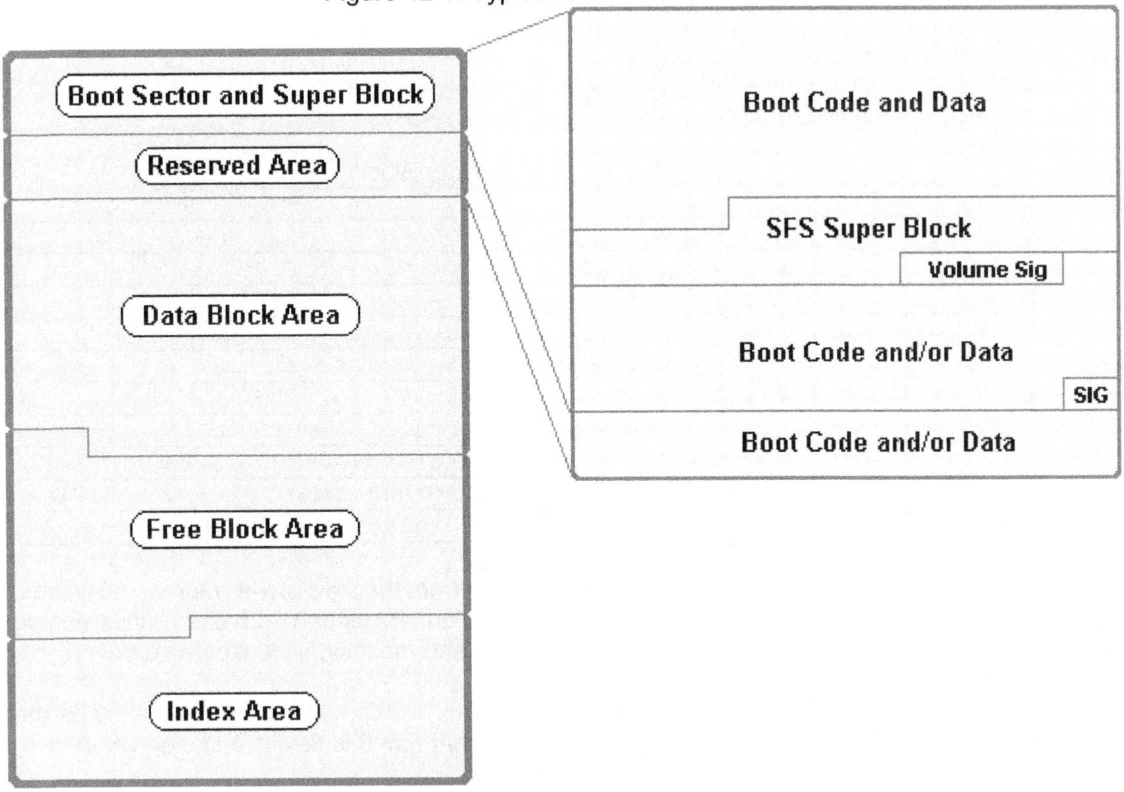

The Boot Code and Data, Super Block, and any remaining boot code and/or data start at LSB 0. Then any remaining sectors reserved for boot code or other data follow, with the Data Block Area, the Free Block Area, and finally the Index Data Area.

The Boot and Reserved Area

The first block contains any necessary code and data to either completely load a capable booting system or simply contains zeros when booting this volume is not required. If booting this volume is an option, the first block and any blocks in the Reserved Area are available for use. The size of the Reserved Area is predetermined and stored in the Super Block, which is stored within this first block of the volume and described next.

If a MBR Partitioning scheme is used, with one or more of these entries pointing to an SFS partition, each of these entries should be assigned the value of 0x53 in the ID field of the partition entry. If a GPT is used, the original author has assigned the GUID: 4EBF0E06-11BF-450C-1A06-534653534653

The Super Block

The Super Block is contained within the first block of the volume and has the format shown below. It must reside at offset 0x18E within this first block.

Table 12-1: SFS Super Block

Simple File System: Super Block		
Offset	Size	Description
00h	8	TimeStamp: Time Stamp of when volume was changed.
08h	8	DataSize: Size of Data Area in blocks.
10h	8	IndexSize: Size of Index Area in bytes.
18h	3	Magic: signature, 'SFS' (0x524653)
1Bh	1	Version: SFS version (0x10 = 1.0, 0x1A = 1.10)
1Ch	8	TotalBlocks: Total number of blocks in the volume.
24h	4	ReservedBlocks: Number of reserved blocks.
28h	1	BlockSize: Log(x+7) of block size. (x = 2 = 512)
29h	1	CRC: Zero sum of bytes in this table.

All LSB pointers in the Super Block are zero based from the start of the volume. All values, including other data structures within this specification, are written and read as little-endian format, with least significant byte read/written first and most significant byte last.

The TimeStamp field's format is explained in a later section and is updated anytime the DataSize or the IndexSize field changes. Remember that this field is a signed value.

The DataSize field is the count of blocks used for the Data Block Area. This is the area used to hold the file contents and is explained later.

The IndexSize field is the size in bytes of the Index Data Area, the area holding the file metadata and is explained later.

The Magic field is a three-character signature field holding 'SFS' (0x534653) indicating that this is a Simple File System Super Block.

The Version field holds the version of the specification this volume supports. The version is stored in BCD format, with the high nibble holding the major version and the low nibble holding the minor version. The version described in this chapter is 1.10, which means this field will hold a value of 0x1A.

The TotalBlocks field holds the 64-bit unsigned integer count of number of blocks in the whole volume. This is the count of all blocks from the block that holds the Super Block to the ending block that holds the last block of the Index Data Area.

The ReservedBlocks field holds the 32-bit unsigned integer count of blocks before the Data Block Area. This includes the block holding the Super Block and any sequential blocks that may be present following this first data block. This field is used to know where the Data Block Area begins. This field's value is relative to the start of the volume.

The BlockSize field is used to calculate the size of a block. This field is calculated as shown below.

```
bytes per block = 2 ^ (block_size + 7)
```

For example, if the block size is 512, the standard size of most media, the BlockSize field will hold a value of 2. For 1,024-byte sectors, a value of 3 is used, and so on.

If I were using the C Language to do this calculation, I would use something similar to the following.

```
unsigned int bytes_per_block = 1 << (super.block_size + 7);
```

The CRC field is a zero-byte check sum of the fields from the Magic field to this field, inclusive, so that when each byte is added, ignoring any carryover larger than a byte, the resulting sum will be zero.

The Data Block Area
The Data Block Area is where all of the file data is stored. Each file starts at a specified block indicated in the Index Data Area and is sequentially stored toward the end of the volume, block by block. Each file starts on a block boundary.

There is no file metadata stored in this area, strictly only the contents of each file. All metadata is stored in the Index Data Area.

This area may grow or shrink depending on the usage of the volume. When a new file is to be added, the host may append to the end of the data area as long as there are enough sequentially spaced blocks to store the file data. Fragmentation of file data is prohibited. If the host deletes a file from the Index Data Area, the count of blocks used to store the file's data within this Data Block Area are said to be free for use. It is outside this specification on how the host is to maintain free blocks within this Data Block Area. No blocks within the SFS volume may be used to store or maintain this information.

Once a host finds that there are free blocks within the Data Block Area with enough sequentially stored blocks to hold the file's data, it may re-use these blocks without having to append to the Data Block Area.

If the host must append to the Data Block Area, it must first check that there is enough free space before the Index Data Area. Once it has found there is enough, it must update the DataSize field in the Super Block to indicate the new size of the Data Block Area.

Note that if the Index Area needs to add a block to store the new file's meta-data, this added block must be accounted for when determining if there is enough room in the free area to store the new file's contents.

The Free Block Area
The Free Block Area is the blocks between the Data Block Area and the Index Data Area. These blocks are free for use to resize the Data Block Area, by adding blocks toward the end of the volume, or to resize the Index Data Area by adding blocks toward the start of the volume.

There are always free blocks in the Free Block Area until the point where the end of the Data Block Area meets the start of the Index Data Area. Once this happens, there are no more free blocks to use for file data unless the host has knowledge of unfragmented blocks within the Data Block Area. However, there is no more room for new unused entries in the Index Data Area.

The Index Data Area
The Index Data Area is where all of the file metadata is stored. This area holds a count of 64-byte entries holding various formats of data for the file system. The Index Data Area size is determined by the IndexSize field in the Super Block and must be a multiple of 64 bytes.

The first entry is at the end of the last block in the volume, with each sequential entry toward the start of the volume.

 Please note that if an Index Block Entry contains continuation entries, explained later, the Index Data Entry associated with the continuation entries will be closest to the start of the volume, with each continuation entry after it, toward the end of the volume.

The first entry in the Index Data Area, remembering that this is the last 64 bytes of the last block of the volume, is the Volume ID entry. The last entry in the Index Data Area, remembering that this is the first 64 bytes of the Index Data Area, is the Start Marker entry.

 Note that if the size of the Index Data Area is not a multiple of the block size, the Start Marker entry may not be at the beginning of the block, but toward the end of the block depending on how many entries are in this first block.

There are eight (8) types of valid entries in the Index Data Area with one more type being a continuation entry. Each of the eight entries has a type field as the first byte of the 64-byte entry as well as a byte check sum. For example, the following table shows the format of the Unused Entry type.

Table 12-2: SFS Index Area -- Unused Entry

Simple File System: Index Area -- Unused Entry		
Offset	Size	Description
00h	1	Type: Type of entry (Unused: 0x10)
01h	1	CRC: Zero sub byte check sum.
02h	62	Reserved and preserved

Each type will start with this single unsigned 8-bit value ranging from 0x01 to 0x1A and shown in the table below.

The Type field must be one of the eight listed below. If it is any other value, it is either an invalid entry or part of a continuation entry, explained later.

The CRC field is the byte sum of all 64 bytes in this entry and if used, all 64 bytes of each continuation entry linked to this entry.

Table 12-3: SFS Index Area – Entry Types

Value	Description
0x01	Volume ID
0x02	Start Marker
0x10	Unused Entry
0x11	Directory Entry

0x12	File Entry
0x18	Unused Entry (Bad Sectors marker)
0x19	Deleted Directory Entry
0x1A	Deleted File Entry

 Please note that even if not all of the bytes are used in the continuation entries for that particular entry type, all 64 bytes of each entry are still calculated within this CRC value and this CRC field only exists in the first entry before any continuation entries.

The Volume ID Entry

The Volume ID entry is as follows and holds the name of this volume as well as a time stamp of when it was created. All SFS volumes must contain this entry and it must be the first entry in the Index Data Area.

Table 12-4: SFS Index Area – Volume ID Entry

Simple File System: Index Area -- Volume ID Entry		
Offset	Size	Description
00h	1	Type: Type of entry (Volume ID: 0x01)
01h	1	CRC: Zero sub byte check sum.
02h	2	Reserved and preserved
04h	8	TimeStamp: Time stamp of when this was created.
0Ch	52	VolumeID: UTF-8 null terminated Volume ID string.

 All reserved fields in any entry type are to be written as zeros at creation time and preserved when later written to.

The TimeStamp field is written to at volume creation time and is then not normally ever changed. This field holds the date and time of day when the volume was created and this format is explained later.

The Name field holds the volume name usually written to at creation time but may change throughout the life of the volume. The format of this field and all character-based fields in any other entry, are explained later.

 Again, this entry, the Volume ID entry, is the last 64 bytes of the last block in the volume and the Start Entry, shown next, is the first 64 bytes of the Index Area closest to the start of the volume.

The Start Marker Entry

The Start Marker entry is as follows and marks the last entry in the Index Data Area.

Table 12-5: SFS Index Area – Start Marker Entry

Simple File System: Index Area -- Start Marker Entry		
Offset	Size	Description
00h	1	Type: Type of entry (Start Marker: 0x02)
01h	1	CRC: Zero sub byte check sum.
02h	62	Reserved and preserved

Remember that the Start Marker Entry is the entry closest to the start of the volume and may or may not be on a block boundary. For example, if the Block Size is 512 bytes and the Index Data Area is 1,408 bytes, the Index Data Area will occupy the last three blocks of the volume. However, the first 128 bytes of the first block, the block closest to the start of the volume, will be unused, with the Start Marker Entry at offset 128 within the block.

Since the Free Block Area cannot use partial blocks, it is usually common for the Index Data Area to use all of the block closest to the start of the volume and have the Start Marker Entry at the start of that block, adding Unused entries as needed.

The Unused Entry

The Unused entry is shown in Table 12-2 on a previous page and is simply an available entry for use as a different type when needed.

The Directory Entry

The Directory Entry is as follows and simply holds the name of a directory contained on the volume.

Table 12-6: SFS Index Area -- Directory Entry

Simple File System: Index Area -- Directory Entry		
Offset	Size	Description
00h	1	Type: Type of entry (Unused: 0x11)
01h	1	CRC: Zero sub byte check sum.
02h	1	NumCont: Number of continuation slots used.
03h	8	TimeStamp: Time Stamp for this entry.
0Bh	53	Name: UTF-8 null terminated directory name string.

This entry only holds a name for a directory existing on the volume. No other information is given since the full path for each file is placed within its respected File Entry.

The NumCont field is an 8-bit unsigned integer of number of continuation entries that follow this entry used to store the name and path if the Name field is not large enough to do so. Continuation entries are stored sequentially after this entry, toward the end of the volume, and are explained later.

The TimeStamp field may be updated by the host when the directory is created or any file or directory within it is also created, moved, renamed, or deleted. It is not part of the specification on when or how often this field is updated.

The Name field holds all or the first part of the full path of this directory using continuation entries as needed.

The File Entry

The File Entry is as follows and holds all of the metadata needed to store the file on the volume.

Table 12-7: SFS Index Area -- File Entry

Simple File System: Index Area -- File Entry		
Offset	Size	Description
00h	1	Type: Type of entry (Unused: 0x12)
01h	1	CRC: Zero sub byte check sum.
02h	1	NumCont: Number of continuation slots used.
03h	8	TimeStamp: Time Stamp for this entry.
0Bh	8	StartBlock: Starting Block in Data Area of file.
13h	8	EndBlock: Ending Block in Data Area of file.
1Bh	8	FileLen: File length in bytes.
23h	29	Name: UTF-8 null terminated file name string.

This entry holds the necessary data to find and read the data contents for this file.

The NumCont field is an 8-bit unsigned integer of number of continuation entries that follow this entry used to store the name and path if the name field is not large enough to do so. Continuation entries are stored sequentially after this entry, toward the end of the volume, and area explained later.

The TimeStamp field is updated by the host when this file is created or modified.

The StartBlock and EndBlock fields indicate the starting block and ending block of the file's contents relative to the start of the volume, the same block that stores the Super Block. If the file does not contain any data, i.e.: the file is a zero-length file, then no blocks within the Data Block Area are used and both these entries are written as zero. The EndBlock field is the last used block of the file. For example, if the block size is 512 and the file's length is 623 bytes, the EndBlock field will be (StartBlock + 1). If the file's length is 512 bytes or less, the EndBlock field will be the same as the StartBlock field.

The Name field holds all or the first part of the full path of this filename using continuation entries as needed.

The Unusable Entry
The Unusable Entry is as follows and holds a starting and ending block number of unusable blocks.

Table 12-8: SFS Index Area -- Unusable Entry

Simple File System: Index Area -- Unusable Entry		
Offset	Size	Description
00h	1	Type: Type of entry (Unused: 0x18)
01h	1	CRC: Zero sub byte check sum.
02h	8	Reserved and preserved
0Ah	8	StartBlock: Starting Block in Data Area of file.
12h	8	EndBlock: Ending Block in Data Area of file.
1Ah	38	Reserved and preserved.

Unusable blocks are blocks that are not usable by the host. For example, there could be bad blocks on the media and this entry is used to indicate which ones. If there are more than one area, non-sequentially linked, you must have one entry for each non-sequential set of unusable blocks.

The Deleted Directory and File Entries
The Deleted Directory and Deleted File Entries are identical to their respective entries except that the type field has changed to a value of 0x19 and 0x1A respectively. See Table 12-6 and Table 12-7.

This is so that you may undelete a file or directory if you so desire. This is where the CRC field comes into play. You must verify that all bytes within this entry and any continuation entries associated with this entry pass the byte-sum check before you undelete a directory or file name.

For example, the host system might see a deleted entry as an unused entry and each continuation entry associated with it as also unused. It then might reassign one of the continuation entries but not the deleted entry.

 Note that if you do not wish to have Undelete capabilities, mark all deleted entries, including the associated continuation entries, as Unused entries. It is not good practice to reassign "deleted" continuation entries without reassigning the deleted parent entry as well.

Note that just because the Deleted Entry is still valid, this doesn't mean that the blocks used to store the deleted file's data are still intact. It is up to the host to determine if they are still intact and any technique used is not part of this specification.

File Names and Directory Names

As other file systems may store directory information within the media's data area, the SFS does not. Each file has its full path name stored within its File Entry. Therefore, there is no need to store directory information elsewhere. However, a Directory Entry is included to simply indicate the name and existence of that directory. It also contains its full path and name.

For example, a file that may be stored in the (virtual) root directory will simply hold the name of the file. If the volume includes a directory name, "foobar" for example, there will be a Directory Entry with that name. Then any file within the directory will have that name followed by a forward slash and then the name of the file as in "foobar/name.txt".

Note that there is no forward slash at the beginning of the path.

There must be a Directory Entry for every directory name used and its entry in the Index table must precede any File entry that uses this directory name in its path.

All names, File, Directory, or Volume IDs, are stored as UTF-8 character strings and are null terminated. All character codes less than 0x0020, codes 0x0080 through 0x009F inclusively, and all of the following codes are invalid and should not be used in any name.

- " (double quote, 0x0022)
- * (asterix, 0x002A)
- : (colon, 0x003A)
- < (less than sign, 0x003C)
- > (greater than sign, 0x003E)
- ? (question mark, 0x003F)
- \ (backward slash, 0x005C)
- DEL (delete, 0x007F)
- NBSP (no break space character, 0x00A0)

This includes forward slashes in file names since forward slashes indicate a path separation.

Continuation Entries

Since the space allocated within a given entry may not be enough to hold the full path and file name, the SFS specification gives the ability to allocate more space by assigning sequentially consecutive entries as continuation entries. These entries must follow the associated entry in the direction toward the end of the volume. The associated entry will indicate how many continuation entries are used.

A continuation entry does not have a type field or any other structured data within it. A continuation entry is just a 64-byte entry to continue the name from the previous entry. With an 8-bit unsigned integer, this allows up to 255 continuation entries to each associated named entry giving a path and name length limit of 16,320 bytes not including the space within the associated entry.

 Note that the continuation entries will be sequentially consecutive in memory, in turn simply turning the short 53-byte directory name field into a 16,373-byte field.

If a continuation entry is not needed, the NumCont field in the associated entry will be zero.

Remember that all name strings must be null terminated, meaning that all strings must end in a 0x0000 code. If the complete path will fit within the room allocated in the associated entry, but is not null terminated, you must still allocate a continuation entry just for the null terminator.

 Note that most ASCII characters are UTF-8 characters and will occupy a single byte per character.

Time Stamp

Some entries and the Super Block contain a 64-bit TimeStamp field. This field is the *signed* integer count of 1/65536ths of a second before or after an EPOC time of midnight, January 1st, 1970. With this in mind, a value of one (1) is roughly 15 microseconds, or a value of 3,932,160 being one minute past midnight.

 This is a much more accurate or precise measurement of time. Usually, with a write-once file system, this is not an issue, but the author decided to use this anyway. Precise time stamps are quite valuable in MAKE instances when a file's time stamp indicates if it needs to be built or not.

Examples
This section contains a list of examples and DEBUG style dumps to show exactly what a volume might look like. The first example is a Super Block from a 1.44Meg floppy disk.

Super Block:
```
00000180                                              00 00
00000190  71 1C FF 61 00 00 EB 07-00 00 00 00 00 00 40 04
000001A0  00 00 00 00 00 00 53 46-53 1A 40 0B 00 00 00 00
000001B0  00 00 01 00 00 00 02 AC
```

offset	contents	description
0000018E	0x000061FF1C710000	Time Stamp (2022/02/05 17:55:13)
00000196	0x00000000000007EB	Data Block Count (2,027 blocks used)
0000019E	0x0000000000000440	Index Size in bytes (1,088 bytes)
000001A6	0x534653	Magic Signature 'SFS'
000001A9	0x1A	Version 1.10
000001AA	0x0000000000000B40	Total Blocks in Volume (2,880 blocks)
000001B2	0x00000002	Reserved Blocks (2)
000001B6	0x02	Block Size (2 = 512)
000001B7	0xAC	Byte Sum CRC

Here is an example of a File Entry that does not need a continuation.

File Entry: (64 bytes)
```
00167C40  12 6D 00 00 00 71 1C FF-61 00 00 79 04 00 00 00
00167C50  00 00 00 32 05 00 00 00-00 00 00 68 73 01 00 00
00167C60  00 00 00 6C 6F 61 64 65-72 2E 73 79 73 00 00 00
00167C70  00 00 00 00 00 00 00 00-00 00 00 00 00 00 00 00
```

offset	contents	description
00167C00	0x12	File Entry Type
00167C01	0x6D	Byte Sum CRC
00167C02	0x00	No Continuation Entries used
00167C03	0x000061FF1C710000	Time Stamp (2022/02/05 17:55:13)
00167C0B	0x0000000000000479	Start Block
00167C13	0x0000000000000532	End Block
00167C1B	0x0000000000017368	File Length in bytes (95,080 bytes)
00167C23	'loader.sys',0	Null terminated name

Now for an (fictitious) entry that uses name continuation.

File Entry: (64 bytes)
```
00167C40  12 EA 01 24 86 52 E1 B9-59 00 00 F3 03 00 00 00
00167C50  00 00 00 F4 03 00 00 00-00 00 00 75 10 00 00 00
00167C60  00 00 00 61 20 6C 6F 6E-67 20 73 74 69 6E 6B 27
```

```
00167C70  6E 20 6E 61 6D 65 20 74-68 61 74 20 6A 75 73 74
00167C80  20 67 6F 65 73 20 6F 6E-20 61 6E 64 20 6F 6E 00
00167C90  00 00 00 00 00 00 00 00-00 00 00 00 00 00 00 00
00167CA0  00 00 00 00 00 00 00 00-00 00 00 00 00 00 00 00
00167CB0  00 00 00 00 00 00 00 00-00 00 00 00 00 00 00 00
```

offset	contents	description
00167C40	0x12	File Entry Type
00167C41	0xEA	Byte Sum CRC
00167C42	0x01	One Continuation Entry used
00167C43	0x00005BA6D89F0000	Time Stamp (2018/09/22 17:04:47)
00167C4B	0x00000000000003F3	Start Block
00167C13	0x00000000000003F4	End Block
00167C1B	0x0000000000000275	File Length in bytes (629 bytes)
00167C23	'a long stink'n name that just goes on and on',0	

Wrap Up

Remember that each File and Directory entry contains the full path within its entry. For example, consider the directory tree shown below.

```
\ (root)
  foo\
  foo\bar.txt
  foo\bar.bin
  bar\
  bar\foo.txt
  bar\foo.bin
```

If this is the only thing on the volume, not counting the Start Marker Entry and the Volume ID Entry, you will have six (6) total entries, two (2) Directory Entries and four (4) File Entries. The File Entry for the last file in the list above, "bar\foo.bin" will have its name entry contain:

'bar/foo.bin',0

Minus the single quotes and comma, of course.

When searching for a file within the Index Data Area, be sure to skip the continuation entries when advancing to the next entry. This means that you have to watch for all FILE, DIR, DEL_FILE, and DEL_DIR entries so that you can see if either have continuation entries and if so, skip them. Even though all type values are considered invalid filename characters, it isn't wise to assume that the first character in a continuation entry will not be a valid type value.

Remember that the Data Area grows from start of volume toward the center of the volume. However, the Index Area starts at the end of the volume and grows to the center of the volume. Any advance through the Index Area starts at the end of this area and moves toward the center of the volume except for continuation entries as shown below.

Figure 12-2: Area Growth Direction

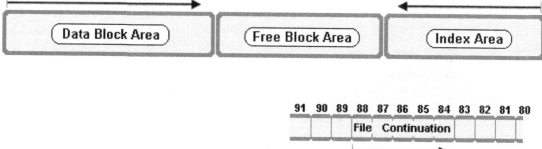

Chapter 13 – The "ISO" File System

All of the other file systems described in this book are for magnetic or flash media, media that can be written to more than once. The file system explained in this chapter is for CD-ROM media, media that is usually only read from. The file system used for most CD-ROM's is the ISO9660 file system. It is also known as the CDFS, or Compact Disc File System, and described in ECMA-119. See Appendix A on how to get this specification.

Since CD-ROM's are/were widely used on multiple machines, there needed to be a portable file system that would work across different platforms.

CD-ROMs were quite popular until flash media became so common and cheap. CD-ROMs could hold a bit less than a single Gig of data, where today's flash drives can hold 128 to 256 Gig quite cheaply. Also, flash drives are easily re-writable, where CD-ROMs are not.

CD-ROMs are still quite popular for new software, software you purchase with a book, product, or utility. A purchase that once you install the needed software, you will probably store away the CD-ROM and never need it again. The advantage of the CD-ROM, the data's integrity will last a lot longer on the CD-ROM than it will on a flash drive or magnetic media.

For this reason, it is good for your operating system to be able to read from an ISO9660 CD-ROM.

You must note throughout this chapter, a sector on a CD-ROM is 2,048 bytes, not 512 bytes. Therefore, watch your buffer sizes when reading sectors. If you use the same virtual file system code to read from a CD-ROM as you do a hard disk drive, make sure the VFS knows about 2,048 sector sizes.

A Typical CDFS Layout

Unlike other media, the first 16 sectors of the CD-ROM may be all zeros. They do not contain any boot code. The first informative sector is sector 16, the 17th sector. It will contain a Volume Descriptor, usually the Primary Volume Descriptor, or PVD.

A Volume Descriptor, such as this PVD, has a 7-byte header to indicate what kind of descriptor, with the remaining 2,041 bytes for the rest of the descriptor.

Table 13-1: CDFS 7-byte Header

Offset	Value	Description
0x00	0 -> 255	Descriptor Type
0x01	'CD001'	Standard Identifier
0x06	0 -> 255	Descriptor Version

The Descriptor Type is an 8-bit value indicating what type of Volume Descriptor follows. It can have one of the five values.

Table 13-2: CDFS Volume Descriptor Type

Value	Description
0	Boot Record Volume Descriptor
1	Primary Volume Descriptor
2	Supplementary Volume Descriptor
3	Volume Partition Descriptor
4->254	Reserved
255	Set Terminator. No more.

The Standard Identifier will always be 'CD001'. This is to verify the block, as with other file systems and their magic numbers.

The Descriptor Version will depend on the descriptor being used, but has not changed since the specification was created. Therefore, all descriptors at this point have a value of one (1).

Figure 13-1 below shows a typical Bootable CD-ROM, while Figure 13-2 shows a non-bootable CD-ROM.

Figure 13-1: Typical Bootable CD-ROM

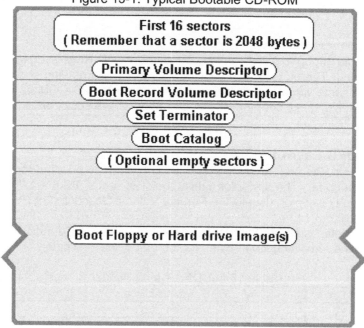

Figure 13-2: Typical Non-bootable CD-ROM

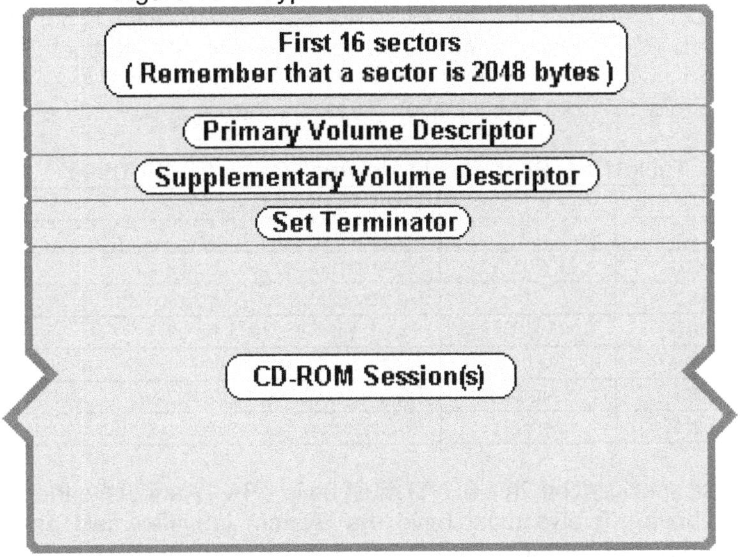

```
┌──────────────────────────────────────────────────┐
│   ╭──────────────────────────────────────────╮    │
│   │          First 16 sectors                │    │
│   │ ( Remember that a sector is 2048 bytes ) │    │
│   ╰──────────────────────────────────────────╯    │
│      ╭───────────────────────────────╮            │
│      │  Primary Volume Descriptor    │            │
│      ╰───────────────────────────────╯            │
│    ╭─────────────────────────────────────╮        │
│    │  Supplementary Volume Descriptor    │        │
│    ╰─────────────────────────────────────╯        │
│         ╭────────────────────╮                    │
│         │   Set Terminator   │                    │
│         ╰────────────────────╯                    │
│                                                    │
│                                                    │
│          ╭──────────────────────╮                 │
│          │   CD-ROM Session(s)  │                 │
│          ╰──────────────────────╯                 │
│                                                    │
└──────────────────────────────────────────────────┘
```

At this point, you have read in 2048 bytes from LBA 16 and have determined what type of Volume Descriptor you have read, usually the Primary Volume Descriptor.

Each of the common descriptor types are described next.

Boot Record Volume Descriptor

When a system that is capable of booting CD-ROM's finds a Boot Record Volume Descriptor, it will start to emulate a floppy or hard drive image depending on the information given. The Boot Record Descriptor points to a Boot Catalog Sector, which stores more information about what type of image to emulate.

The Boot Record Volume Descriptor (BRVD) has the following format.

Table 13-3: Boot Record Volume Descriptor

Offset	Value	Description
0x00	0	Descriptor Type
0x01	'CD001'	Standard Identifier
0x06	1	Descriptor Version
0x07	Varies	System Identifier
0x27	Varies	Identifier
0x47	Varies	System Use to end of sector

From offset 0x47 to the end of the sector is used by the system and this area is defined in the "El Torito" Boot Specification. The "El Torito" Boot Specification is not part of the ISO standard of the CD-ROM. It was added to be able to use the ISO to boot CD-ROM's.

Therefore, the "El Torito" Boot Specification gives the format described below.

Table 13-4: Boot Record Volume Descriptor: 'El Torito'

Offset	Value	Description
0x00	0	Descriptor Type
0x01	'CD001'	Standard Identifier
0x06	1	Descriptor Version
0x07	Specified	System Identifier
0x27	zeros	Identifier
0x47	varies	LBA of Boot Catalog
0x4A	zeros	Reserved to end of sector

For the "El Torito" specification, this BRVD must be in LBA 17 and have the format defined in Table 13-4 above. It also must have the System Identifier field as 'EL TORITO SPECIFICATION' padded with NULLs. The field at offset 0x47 is the 32-bit sector number of the Boot Catalog.

The Boot Catalog Sector contains as many sectors as needed and holds sixty-four 32-byte entries in each sector. Five types of entries are allowed. The first 32-byte entry must be a Validation Entry to verify that this is actually a valid Boot Catalog, and has the following format.

Table 13-5: 'El Torito': Boot Catalog: Validation

Offset	Value	Description
0x00	1	Header ID
0x01	0, 1, 2	Platform
0x02	Zero	Reserved
0x04	Varies	Manufacturer Identifier
0x1C	CRC	2-byte zero word check sum
0x1E	0x55	Key Byte
0x1F	0xAA	Key Byte

This entry is used to verify the remaining entries to be valid. The Platform field may contain one of the following three values.

Table 13-6: 'El Torito': Boot Cat: Platform

Value	Description
0	80x86
1	PowerPC
2	Mac

The Manufacturer Identifier field is a string containing the manufacture, vendor, or developer of the product on the CD-ROM.

The Word Checksum is a zero word-check sum. This field contains a value to make all 16-bit words in this entry add up to zero.

The next entry is the Initial Entry and has the following format.

Table 13-7: El Torito: Boot Catalog: Initial

Offset	Value	Description
0x00	0x00, 0x88	Boot Indicator
0x01	0 -> 4	Media Type
0x02	0x07C0	Load Segment of image
0x04	Varies	Partition Type
0x05	Zero	Reserved
0x06	Varies	Sector Load Count
0x08	Varies	Starting LBA of Sector to Load
0x0C	Zero	Reserved (to end of entry)

The Initial Entry is considered the default entry. If there are any additional entries, this Initial entry would normally hold a bootable floppy disk image that might boot to a boot menu, allowing the user to pick any one of the remaining bootable images. If there are no additional entries, this entry holds the only bootable image, floppy or hard drive. See Appendix H for more information on this technique.

The Boot Indicator field is set to 0x00 if the initial/default entry is not bootable. It is set to 0x88 if it is bootable.

The Media Type field has five possibilities. If this media type is set to zero, no emulation is done. The image is loaded to the segment specified with a count of sectors also specified, and then the BIOS jumps to that segment. The CD-ROM is still just that, a CD-ROM, and is not accessible via INT 13h emulation, but is accessible via the Extended BIOS INT 13h read services. Any of the other media types are emulated as that type and INT 13h emulation is available.

Table 13-8: El Torito: Boot Cat: Media Type

Value	Description
0	No Emulation
1	1.20 Meg Floppy
2	1.44 Meg Floppy
3	2.88 Meg Floppy
4	Hard Drive Image

Just because the BIOS is emulating the CD-ROM as a floppy or hard disk image doesn't mean your boot code can't load an ATAPI driver and read the whole CD-ROM as a standalone CD-ROM. Once you load a driver, you can read the whole CD-ROM, just not with INT 13h (when it is emulating another disk type).

The Load Segment field is the value it will provide in the CS register. This is usually 0x0000. This will tell the system to use the traditional value of 0x07C0.

The Partition Type field is a copy of the Partition Type value from the emulated Hard Drive image's Master Boot Record Partition Table entry.

The Sector Load Count field indicates to the system how many 512-byte sectors you would like the BIOS to load for you.

The Starting LBA field is the 32-bit LBA of the first sector of the image to load from the CD-ROM.

 It has been known that some older BIOSes will only load one sector no matter the count in the Sector Load Count field. To work around this, you can place a magic number at the first of the second (emulated) sector. Then at the first of your code, find this magic number. If found, the BIOS loaded more than one sector. If this value is not found, you will need to find and read this Boot Catalog entry, calculate how many more sectors to read, and then read the remaining sectors, all within the first 512 or 2048 bytes of your boot code. However, you can pretty much assume any BIOS made in the year 2000 or later will read in all of your code.

Section Header Entry

The next entry in the Boot Catalog is the Section Header entry. It will describe how many more entries there are.

Table 13-9: El Torito: Boot Catalog: Section Header

Offset	Value	Description
0x00	0x90, 0x91	Header Indicator
0x01	0 -> 2	Platform ID
0x02	Varies	Number of Entries Following
0x04	Varies	ID String (uses remaining bytes)

The Header Indicator field indicates to the system if there are any more entries following. If there are not, a value of 0x90 should be used and the remaining fields are ignored. If there are entries following, a value of 0x91 is used.

The Platform field is identical to Table 13-6 and used to indicate what platform the following entries are compatible with.

The Number of Entries field indicates how many total entries are in this section.

The ID String field uses the remaining of the 32-byte header and is an identifying string identifies this section.

Each entry in this section has the same format, allowing for multiple options. This provides a multi-boot environment as long as the BIOS/booting software understands the specification.

A Section Entry has the following format.

Table 13-10: El Torito: Boot Catalog: Section Entry

Offset	Value	Description
0x00	0x00, 0x88	Boot Indicator
0x01	Varies	Media Type
0x02	0x07C0	Load Segment of image
0x04	Varies	Partition Type
0x05	Zero	Reserved
0x06	Varies	Sector Load Count
0x08	Varies	Starting LBA of Sector to Load
0x0C	0, 1	Criteria Type
0x0D	Varies	Vendor Specific

The Section Entry is very similar to the Initial Entry detailed in Table 13-7 with the following additions.

The Media Type field uses bits 3:0 to indicate the media type as listed in Table 13-8. However, it now uses the remaining four bits. Bit 4 is reserved, bit 5, when set, indicates that there is an Extended Entry following (see below), bit 6 indicates that the image contains an ATAPI driver, and bit 7 indicates that the image contains a SCSI driver.

The Criteria Type field allows a value of 0x00, 'No Selection', or a value of 0x01 used by IBM hardware.

The Vendor Specific field allows for any kind of data to be stored that is specific to this entry. If there is not enough room in this field to store all needed data, this is where bit 5 of the Media Type field comes in. If this bit is set, then there is an Extension Entry to follow and has the format shown on the next page.

Table 13-11: El Torito: Boot Catalog: Extension Entry

Offset	Value	Description
0x00	0x44	Extension Indicator
0x01	0x00, 0x20	Final Extension Indicator
0x02	Varies	Vendor Specific

The Section Entry may have as many of these Extension Entries as needed. To include Extension Entries, make sure bit 5 is set in byte 0x01. The last used Extension Entry should have its byte 0x01 clear.

A final Section Header Entry should follow, with a Header Indicator of 0x90 to indicate no more entries.

An advantage to this technique is that there can be multiple sections, each section listing different options for a specific platform. For example, if your product supports two platforms, with multiple boot options each, you can have two used sections with multiple boot entries each, all on one CD-ROM. No need to include multiple CD-ROMs to support multiple platforms.

Figure 1 on Page 6 of the "El Torito" Bootable CD-ROM Format Specification, Version 1.0, January 25, 1995, shows a good example of using this technique. See Appendix A at the end of this book on how to get this specification.

Primary Volume Descriptor

Every CD-ROM must have a Primary Volume Descriptor, or PVD. It is the descriptor that describes the volume. This descriptor must be at LBA 16. This descriptor describes the volume, how many sectors it contains, where the root starts, and all the other items needed to read from the volume.

Since the CDFS is to be portable across platforms, most values larger than an 8-bit byte are stored twice, once in little-endian and then again in big-endian. The Primary Volume Descriptor has the following format.

Table 13-12: Primary Volume Descriptor

Offset	Value	Description
0x000	1	Descriptor Type
0x001	'CD001'	Standard Identifier
0x006	1	Descriptor Version
0x007	Zero	Reserved
0x008	Varies[2]	System Identifier
0x028	Varies[3]	Volume Identifier
0x048	Zeros	Reserved

0x050	Varies[1]	Volume Space Size
0x058	Zeros	Reserved
0x078	Varies[1]	Volume Set Size
0x07C	Varies[1]	Volume Sequence Number
0x080	Varies[1]	Logical Block Size
0x084	Varies[1]	Path Table Size
0x08C	Varies[1]	L Path Table Location
0x090	Varies[1]	Optional L Path Table Location
0x094	Varies[1]	M Path Table Location
0x098	Varies[1]	Optional M Path Table Location
0x09C	Varies	Root Directory Record
0x0BE	Varies[3]	Volume Set Identifier
0x13E	Varies[2]	Publisher Identifier
0x1BE	Varies[2]	Data Preparer Identifier
0x23E	Varies[2]	Application Identifier
0x2BE	Varies[3]	Copyright File Identifier
0x2E3	Varies[3]	Abstract File Identifier
0x308	Varies[3]	Bibliographic File Identifier
0x32D	Varies	Volume Creation Date & Time
0x33E	Varies	Volume Modification Date & Time
0x34F	Varies	Volume Expiration Date & Time
0x360	Varies	Volume Effective Date & Time
0x371	1	File Structure Version
0x372	Zero	Reserved
0x373	Varies	Application Use
0x573	Zeros	Reserved

[1]Stored Little-endian then Big-endian
[2]Stored as a-characters
[3]Stored as d-characters

When a numerical value is stored Little-endian then Big-endian, each value occupies half of the space provided. If there are 4 bytes provided, each value is a 2-byte value and stored in their respective formats. a-characters and d-characters are defined in Appendix A of the ECMA-119 specification. d-characters are all capital letters of the alphabet, the 10 digits zero to nine, and the underscore character. a-characters are all of the d-characters plus a space and most general punctuation and arithmetic characters.

The Type field of this descriptor is one (1). It is the Primary Volume Descriptor and will always be in LBA 16 of the volume. As with other descriptors, the Standard Identifier is 'CD001' and the Version is 1.

The System Identifier field gives an identification of a system, which can recognize the content in the first 16 sectors of the volume. If there are any values within the first 16 sectors of the disc, this named identifier will be able to understand their meaning.

The Volume Identifier field is to identify the volume. It is a volume label. Note that it may or may not be NULL terminated.

The Volume Space Size field is the count of 2,048 sectors within this volume. Remember that most values in this descriptor are stored as two 2- or 4-byte values, the first Little-endian and the second Big-endian.

The Volume Set Size field is the number given to this set of volumes, usually 1, while the Volume Sequence Number field is the ordinal number of this volume within this set, also usually 1.

The Logical Block Size field is the size of a sector, usually containing a value of 2,048.

The Path Table Size field is the size in bytes of the Path Table. This is usually a multiple of a sector size.

The L Path Table Location and L Optional Path Table Location fields each contain a value of the LBA sector containing the Path Table and Optional Path Table respectively. The next two fields, only differ in name by the 'M', are identical but stored in Most Significant byte first, or Big-endian while the 'L' named fields are Little-endian, or Least Significant byte first.

The Root Directory Record is a structure holding information for the Root Directory and as with all Directory Records, has the following format.

Table 13-13: Directory Record

Offset	Size	Value	Description
0x00	1	Varies	Length of Directory Record
0x01	1	Varies	Extended Attribute Record Len
0x02	8	Varies	Location of Extent
0x0A	8	Varies	Data Length (in bytes)
0x12	7	Varies	Date and Time
0x19	1	Varies	File Flags
0x1A	1	Zero	File Unit Size
0x1B	1	Zero	Interleave Gap Size
0x1C	4	Varies	Volume Sequence Number

0x20	1	Varies	Length of File Identifier (LEN_FI)
0x21	LEN_FI	Varies	File Identifier (File Name)
+LEN_FI	0 or 1	Zero	Padding Field
+0 or 1	Varies	Varies	System Use

The Length of Directory Record field is the length of the whole record used. It may vary depending on the length of the File Identifier, Padding, and System Use fields. For the record within the PVD, this will have a length of 34 since the Root Directory doesn't have a name.

The Extended Attribute Record Length field indicates the length of the assigned Extended Attribute Record or zero if none given.

The Location of Extent field gives the LBA sector number of the first sector of the Directory Block or File Section.

The Data Length field gives the length in bytes of this Directory Block or File Section. This value does not include the length of any Extended Attribute Record.

The Date and Time field is stored as seven values and has the following format.

Table 13-14: Date and Type Storage: Numeric

Offset	Value	Description
0x00	0 -> 255	Number of years since 1900
0x01	1 -> 12	Month of Year
0x02	1 -> 31	Day of Month
0x03	0 -> 23	Hour of Day
0x04	0 -> 59	Minute of Hour
0x05	0 -> 59	Second of Minute
0x06	-48 -> +52	GMT offset in 15-minute intervals

 Other than to possibly save space, I don't know why the creators decided to use two different date and time formats. One in the Directory Record and the other in the Primary Volume Descriptor.

The File Flags field of the Directory Record is an 8-bit field and has the following bit format.

Table 13-15: Directory Record: File Flags

Bit	Description
7	Set indicates more records needed
6:5	Reserved
4	Owner and Group Identification
3	Set indicates Record Format Field

2	Set indicates is an Associated File
1	Set indicates is a Directory Record
0	Set indicates is a Hidden Record

The Unit Size field indicates the size of a unit in the file section if Interleaving is used and is usually zeroed. The Interleave Gap Size field is also used for Interleaving and is usually zeroed.

The Volume Sequence Number field is the ordinal number of the volume set this Extent it recorded on.

The Length of File Identifier field, LEN_FI, indicates the length of the file name, the File Identifier field.

The File Identifier field holds the file name of the file. If it is not a directory name, bit 1 is clear in the File Flags field, this field may contain the d-character file name of the file. If this is a directory, the name may also contain a single zero or one value. These two additions are used in the root directory record entry in the PVD.

The Padding Field is only used if the Length of the File Identifier field is an even number. If LEN_FI is an even number, then this Padding Field should be a size of one and have a value of zero. If the LEN_FI field is an odd number, the Padding Field does not exist.

The Volume Set Identifier field in the Primary Volume Descriptor holds the label of this volume's set. If there are multiple sets, this is the label for this set.

The Publisher Identifier field is the identifier of the user who specified what should be recorded. If the first byte of this field is 0x5E, then there is an 8.3 DOS type file name following that points to a file in the Root Directory holding this information. If all bytes in this field are 0x20, then there is no user specified.

The Data Preparer field holds the identification of who is in control of the preparation of the data and is stored identical to the Publisher Identifier field.

The Application Identifier specifies of the specification used to store the data and also uses the same form of storage as the previous two fields.

The Copyright, Abstract, and Bibliographic File Identifier fields each hold a DOS type 8.3 file name that resides in the Root Directory, each file holding the respective type's data. If the field is filled with 0x20, then no file is specified.

The Volume Creation, Modification, Expiration, and Effective Date and Time fields hold their respective date and time values. Each field has the format shown on the next page.

Table 13-16: Date and Type Storage: Digits

Offset	Size	Value	Description
0x00	4	1 -> 9999	Year
0x04	2	1 -> 12	Month of Year
0x06	2	1 -> 31	Day of Month
0x08	2	0 -> 23	Hour of Day
0x0A	2	0 -> 59	Minute of Hour
0x0C	2	0 -> 59	Second of Minute
0x0E	2	0 -> 99	Hundredths of a Second
0x10	1	-48 -> +52	GMT offset in 15-minute intervals

All fields in the first 16 bytes are stored as d-characters with the last byte stored as a signed byte offset from Greenwich Mean Time. Take the value and multiply it by 15 minutes to get the value needed. If all fields are zero, the character '0' or the value zero for offset 0x10, then no date or time is specified.

The File Structure Version field indicates the version of the structures used in the Path Tables and Directory Records. It must contain a value of one (1).

The Application Use field is not specified by this file system and may be used to store data specific to the application of the data on the CD-ROM.

Supplementary Volume Descriptor

A Supplementary Volume Descriptor is very similar to the Primary Volume Descriptor and is used when the string items and names within this descriptor and the Directory Blocks on this volume need to be UCS-2 (Universal Character Set-2) encoding.

UCS-2 encoding was created before UTF-16 encoding, but is very similar. UCS-2 is simply an UTF-16 in a 2-byte fixed field for code points 0x0000 -> 0xFFFF.

It also points to a different Path Table and Directory Block which will now also use these character sets. Each Directory Record within these new Directory Blocks will point to the same file data as the ones pointed to by the Primary Volume Descriptors Directory Blocks. i.e.: This descriptor gives a new set of names all encoded to use a different character set but each new entry points to the same data block as its respective 8-bit ASCII directory entry.

Besides a different Descriptor Type value, there are two new fields within this descriptor. These two fields use previously reserved fields and are listed on the next page.

Table 13-17: Supplementary Volume Descriptor

Offset	Value	Description
0x000	2	Descriptor Type
...		
0x007	Varies	Flags
...		
0x058	Varies	Escape Sequences

The Flags field uses bit 0 to indicate whether the escape sequences are registered according to ISO 2375. If bit 0 is set, then at least one escape sequence is not registered according to ISO 2375.

The Escape Sequences field gives a list of escape sequences to indicate what form of encoding is used to store the characters. The three allowed escape sequences are listed below. The Level gives different levels of additions to the specification.

```
Level 1      0x25, 0x2F, 0x40      '%\@'
Level 2      0x25, 0x2F, 0x43      '%\C'
Level 3      0x25, 0x2F, 0x45      '%\E'
```

This descriptor is used with the Joliet version of the ECMA-119 specification. Any Joliet compatible system should check for this descriptor and use it instead of the Primary Volume Descriptor if long file names and wide character sets are desired.

Other than the new character set usage, everything else is identical to the Primary Volume Descriptor and the descriptions within this chapter. Therefore, I will not discuss the Joliet version any further than what is in this section. For more information on the Joliet specification, see Appendix A.

Volume Partition Descriptor

The Volume Partition Descriptor is used to show a partition volume within the CD-ROM volume. This descriptor is shown in the EMCA-119 specification at Section 8.6, and not needed or discussed further within the scope of this book.

Volume Descriptor Set Terminator

The Volume Descriptor Set Terminator descriptor is used to indicate to the system that there are no more descriptors to follow. Each volume must contain a terminating descriptor and it must have the format listed on the next page.

All Volume Descriptors must be before this descriptor. Any sectors after this descriptor are then available for use by the volume. For example, the "El Torito" Boot Catalog must be after this Terminator Descriptor, even though the Boot Descriptor is before.

Table 13-18: Volume Descriptor Set Terminator

Offset	Value	Description
0x00	255	Descriptor Type
0x01	'CD001'	Standard Identifier
0x06	1	Descriptor Version
0x07	Zeros	Reserved to end of sector

Example Layout

The figure on the next page shows two examples of what a bootable CD-ROM might look like. With the first example, only the Initial Entry is used. Then a single Section Header entry marked with a 0x90 meaning no more entries. The second example shows an entry in the Initial Entry and then three addition entries with a Section Header, followed by another Section Header to indicate no more.

Root Directory

Whether you have a boot image or a group of boot images, all CD-ROM's may have a data area to hold files and directories. This area is pointed to by the Root Entry in the PVD.

Even if your CD-ROM is bootable and only needs that bootable file, it is still a good idea to create a Root Directory with at least one file. If the CD-ROM is ever read by a different platform, meaning it wasn't booted, this file could be used to explain what the CD-ROM is for, who created it, and other similar type information.

Along with that idea, the bootable image could be solely to boot to a known state and then read the data from the CD-ROM's root directory, holding many files.

As with most file systems, the Root Directory on a CD-ROM is just a block of memory with a consecutive list of Directory Records. However, these Directory Records are not a fixed size like other file systems. Therefore, the first entry of the record gives the length of this record. The next record follows. The format of this record is shown in Table 13-13 earlier in this chapter.

Figure 13-3: Example Bootable CD-ROM

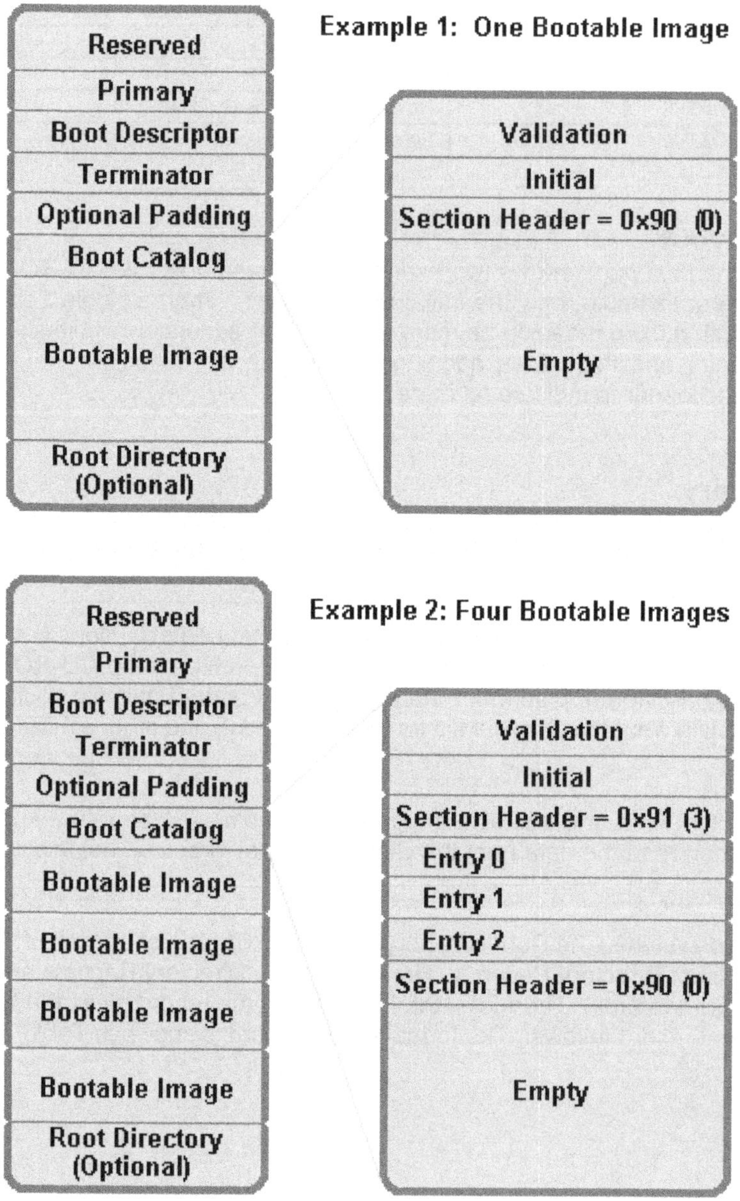

Example 1: One Bootable Image

Reserved
Primary
Boot Descriptor
Terminator
Optional Padding
Boot Catalog
Bootable Image
Root Directory (Optional)

Validation
Initial
Section Header = 0x90 (0)
Empty

Example 2: Four Bootable Images

Reserved
Primary
Boot Descriptor
Terminator
Optional Padding
Boot Catalog
Bootable Image
Bootable Image
Bootable Image
Bootable Image
Root Directory (Optional)

Validation
Initial
Section Header = 0x91 (3)
Entry 0
Entry 1
Entry 2
Section Header = 0x90 (0)
Empty

An example root directory with three records might look like the following.

Listing 13-1: Root Directory Example

```
              Length: 78
       Extended Attr: 0x00
     Extent Location: 0x00001234
         Data Length: 0x00004321
                Date: 2014/06/22 01:23:45 gmt offset: -7
               Flags: 0
           Unit Size: 0
            Gap Size: 0
        Sequence Num: 1
     File Name Length: 12
           File Name: TEMP01.TXT;1
            Pad Byte: 0x00
 00 00 00 00 00 00 00 00-00 00 00 00 00 00 00 00
 00 00 00 00 00 00 00 00-00 00 00 00 00 00 00 00


              Length: 76
       Extended Attr: 0x00
     Extent Location: 0x0000DEAD
         Data Length: 0x0000BEAF
                Date: 2014/06/22 01:23:45 gmt offset: -7
               Flags: 0
           Unit Size: 0
            Gap Size: 0
        Sequence Num: 1
     File Name Length: 11
           File Name: TEMP2.BIN;1
 00 00 00 00 00 00 00 00-00 00 00 00 00 00 00 00
 00 00 00 00 00 00 00 00-00 00 00 00 00 00 00 00


              Length: 76
       Extended Attr: 0x00
     Extent Location: 0x00008AA8
         Data Length: 0x0000A88A
                Date: 2014/06/22 01:23:45 gmt offset: -7
               Flags: 0
           Unit Size: 0
            Gap Size: 0
        Sequence Num: 1
     File Name Length: 11
           File Name: TEMP3.ZIP;1
 00 00 00 00 00 00 00 00-00 00 00 00 00 00 00 00
 00 00 00 00 00 00 00 00-00 00 00 00 00 00 00 00
```

The Directory Record allows for System Use space after the file name. To do this, create a record with a Record Length larger than the amount needed for the record and the file name. The extra space after the file name is available for use by the system reading the record.

This has the advantage, for example, that you may give the file a much longer file name and use lowercase names. However, only the systems that wrote the extra data may be able to understand what it is. The section below shows this advantage.

System Use Sharing Protocol

This is where the "System Use Sharing Protocol" came into play. It uses the System Use area of the Directory Record to store additional information about the file, also called File metadata. See Appendix A for information on getting the "System Use Sharing Protocol" specification.

The "System Use Sharing Protocol" contains small blocks of memory with each type containing the following header at the beginning.

Table 13-19: System Use Entry

Offset	Size	Value	Description
0x00	2	Sig	Signature (0x?? 0x??)
0x02	1	Varies	Length of block
0x03	1	1	Version
0x04	Len - 4	Varies	Remainder of entry

The Sig field above, holds the type and the following table lists the types allowed.

Table 13-20: System Use Entry Types

Value	Description
System Use Sharing Protocol	
CE	Continuation Area
ER	Extensions Reference
ES	Extension Selector
PD	Padding
SP	System Use Sharing Protocol Indicator
ST	System Use Sharing Protocol Terminator
Rock Ridge Interchange Protocol (POSIX)	
CL	Child Link
NM	Alternate Name
PL	Parent Link
PN	POSIX Device Numbers
PX	POSIX File Attributes
RE	Relocated Directory

RR	Rock Ridge Extensions In-use Indicator[1]
SF	Sparse File Data
TF	Time Stamp
Other Known Entry Types	
AA	Apple Extension, preferred
AB	Apple Extension, old
AS	Amiga File Properties

[1]RR was dropped from the standard after v1.09

For example, since the standard ISO only allows capital letters in the file name, you could include the NM type System Use entry and give it a longer file name with mixed case characters.

Listing 13-2: Root Directory Example: NM Type

```
            Length: 98
     Extended Attr: 0x00
   Extent Location: 0x00001234
       Data Length: 0x00004321
              Date: 2014/06/22 01:23:45 gmt offset: -7
             Flags: 0
         Unit Size: 0
          Gap Size: 0
      Sequence Num: 1
  File Name Length: 12
         File Name: TEMP01.TXT;1
          Pad Byte: 0x00
 4E 4D 34 01 00 41 20 54-65 6D 70 20 46 69 6C 65
 20 4E 61 6D 65 20 57 69-74 68 20 4D 69-78 65 64
 20 43 61 73 65 20 43 68-61 72 61 63 74-65 72 73
 2E 74 78 74
```

The above example now gives an Alternate Name entry with the new name as 'A Temp File Name With Mixed Case Characters.txt'.

File Names

This file system does have a few drawbacks when it comes to file names. As you probably have noticed, a lot of the structures shown have version numbers. The creators decided to add a version number to the file names too. This is where the ';1' comes in. At the end of each file name, you place the semicolon separator, and then the version of the file, in most cases, one. The version number can be any number from 1 to 32767.

Don't assume that all file names will have this version suffix. Some Windows implementations took this feature as optional and didn't include the suffix.

The file name has the following format.

```
name[SEPARATOR 1]ext[SEPARATOR 2]NNNNN
```

There are a few restrictions to this file name's length. The total length of the file name, the value that is in the File Name Length field, cannot exceed 18 bytes. This includes the file name, the period (SEPARATOR 1), the extension, the semi-colon (SEPARATOR 2), and the version number digits. The file name must follow the DOS file name technique. The name cannot exceed 8 characters and the extension cannot exceed 3. Directory names do not have an extension, therefore can only be 8 characters in length.

Even though the ECMA-119 specifications allow for up to a 37-byte file name, the decision to only allow 8.3 file names was made since that was the norm at the time.

Also, directories are limited to a depth of eight, including the root directory. Another limit is on how many directories you can have, due to the Path Table.

In UCS-2 encoding, all code points from 0x0020 to 0xFFFF are allowed except for 0x002A (asterisk), 0x002F (forward slash), 0x003A (full-colon), 0x003B (semi-colon), 0x003F (question mark), and 0x005C (back slash).

Path Table

The Path Table is used to quickly and easily find a directory location. For example, without the path table, if you had the following path

```
root\utils\make_hdr
```

You would have to find the 'utils' directory entry in the root directory block, read in the 'utils' directory block, and find the 'make_hdr' in that block, then read in that directory's block. This is a lot of jumping around and reading of directory blocks.

With the Path Table, you can read only one block, the Path Table, and find the directory block of the 'make_hdr' directory without having to read each consecutive path.

To do this, the Path Table contains a list of all the directories, their names and locations, in a single list. This list is of ascending order of directory level, with each directory level's list in alphabetical order.

The figure on the next page shows an example of a Path Table. The column under the 'List' heading is the actual list of entries in the Path Table.

Figure 13-4: Example Path Table

Actual	Entry Num	List	Parent Num
root	1	root	1
docs	2	bochs	1
bochs	3	docs	1
source	4	images	1
fysfs	5	source	1
include	6	utils	1
kernel	7	embr	5
embr	8	fysfs	5
mbr	9	include	5
loader	10	kernel	5
utils	11	loader	5
include	12	mbr	5
list_mbr	13	a20	6
vid_info	14	diskinfo	6
make_hdr	15	include	6
mem_info	16	list_mbr	6
mpart	17	make_hdr	6
diskinfo	18	mem_info	6
mputimg	19	mfysfs	6
msectcpy	20	mpart	6
a20	21	mputimg	6
nbasmide	22	msectcpy	6
mfysfs	23	nbasmide	6
rdtsc	24	rdtsc	6
images	25	vid_info	6

The list on the left in the figure above, is an example of the actual directory listing of the CD-ROM that is included with "FYSOS: The System Core", another book in this series. The right half shows the Path Table listing. The first column of numbers is the entry number for the name to its right. The column of numbers on the right is the Parent Number of this entry. For example, the entry 'make_hdr' is in entry 17 and has a parent number of 6, which means that its parent directory is 'utils'. The 'utils' entry has a Parent Number of 1, which is the Root Directory.

By reading in only the Path Table, which your driver might do only once at mount time, you can quickly find the 'make_hdr' Path Table entry.

One way to do so would be to search the list for 'make_hdr' and save its location in the list. Then see if its parent entry is 'utils'. If so, then see if its parent entry is 'root'. If so, you have found the correct 'make_hdr' directory entry.

If at any time, the parent is not the correct parent you are looking for, continue looking for the next 'make_hdr' entry, checking its parent line back to root. Once you have found the correct line back to root, you have the correct directory entry.

I am sure there are other maybe more efficient ways to parse this table, but this gives you an idea of how it is made up.

The format of an entry within the Path Table is listed below.

Table 13-21: Path Table Entry

Offset	Size	Value	Description
0x00	1	Varies	Ident Length (ID_LEN)
0x01	1	Varies	Extended Attribute Len
0x02	4	Varies	Extent to Directory Block
0x06	2	Varies	Parent Table Entry Num
0x08	ID_LEN	Varies	Directory Name
ID_LEN + 8	1	0	Padding if ID_LEN is odd

The Ident Length field (ID_LEN) is the length of the identifier within this entry. The identifier is the name of the directory this entry refers to.

The Extended Attribute Len field is used to identify the length in bytes of the Extended Attribute of this directory, if it exists.

I have not seen any use of the Extended Attribute feature. In fact, I have seen reference that this feature is not to be used. If it were used, the EA would occupy the first sector(s) of the data block for this file or directory block. i.e.: if this feature was used, the first sector of the file/directory block would contain the EA's and the actual data would start on the next sector. With only an 8-bit field in the Path Table Entry, this means the very next sector. However, I have seen documents state that this feature is not to be used.

The Extent to Directory Block field is the 32-bit sector number to the directory block holding this directory's Directory Records. The format of this field depends on which pointer you used from the Volume Descriptor, either Little-endian, or Big-endian.

The Parent Table Entry Num field is a 1-based number to the entry within this Path Table, which is the parent directory of this directory. If this directory is in the root, this value is 1. The format of this field will be Little-endian or Big-endian depending on the Volume Descriptor pointer used.

There is a limiting factor with this field. With only 16 bits to work with, this limits the table to about 65,535 entries. If you have more than 65,535 directories and one of these directories is a parent to another, the child directory's Parent Number field will no longer hold the correct value due to the truncation to 16 bits. Personally, I have not seen a CD-ROM with that many directories, though it is quite possible to have that many entries.

The Directory Name field holds the name of the directory. If this is the Path Table from the Primary Volume Descriptor, this name is ASCII 8-bit characters. If this is the Path Table from the Supplementary Volume Descriptor, this name is UCS-2 encoded characters.

The Padding field is only present if the Directory Name field has an odd numbered length. This is to pad the entry to an even byte. If this padding is necessary, it is a zero value byte.

 Since the Parent Directory information is stored within the directory itself, the Path Table is not needed. Most modern operating systems no longer use the Path Table due to the limit of its 16-bit sized Parent field.

Joliet

See the section on the Supplementary Volume Descriptor earlier in this chapter on how the Joliet specification extension is defined.

 The Joliet extension specifies file names to be at most 64 2-byte characters. However, the size of the Directory Record allows for 103 2-byte characters. Some modern systems account for this and allow the 103- character size.

ECMA-168 and Sessions

A CD-ROM may also have multiple sessions. Since CD-ROM's are not re-writable, a session will only occupy part of the disc. Then when there needs to be a modification to the disc, an unused part of the disk can contain another session.

Sessions are used to store new, modified Path Tables and Directories, and possibly modified or additional files. If you need to only modify one file on the disc, a new session can be written that has the newly updated and complete Path Table and Directory blocks, then only the one new file needs to be saved to the disc. The new complete Path Table entries and Directory Records will all point to the previous session's data blocks, but with the one modification of the new or modified file, which is stored within the new session. This allows for an emulated modification of files, at least until the disc is used up.

To do so, the system needs to read in the 16th sector from the first track of the last session, rather than the physical 16th sector of the disc. The new 16th sector contains a new set of Volume Descriptors, which point to new Path Tables and Directory Blocks.

I won't go into much more detail about sessions within this book, though please see the ECMA-168 specification for more on sessions. Appendix A in this book has a link to more information on this subject.

Wrap up

CD-ROM's, especially file images of CD-ROM's are still used to transport data. If you are going to create a system to read media, reading from CD-ROM's should be a priority.

A couple of last thoughts include if you see a reference to a specification "ISO 2735", please note that this is a typo in the ISO specification and it should be "ISO 2375".

Also, when it comes to the Primary and Supplementary Volume Descriptors, in theory, a system could point the Little-endian values to one set of path tables and directories and the Big-endian values to another complete set. In the specification, the two should point to the same set. However, there is nothing wrong with them being different, though why would you want to.

Intentionally Left Blank

Intentionally Left Blank

Appendix A - Source Code Repository Contents

The freely available repository contains all the mentioned source code, utilities, and other mentioned items within this book and can be found at the URL below. The following list shows its layout.

https://github.com/fysnet/FYSOS/tree/master/main

readme.md	main readme file
main	main folder for all books in this series
main\filesys	main folder for this book
readme.md	main readme file
main\filesys\docs	The documents files folder
fysfs.pdf	The FYSFS file specification
sfs.pdf	The SFS file specification
main\filesys\images	The Images files folder
a.img	Floppy Image of FYSOS
bootcd.iso	Bootable CD ISO image
fat12.img	FAT 12 hard drive image
fat16.img	FAT 16 hard drive image
fat32.img	FAT 32 hard drive image
fysfs.img	FYSFS file system hard drive image
leanfs.img	LEAN file system hard drive image
sfs_f.img	Simple File System floppy image
sfs_hd.img	Simple File System hard drive image
main\filesys\source	The Source File Folder
main\filesys\source\cd_menu	The Source for CD_MENU boot image
cd_menu.asm	ASM source file for CD_MENU boot image
cd_menu.inc	ASM Include file for CD_MENU boot image
main\filesys\utils	The Utilities Folder
main\filesys\utils\dump	The DUMP folder
dump.exe	WinXP dump application
readme.txt	readme file
main\filesys\utils\include	The Include folder for the utilities
ctype.h	C++ include file for utilities
misc.h	C++ include file for utilities
main\filesys\utils\lean_chk	The Lean Check Utility folder
lean_chk.cpp	C++ source file for LEAN Check app
lean_chk.h	C++ include file for LEAN Check app
main\filesys\utils\mbootcd	The Make Boot CD app
files.txt	Resource File for Make Boot CD app
mbootcd.cpp	C++ source file for Make Boot CD app
mbootcd.h	C++ include file for Make Boot CD app
main\filesys\utils\mfysfs	The Make FYS File System app
files.txt	Resource File for Make FYSFS app
floppy.txt	Resource File for Make FYSFS app
mfysfs.cpp	C++ source file for Make FYSFS app

mfysfs.h	C++ include file for Make FYSFS app
main\filesys\utils\mkdosfs	The Make DOS File System app
fat12.txt	Resource File for Make DOS FS app
fat16.txt	Resource File for Make DOS FS app
fat32.txt	Resource File for Make DOS FS app
mkdosfs.cpp	C++ source file for Make DOS FS app
mkdosfs.h	C++ include file for Make DOS FS app
main\filesys\utils\mksfs	The Make Simple File System app
floppy.txt	Resource File for Make SFS app
harddisk.txt	Resource File for Make SFS app
mksfs.cpp	C++ source file for Make SFS app
mksfs.h	C++ include file for Make SFS app
main\filesys\utils\mleanfs	The Make Lean File System app
files.txt	Resource File for Make LEANFS app
mleanfs.cpp	C++ source file for Make LEANFS app
mleanfs.h	C++ include file for Make LEANFS app
main\filesys\utils\ultimate	The Windows Ultimate File Viewer app
*.cpp	C++ source files for Ultimate app
*.h	C++ include files for Ultimate app
misc	Misc files for Ultimate app

Finding the Specification Files

Since most of the specifications mentioned in this book are not to be distributed by anyone outside the company that owns the specification, I have not included them here. However, I will include information on where you can find them.

"El Torito" Bootable CD-ROM Format Specification Version 1.0
   https://pdos.csail.mit.edu/6.828/2017/readings/boot-cdrom.pdf

Volume and File Structure of CD-ROM for Information Exchange
   https://www.ecma-international.org/publications/standards/Ecma-119.htm

Microsoft Extensible Firmware Initiative FAT32 File System v1.03
   https://www.fysnet.net/docs/fatgen103.pdf

FYSFS File System
   https://www.fysnet.net/docs/fysfs.pdf

System Use Sharing Protocol
   http://fileformats.archiveteam.org/wiki/System_Use_Sharing_Protocol

Rock Ridge (Almost same doc as above)
   http://www.ymi.com/ymi/sites/default/files/pdf/Rockridge.pdf

Joliet extensions to the CD-ROM
  https://www.pismotechnic.com/cfs/jolspec.html

Multi-session CD-ROM's
  https://en.wikipedia.org/wiki/ISO_13490

More FAT information
  https://en.wikipedia.org/wiki/Design_of_the_FAT_file_system

Finding an Emulator

If you do not have a physical test machine, and/or would rather test your code in an emulator, here is a small list of the most popular free emulators. Each are available for most modern machines and operating systems.

Bochs Emulator   https://bochs.sourceforge.io/

QEMU   https://www.qemu.org/
QEMU for Windows   https://qemu.weilnetz.de/

VirtualBox   https://www.virtualbox.org/

Appendix B - Included Utilities/Source Code

The following appendix will describe and show an example output of some of the utilities included in the repository.

Source code for all the utilities is included and should be portable to most any platform, except for the Ultimate application. They do not use platform specific items and should be able to be compiled on a DOS, Windows DOS session, Linux, or other platform with minimal modifications.

Obtaining a C/C++ Compiler

Unless otherwise noted, most of the C source code is compiled with the GCC ported C Compiler named DJGPP found at http://www.delorie.com/djgpp/. Go to the "Zip Picker" at http://www.delorie.com/djgpp/zip-picker.html and select a FTP site, "Build and Run programs with DJGPP", the operating system you will use (Windows2000/XP), choose where you want to read the online documentation, then make sure that "C", "C++", "Objective C", and "Assembler" are checked. Then choose the remaining items as you would like and click on "Tell me which files I need". This will give you a list of files, with links, and instructions on how to install and configure the compiler.

Obtaining an Assembler

You will need an assembler for one of the source files included. You may obtain a free x86 assembler from the author's website at https://www.fysnet.net/newbasic.htm. This assembler is free to use for non-profit use and has documentation and example source code. This assembler comes with an Integrated Development Environment (IDE) called NBASMIDE. It can load numerous files at a time, including projects, has color syntax, integrated build options, along with numerous other options to help your development. The author used this IDE for some of the development of this series of books.

Dump - Dump a file's contents - v1.75.00

This utility is a WinXP app that allows you to dump a file's contents into many different formats for debugging the file. For more information, please go to the following URL.

https://www.fysnet.net/win_dump.htm

Lean_chk - Check a LeanFS Image – v2.02.00

This utility will check a disk image that is formatted with the Lean file system. It will check all the structures and other objects of the file system and display any errors it finds.

Running lean_chk.exe will produce something like the following example. The example is a check of the image in the IMAGES\ directory of the disc. Since the image contains the LeanFS partition at base 63, you must specify with the /B:63 parameter.

```
D:\...\FILESYS\UTILS\LEAN_CHK\>lean_chk leanfs.img /B:63<enter>

  LEAN_CHK  v2.02.00    Forever Young Software 1984-2022
  Using a base LBA of 63
   Super found at LBA 16 with a checksum of 0x2DE4B6DA.
   Found version number 0.7.
   PreAllocate Count is 7
   Logical blocks per band is 12 (4096 blocks per band)
   State is 0x00000001
   Volume block count is 10080
   Free block count is 7696
   Bitmap starts at 17
   Super indicates root Inode is at 18
   Super indicates bad block Inode is at 0
   Super indicates Journal Inode is at 0
   Super indicates Block Size is 512
   Checking the backup Super Block block...
    Found backup super at block: 4095
   Total bands found: 3
   Each bands bitmap size in blocks: 1
   Counted 7696 free blocks.  Super reported 7696 free blocks
   Checking: \
  Inode Number: 18
   Checking: \.
   Checking: \..
   Checking: \bsod.sys
  Inode Number: 34
   Checking: \kernel32.sys
  Inode Number: 41
   Checking: \kernel64.sys
  Inode Number: 1017
   Checking: \loader.sys
  Inode Number: 2161
   Checking: \system.sys
  Inode Number: 2348
   Found 0 orphand blocks.
   Found 0 unmarked blocks.

   Extent Blocks used: 2363
      Total Directors: 1
          Total Files: 5

      Errors Found: 0
  Diagnostics Found: 0
```

You can also give the /V parameter to show even more information about the image. If you use the /R parameter, it will ask you if you would like to repair found errors.

MBootCD -- Create a Bootable CD-ROM Image

This utility will create a bootable ISO CD-ROM image, inserting bootable floppy or hard drive images. This utility will create all the necessary objects of the ISO image to allow for multiple bootable images to be included.

You give a file name to a resource file, which contains information for this image to process.

 Most of the utilities included on this disc use the same resource file parser. Therefore, there are ignored entries in the example files.txt file in the MBOOTCD directory. Only the 'imgfile=' parameter is needed, then any listing of included files to insert. Other utilities use more of the parameters within the resource files. See the MFYSFS utility section for more information.

The following is an example output produced by this utility.

```
Writing D:\fysos\main\filesys\source\cd_menu\cd_menu.img to LBA 22
Writing D:\fysos\main\filesys\images\a.img to LBA 742
Writing D:\fysos\main\filesys\images\fat12.img to LBA 1462
Writing D:\fysos\main\filesys\images\fat16.img to LBA 3976
Writing D:\fysos\main\filesys\images\fat32.img to LBA 6490
Writing 16 sectors to reserved area at LBA 0
Writing Primary Volume Descriptor at LBA 16
Writing Boot Volume Descriptor at LBA 17
Writing Supplementary Volume Descriptor at LBA 18
Writing Terminate Set Volume Descriptor at LBA 19
Writing 2 sector(s) of Boot Catalog at LBA 20
Writing 1 sector(s) of PVD Path Table at LBA 9003
Writing 1 sector(s) of Root Table at LBA 9004
Writing 1 sector(s) of SVD Path Table at LBA 9005
Writing 1 sector(s) of Root Table at LBA 9006
Writing 1 sector(s) of Temp File at LBA 9007
Wrote 9008 sectors (17.594 Meg) to
                            D:\fysos\main\filesys\images\bootcd.iso
```

MFYSFS -- Make an FYS File System – v2.00.10

This utility is used to create an FYSFS file system on a given image. It can create a new image and include a MBR, or it can create the file system in a partition on an existing image.

To create this file system as a new image file, use the following command line.

```
D:\FYSOS\MAIN\FILESYS\UTILS\MFYSFS\>mfysfs files.txt<enter>
```

To create this file system in a partition of an existing image, add the /E parameter.

D:\FYSOS\MAIN\FILESYS\UTILS\MFYSFS\>mfysfs files.txt /E<enter>

The 'files.txt' parameter is a filename to a resource file that contains information on how to create the file system. A typical resource file will look like the following.

```
# Resource file used with MFYSFS for the FILESYS book
#          by Benjamin David Lunt
#  Copyright 1984-2022  All Rights Reserved
#
#  mbrfile=filename    - This is the path/filename of the mbr file
#                          to use (should be 1 sector in length)
#  bootfile=filename   - This is the path/filename of the boot code
#                          file to use (should be 16 sectors in length)
#  imgfile=filename    - This is the path/filename of the target file
#                          to create/modify
#  base_lba=0          - Base LBA to write the Super Block to
#  tot_sects=0         - Total sectors to "allocate"
#  param0=             - Ignored
#  param1=8            - Sectors Per Cluster
#  heads=16            - heads per cylinder
#  spt=63              - sectors per track
#   path_to_source_file0, filename_to_use0, 0
#   path_to_source_file1, filename_to_use1, 0

# If you don't give the /E parameter on the command line, this app
#  will create an image that contains a MBR and the 16 sector boot
#   code, specified by the parameters below.
# If you do give the /E parameter, the mbrfile and bootfile parameters
#  are ignored, and the first sector written is the SuperBlock.
#mbrfile=  D:\fysos\main\filesys\source\mbr\mbr.bin
#bootfile= D:\fysos\main\filesys\source\fysfs\fysfs.bin
imgfile=   D:\fysos\main\filesys\images\fysfs.img


# When /E is used:
#   Base_lba is the LBA with in the existing image to write the
#     Super Block to.
#   Everything from this LBA to LBA+tot_sects-1 will be modified
#   tot_sects does not include MBR or 16 sector boot
# When /E is not used:
#   Base_lba should be 63, but is not required.
#   tot_sects includes MBR, 16 sector boot, and all remaining sectors
# You may use decimal or hexadecimal numbers
base_lba= 63          # Base LBA of partition
                      #   (LBA of 1st sector of boot code)
tot_sects= 10080      # Total number of sectors in partition
param1= 8             # Sectors Per Cluster
heads= 16             # heads per cylinder
spt= 63               # sectors per track
```

```
# The remaining list of files are the files that this app
#  should find and write to the root directory of the image.
#  First parameter is the full path name of the file to copy,
#  second parameter is the name of the file to use in the
#  image's root directory.
# The third parameter is a dummy parameter, not used, but
#  needed for the parser.
# You may have as many or as few as you wish.  Please note
#  that this app does not check for out of bounds due to too
#  many root directory entries specified below.
files.txt, files.txt, 0
floppy.txt,a_file_name_that_has_a_long_file_name_to_use_multiple_
        directory_slots_to_show_how_to_use_a_continuation_slot.txt, 0
```

See the 'files.txt' file in the utils\mfysfs directory on the disc.

The mbrfile= parameter gives the full path to the MBR binary file to use within the image. This file should be 512 bytes and be a valid MBR. This parameter is only used with new image creation.

The bootfile= parameter gives the full path to the FYSFS boot code binary file to use within the image. This file should be sixteen (16) 512-byte sectors. This parameter is only used with new image creation.

The imgfile= parameter is the file to create/use to make the files system. If this will be a new image file, this indicates the file to create. If this is an existing image (using the /E parameter), this is the image file to write to.

The base_lba= parameter is the base LBA of the boot code. For example, if you are creating a new image, the MBR will be at LBA 0, have one partition entry, and its base pointing to 63. Therefore, this base_lba= parameter should be set to 63. This utility will then write the image file pointed by the bootfile= parameter to LBA 63.

If this is an existing image, the use of the /E parameter, this is still the LBA of the 16-sector boot code. However, this utility will not use the bootfile= parameter, nor modify the 16 sectors at this base. It is up to you to write these 16 sectors.

The tot_sects= parameter is the count of total sectors within this image. This is the count of sectors from LBA 0, including base_lba, to the last sector in the partition.

The remaining lines are in pairs. You provide a full path name to a file you would like added to the file system and then its filename. This utility will copy that file to the root directory of the file system, giving it the name specified in the second parameter of the pair, and update the root directory and bitmap. You may include as many path names and file names as you would like. The path name and file name must be separated by a comma and each pair must be separated from another pair by an end of line. The file name must not include a path. All files will be placed in the root directory.

Please note that this utility does not check for overflow. i.e.: it will not check to see if the root directory is full, nor will it check to see if it writes past end of partition. This utility is currently coded for a total of 128 root entries.

The resource file may contain blank lines and comments. Comments are indicated by a '#' character. Anything from the '#' to the end of that line is considered a comment and is ignored.

The fysfs file system will allow 64-bit sector fields. To indicate to this utility that you would like to use 64-bit fields, use the /L parameter.
See the \FYSOS\MAIN\FILESYS\DOCS folder for the fysfs specification or visit http://www.fysnet.net/fysfs.htm for the latest version.

Running mfysfs.exe will produce something like the example on the next page.

```
D:\FYSOS\MAIN\FILESYS\UTILS\MFYSFS\>mfysfs files.txt /E<enter>

  MFYSFS  v2.00.10    Forever Young Software 1984-2022
   Writing SuperBlock to LBA 79
   Writing files.txt to LBA 122
   Writing a_file_name...........ntinuation_slot.txt to LBA 130
   Writing rest of partition to LBA 138 (9941 sectors)
   Writing backup SuperBlock to LBA 10071
   Writing bitmaps to LBA 80
   Writing root directory to LBA 90
```

Please note that this is an updated version from the same utility included with the previous volume of this series. This one fixes a minor bug and includes easier use.

MKDOSFS -- Make a DOS FAT file system – v2.00.11
This utility will take a resource file and create a specified FAT file system image from parameters within that resource file.

See the description for the MFYSFS utility for more on the resource file format.

Running mkdofs.exe will produce something like the following example.

```
D:\FYSOS\MAIN\FILESYS\UTILS\MKDOSFS\>mkdosfs fat12.txt<enter>
```

```
Make DOS Image  v02.00.11    Forever Young Software 1984-2022

Writing MBR to LBA 0
Writing Padding between MBR and Base LBA...
Writing Boot Sector(s) to LBA 63
 0: Writing fat12.txt to LBA 88
 1: Writing fat16.txt to LBA 96
 2: Writing fat32.txt to LBA 104
Writing FAT(s) to LBA 64
Writing Root to LBA 80
Writing rest of partition to LBA 112, 9968 sectors....
```

Using the 'param0=' parameter in the resource file, you can specify to make a 12-, 16-, or 32-bit FAT file system. See the three resource files included in the MKDOSFS\ directory for more information on the resource file format. Also, you can specify the /1 command line parameter and it will only create one FAT table instead of the normal two.

MKSFS -- Make a SFS file system – v2.00.10

This utility will take a resource file and create a SFS file system image from parameters within that resource file.

 See the description for the MFYSFS utility for more on the resource file format.

Running mksfs.exe will produce something like the following example.

```
D:\FYSOS\MAIN\FILESYS\UTILS\MKSFS\>mksfs floppy.txt<enter>

MKSFS  v2.00.10    Forever Young Software 1984-2022
Writing "kernel64.sys" to LBA 1
Writing "loader.sys" to LBA 1146
Writing "system.sys" to LBA 1332
 Adding "/system"
 Adding "/system/fonts"
Writing "system/fonts/arial.fnt" to LBA 1365
Writing "system/fonts/couriernew.fnt" to LBA 1370
Writing "system/fonts/lucidac.fnt" to LBA 1375
Writing "system/fonts/sansserf.fnt" to LBA 1383
Writing "system/fonts/simple.fnt" to LBA 1395
Writing "system/fonts/System128.fnt" to LBA 1400
Writing "system/fonts/System256.fnt" to LBA 1407
 Adding "/system/grfx"
Writing "system/grfx/hallway.gif" to LBA 1421
Writing "system/grfx/images.sys" to LBA 1689
Writing free space at LBA 2029 (849 blocks)
Updating Super block...
```

See the chapter on the Simple File System for more information on what this utility will do.

MLEANFS -- Make a Lean file system – v2.10.10

This utility will take a resource file and create a Lean file system image from parameters within that resource file.

See the description for the MFYSFS utility for more on the resource file format.

Running mleanfs.exe will produce something like the following example.

```
D:\FYSOS\MAIN\FILESYS\UTILS\MLEANFS\>mleanfs files.txt<enter>

  MLEANFS  v2.10.10    Forever Young Software 1984-2022

   Writing MBR to LBA 0
   Writing Padding between MBR and Base LBA...
   Writing Boot Sector(s) to LBA 63
    0: Writing bsod.sys to block 97
    1: Writing kernel32.sys to block 104
    2: Writing kernel64.sys to block 1080
    3: Writing loader.sys to block 2226
    4: Writing system.sys to block 2413
   Writing folder '/' to block 81
   Writing Super Block to block 79
   Writing Backup Super Block to block 4158
   Writing Bitmap #1 to block 80
   Writing Bitmap #2 to block 4159
   Writing Bitmap #3 to block 8255

      Total space used: 23%
   Total bytes remaining: 3940352   (4 Meg)
```

See the chapter on the Lean File System for more information on what this utility will do.

ULTIMATE – The Ultimate Image Utility – v0.56.00

This utility is written for a Windows XP or Windows 10 system and combines all of the utilities here into one easy to use GUI application. It supports a few more file systems and easily allows you to add or remove files and folders, modify the partition scheme, and create new images. Please see the following link for more information. Source code is included on the repository.

https://www.fysnet.net/ultimate/index.htm

Wrap Up

All utilities listed here are available for your use when building your project(s). You may use them and modify them for your needs. However, please do not distribute them without the authors written permission.

Appendix C - List of Tables and Figures

Tables

Figures

Listings

Outlines

Appendix D – UTF-8/16

A lot of the newer file systems use some sort of character encoding so that they can use different languages within the same structures without having to redesign the structure to accommodate a different language.

One of the most common used is Unicode in 8- and 16-bit forms. For example, the FAT Long File Name system uses the 16-bit format, while the Lean file system uses 8-bit format.

In this appendix, I will discuss how to use each form.

UTF-8

Unicode characters may have a value from 0x000000 to 0x10FFFF. Since we will discuss the English language here and will use ASCII characters that use no more than 8 bits, if we used a character width that allowed a value of up to 0x10FFFF, we would have to have a minimum of 24 bits per character. Since values are usually 8-, 16-, or 32-bits, each character would actually use 32-bits to store this 8-bit character. If we support a character value of up to 0x10FFFF, every string would be four times as long as usual.

This is why the 8-bit form of the Unicode string was created. It allows up to 31 bits of character data to be stored in one to six bytes. If the character value is less than 8 bits wide (is less than or equal to a value of 127), then you can use a single byte to represent this character. If a character has a value greater than 127, you may use two or more bytes to store that character. With this form, you only need enough bytes to store the value and each character in the string may use a different number of bytes to do so.

With most character strings in the English language, one or two bytes is all that is needed. However, using UTF-8, you can always support more without any modification needed.

To indicate how many bytes are used for the current character, UTF-8 uses the top most bits. If the top most bit, bit 7, is zero, then this is the only byte used and the value will be 127 or less in value, given in the lower seven bits. If the top most bit is set, then the remaining set bits up to a zero bit indicates the number of bytes that follow, with each additional byte having six bits used for the value.

For example, if bit 7 and bit 6 are set and bit 5 is clear, there are a total of two bytes in this character. Two bits set means two bytes used. If bits 7:4 are set, bit 3 bits clear, this means four bytes are used. Four bits are set, four bytes used.

Then, combining bits 6:0 of any remaining bytes *and* the remaining bits of the first byte after the first cleared bit, you make up the value. See the figure on the next page for a Code Point that uses two bytes, this two-byte Code Point allowing a value up to 0x7FF, using 11 bits to represent this value.

Figure D-1: A two-byte 8-bit UTF Encoding

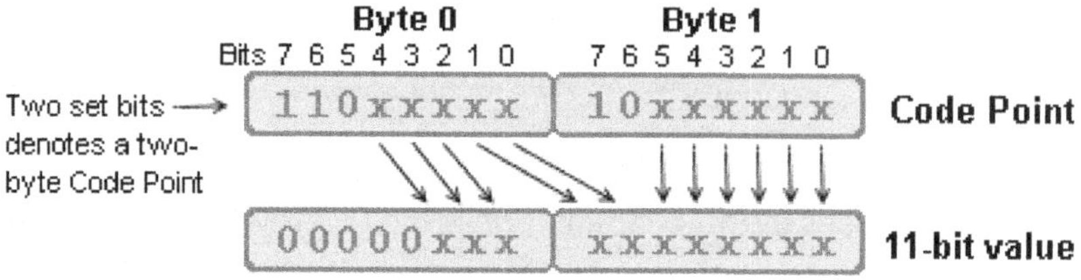

See the table below for another representation. The value to encode is called a Code Point. For example, if the value 0x00100F was to be encoded, it needs 13 bits to encode it, since the remaining high order bits are implied as zeros. Therefore, you find the entry in the table below, that will hold this 13-bit Code Point and use that encoding.

Table D-1: 8-bit UTF Encoding

Bits	1st C-Point	Last C-Point	Byte #1	Byte #2	Byte #3	Byte #4	Byte #5	Byte #6
7	00	7F	0xxxxxxx					
11	80	7FF	110xxxxx	10xxxxxx				
16	800	FFFF	1110xxxx	10xxxxxx	10xxxxxx			
21	10000	1FFFFF	11110xxx	10xxxxxx	10xxxxxx	10xxxxxx		
26	200000	3FFFFFF	111110xx	10xxxxxx	10xxxxxx	10xxxxxx	10xxxxxx	
31	4000000	7FFFFFFF	1111110x	10xxxxxx	10xxxxxx	10xxxxxx	10xxxxxx	10xxxxxx

A First Code Point is the lowest value that can use this form of encoding, with the Last Code Point being the highest value that will fit in this encoding.

Remember that the Unicode Specification only allows a value up to 0x10FFFF even though you can code up to 0x7FFFFFFF. Also, after decoding a Code Point, for example using two bytes indicated by two high bits being set, if you find an additional continuation byte (third byte of the sequence), a byte with the top two bits as 10b, the string is in error and you will need to search for the next non-continuation byte.

With this encoding, you can store the normal ASCII 8-bit strings and when needed, store 31-bit character strings. Also, if one character needs 21 bits to store it, that doesn't mean another character in the same string has to use the same encoding, it may use less bytes if needed.

UTF-16

Sixteen-bit Unicode is stored differently. Each character must use either 16 or 32 bits to encode a string. If the character only needs 16 bits, i.e., it is less than 0x10000, use a 16-bit encoding and store the value as is. If the value is 0x10000 or greater, then use a 32-bit encoding as described on the next page.

Since a value of 0x10000 or more needs more than 16 bits, we now need to use a 32-bit value to encode it. However, since a value larger than 0x10FFFF is illegal, if we subtract 0x010000 from it, you only need 20 bits to store it. 0x10FFFF − 0x010000 = 0x0FFFFF. Now create two 16-bit values, high word initialized as shown below, and insert this 20-bit value into it as shown.

```
Character = 0x10FFFF - 0x010000 = yyyyyyyyyyxxxxxxxxxx
WORD1 = 110110yyyyyyyyyy
WORD2 = 110111xxxxxxxxxx
```

When storing to memory or disk, store WORD1 first, then WORD2.

This works because a character between 0xD800 and 0xDFFF is considered reserved in the Unicode Specification.

 Remember when reading in a 16-bit Unicode, check to see if the 16-bit word read is 0xD800 through 0xDFFF. If it is, read in the next 16-bit word, combine the lower 10 bits of each and be sure to add 0x010000 to the result.

Appendix E – One Physical Floppy, Two Logical Drives

Back in the day when floppy drives were a common use, it was common to have one floppy drive and have the operating system simulate two drives. This was by design.

For example, the user often wanted to copy a file from one floppy disk to another and do it often. With only one physical drive, you might have had to copy the file from the floppy to the hard drive, eject the floppy and insert the other, copy the file from the hard drive to the newly inserted floppy, and finally delete the file from the hard drive.

This made for extra work and assumed you had a hard drive and available room on that hard drive for the file(s).

By the operating system simulating two floppy drives, 'A:' and 'B:' for example, you could use the following command to copy a file from 'A:' to 'B:'.

```
copy a:\filename.txt b:\
```

The operating system would execute the 'copy' command as usual. 'Copy' would read in a number of sectors from the 'A:' drive, then request the operating system to write these bytes to the 'B:' drive. As far as the 'copy' command was concerned, there are two physical floppy drives installed.

However, this is where the simulation comes in to play. The operating system, as soon as it found a request to write to the 'B:' drive, it would mark the A: logical drive as inactive, mark the B: logical drive as active, ask the user to swap disks, and continue the process. Each logical drive would use the same physical drive.

However, since a disk has been removed and inserted, the floppy drive indicates that there has been a disk change. If this is the first time it accesses the 'B:' disk for the copy command, it will mount the file system on that floppy disk, and process the request.

As soon as the copy command again requested to read from the 'A:' drive, the operating system would do the same process, switching from 'B:' to 'A:', asking the user to swap the disks again.

However, it now needs to check that the disk in drive 'A:' is the same disk it expects to read from. If it is not, it will abort the 'copy' command and display an error on the screen.

This is actually a little complicated to implement correctly, but your VFS driver needs to keep this in mind if it finds a floppy drive and this is the only floppy drive.

The best way to implement this is that every time you mount a floppy disk, you keep track of the disk using an identification of some kind. This ID is checked every time the disk is accessed. When a command is using the disk and the VFS sees a disk change notice, it needs to compare the new disk with the identification of the old disk. If it is the same disk, continue on with no interruption. However, if it is now a new disk, display an error and abort the command.

Also, now that a new disk is in the drive, you need to unmount the old disk and mount the new one.

If you don't plan to support floppy disks, which is very common now, all of this work can be ignored.

Appendix F – File System Detection

Once you have found a partition on a form of media, you will need to try to detect the file system that is on that partition. You must detect it correctly and accurately to be sure that you do not corrupt the current file system that resides on that media.

Therefore, it is critical to make sure and detect the correct file system and the correct version of that file system before you mount the partition.

This Appendix shows in detail, the steps to take for each of the five file systems discussed in this book.

FAT File System Detection

There are three different versions, or types to the FAT file system, the 12-, 16-, and 32-bit FAT types. Once you detect what size the FAT cluster numbers are, you may then read and write from the file system.

There are a few things in the FAT BPB that could indicate the FAT size of the volume, especially the System Type field. If you remember from Chapter 9, the System Type field had a string that showed the type of FAT installed, 'FAT12 ' for a 12-bit FAT. However, it is highly recommended that you do not rely on this field to determine the FAT size, alone.

The correct way to calculate the FAT size is by counting the clusters. The FAT specification gives a detailed description of how to figure the FAT size, and is described below. Once you have determined the size, then verify that it matches the System Type field. If it does not, do not mount the partition.

To determine the FAT size, we start by getting the sector count used by the Root Directory.

```
RootSz = ((BPB_RootCnt * 32) + (BPB_BytesSec - 1)) / BPB_BytesSec;
```

Note that on a 32-bit FAT system, this will return zero. Next, we determine how many sectors there are in the data section of the disk.

```
DataSz = TotSects - (Resvd + (NumFATS * FATsz) + RootSz);
```

Remember to calculate the Total Sectors from the two fields in the BPB, along with the correct FAT Size field. Once we have these values, we can now calculate how many clusters there are.

```
Clusters = DataSz / BPB_SectsCluster;
```

Remember to round down or drop the decimal part of the division above.

Now that we have the cluster count, we can figure the FAT type with a simple compare. If the count is less than 4,085 it is a 12-bit FAT. If the count is equal to or greater than 4,085 but less than 65,525, then it is a 16-bit FAT. If the count is equal to or greater than this 65,525, then we have a 32-bit FAT.

The check above works correctly every time, assuming that the creation of the volume followed that same formula, as defined by the FAT specification.

Technically, a 12-bit FAT should never have more than 4,084 clusters; a 16-bit FAT should never have less than 4,085 or more than 65,524 clusters; and therefore a 32-bit FAT should never have less than 65,525 clusters. Any other count is considered an invalid FAT file system. However, even though it would be considered invalid, a 1.44M floppy disk, which has no more than 2,880 clusters, may have a perfectly performing 16- or 32-bit FAT file system installed.

Since the above is known to happen, we must do another check to verify that we are still valid. When the utility that formatted this volume created the BPB, hopefully it put the correct value in the System Type field. Therefore, check this field to see if it matches the first check above. If it does not match, you should not mount the FAT system, and you should indicate an invalid FAT to the user.

This is all and good, but what if this partition is formatted with a different file system and the values read from the positions we assume are FAT members, just so happen to calculate to a known FAT size?

Therefore, we must first determine that the known members of the BIOS Parameter Block are actually part of the BPB. Once we do this, then we can compute the FAT size.

The two pseudo code listings starting below show the technique used by the FYSOS Virtual File System FAT detection routine.

This pseudo code assumes you have read in the first sector of the partition, placed it into a buffer and have pointed a member named 'bpb' to it, then using that buffer as if it were a valid BPB.

Listing F-1: FAT FS Detection

```
/* Check the JMP instruction */
IF (BPB->JMP[0] == 0xEB) AND (BPB->JMP[2] == 0x90)
   OR
   (BPB->JMP[0] == 0xE9) AND (BPB->JMP[1 & 2] < 0x1FE)
   CONTINUE
ELSE
   RETURN FALSE

/* Check that BYTES_PER_SECTOR is a power of 2
     from 128 -> 4096 */
```

```
IF (BPB->BYTES_PER_SECT < 128)
  OR
   (BPB->BYTES_PER_SECT > 4096)
  OR
    BPB->BYTES_PER_SECT IS NOT A POWER_OF_TWO
  RETURN FALSE
ELSE
  CONTINUE

/* Check that SECT_PER_CLUST is a power of 2
   with a range of 1 -> 128 */
IF (BPB->SECT_PER_CLUST == 1)
  CONTINUE
ELSEIF (BPB->SECT_PER_CLUST < 1)
  OR
   (BPB->SECT_PER_CLUST > 128)
  OR
    BPB->SECT_PER_CLUST IS NOT A POWER_OF_TWO
  RETURN FALSE
ELSE
  CONTINUE

/* Check that SEC_RESERVED > 0 */
IF BPB->SECT_RESERVED == ZERO
  RETURN FALSE
ELSE
  CONTINUE

/* Check that NUM_FATS > 0 */
IF BPB->FATS == ZERO
  RETURN FALSE
ELSE
  CONTINUE

/* Check BPB->SECTORS or BPB->SECT_EXTND is non zero */
IF (BPB->SECTORS == ZERO)
  AND
   (BPB->SECT_EXTND == ZERO)
  RETURN FALSE
ELSE IF (BPB->SECTORS != ZERO)
  AND
   (BPB->SECT_EXTND != ZERO)
  RETURN FALSE
ELSE
  CONTINUE
```

```
/* Check that the Media Descriptor matches a known value */
IF BPB->DESCRIPTOR IS ONEOF
    0x00, 0x01, 0xF0, 0xF8, 0xF9, 0xFA,
    0xFB, 0xFC, 0xFD, 0xFE, 0xFF
  CONTINUE
ELSE
  RETURN FALSE

/* If we make it here, we found a valid BPB */
  RETURN TRUE
```

Once we have found a valid BIOS Parameter Block, we can then check the FAT size.

The reason we go through more checks within this code is because a 1.44Meg floppy might and could be perfectly formatted with a 16- or 32-bit FAT size, even though per the specification, it would be invalid. I have formatted a floppy with both 16- and 32-bit FAT sizes, just to see if they work.

Listing F-2: FAT Size Detection

```
/* This code does the following three checks
 *  1. checks the size per the MS specification.
 *  2. checks the type field in the BPB.
 *  3. checks the first two DWORDS in the FAT(s)
 *      if the value is: Fi FF FF xx xx xx xx xx = FAT12
 *      if the value is: Fi FF FF FF xx xx xx xx = FAT16
 *      if the value is: Fi FF FF 0F FF FF FF 0F = FAT32
 *    #3 will only correctly identify a FAT32 volume.
 *     The xx's in a fat16 or fat12 may be eof markers
 *      and be 0xFF's, where there would be no way
 *      of telling if it was a fat12 or fat16 fat table.
 */

/* #1:  This is per the specification
LET FAT12 = ZERO, FAT16 = ZERO, FAT32 = ZERO

LET ROOT_DIR_SECTS = ((BPB->ROOT_ENTRYS * 32)
                  +  (BPB->BYTES_PER_SECT - 1))
                  /   BPB->BYTES_PER_SECT

LET FAT_SIZE =
  IF (BPB->SECT_PER_FAT != 0)
    BPB->SECT_PER_FAT
  ELSE
    BPB->SECT_PER_FAT32
```

```
LET TOTAL_SECS =
  IF (BPB->SECTORS != 0)
    BPB->SECTORS
  ELSE
    BPB->SECT_EXTND

LET DATA_SEC =  TOTAL_SECS
             - (BPB->SECT_RESERVED
             + (BPB->FATS * FAT_SIZE)
             +  ROOT_DIR_SECTS)

LET CLUSTERS = (DATA_SEC / BPB->SECT_PER_CLUST)

IF (CLUSTERS < 4085)
  INCREMENT FAT12
ELSE IF (CLUSTERS < 65525)
  INCREMENT FAT16
ELSE
  INCREMENT FAT32
/* Now let's check BPB->FS_TYPE
IF (BPB->SYS_TYPE == "FAT12   ")
  INCREMENT FAT12
ELSE IF (BPB->SYS_TYPE == "FAT16   ")
  INCREMENT FAT16
ELSE IF (BPB->SYS_TYPE == "FAT32   ")
  INCREMENT FAT32

/* Load the first FAT of this partition and compare
 * the first two dwords with known values of a fat32
 * type fat.  If it is Fi FF FF 0F FF FF FF 0F, then FAT32
 */
LET DWORD0 = FIRST DWORD OF SECTOR
LET DWORD1 = SECOND DWORD OF SECTOR

IF (DWORD0 == 0x0FFFFFF0) AND (DWORD1 == 0x0FFFFFFF)
  INCREMENT FAT32

/* If more than one flag is non zero, we have an error
IF (FAT12 AND NOT FAT16 AND NOT FAT32)
  RETURN IS FAT12
ELSE IF (NOT FAT12 AND FAT16 AND NOT FAT32)
  RETURN IS FAT16
ELSE IF (NOT FAT12 AND NOT FAT16 AND FAT32)
  RETURN IS FAT32
ELSE
  RETURN UNKNOWN SIZE
```

FYSFS File System Detection

Unlike the FAT File System, the FYSFS File System has a few signatures and a version number we can check. This will make it a bit easier to verify the file system along with which version of the file system to support.

Once you have loaded LSN 16 from the partition, do the following checks.

Listing F-3: FYSFS File System Detection

```
/* Check the Super Block Signature */
IF (SUPER->SIG == "FYSFSUPR")
  CONTINUE
ELSE
  RETURN FALSE


/* Check that SECT_PER_CLUST is a power of 2
    with a range of 1 -> 512 */
IF (SUPER->SECT_PER_CLUST == 1)
  CONTINUE
ELSEIF (SUPER->SECT_PER_CLUST < 1)
  OR
   (SUPER->SECT_PER_CLUST > 512)
  OR
   SUPER->SECT_PER_CLUST IS NOT A POWER_OF_TWO
  RETURN FALSE
ELSE
  CONTINUE


/* Check that ROOT_ENTRIES is a multiple of 4
    with a range of 128 -> 65532 */
IF (SUPER->ROOT_ENTRIES IS A MULTIPLE OF 4)
  AND
   (SUPER->ROOT_ENTRIES >= 128)
  AND
   (SUPER->ROOT_ENTRIES <= 65532)
  CONTINUE
ELSE
  RETURN FALSE


/* Make known fields are within known ranges */
IF (SUPER->ENCRYPTION > 1)
  OR
   (SUPER->BITMAPS < 1)
  OR
   (SUPER->BITMAPS > 2)
  RETURN FALSE
```

```
ELSE
  CONTINUE

/* Check that the Bitmap fields are valid */
IF (SUPER->BITMAP_FLAG IS USE_SECOND_BITMAP)
  AND
    (SUPER->BITMAPS IS NOT 2)
  RETURN FALSE
ELSE
  CONTINUE

/* Check the that data regions are in order */
IF (SUPER->ROOT IS BEFORE SUPER->DATA)
  OR
    (SUPER->ROOT IS AFTER SUPER->DATA)
  RETURN FALSE

/* Now check the version field. */
IF (SUPER->VERSION IS NOT CUR_SUPPORTED_VERSION)
  RETURN FALSE

/* If we get here, we have a valid FYSFS File System */
RETURN TRUE
```

Lean File System Detection

The Lean File System contains items just like the FYSFS file system that make it simple and accurate to detect. These items include a checksum that verifies its correctness.

Since the Lean File System's Super Block is not located in a fixed location, you must check all blocks from Block 1 to Block 33 until you detect the Super Block. However, until you find and read the Super Block, you don't know the size of a block.

Therefore, you must test for a Super Block on every block with a minimum size allowed for the file system. Since the file system allows a block size to be as small as 256 bytes, you must check every 256-byte block starting from the second 256-byte block, which could be the second half of the first 512-byte sector of the partition.

With this in mind, imagine that the block size used is 4096 bytes, though at this point, you don't know this. With a block size of 4096 bytes each, allowing the Super Block to be as high as Block 33, you must check at most the first 513 of these 256-byte blocks.

There are sixteen 256-byte blocks in a 4096-byte block and there are up to 512 of these 256-byte blocks *before* that last block you must check.

Therefore, read 513 of these 256-byte blocks, or a 256 count of 512-byte sectors, and check for a Super Block at every 256-byte offset.

The count of blocks to check gets even higher when larger block sizes are used.

Listing F-4: Lean File System Detection

```
// this code assumes a block size of no more than 65536 bytes

// calculate count of actual sectors to read
LET SECT_SIZE = ACTUAL_SECTOR_SIZE
LET COUNT = (131072 + 65536 + (SECT_SIZE - 1)) / SECT_SIZE
LET BUFFER = ALLOCATE_MEMORY(COUNT * SECT_SIZE)
READ_FROM_FIRST_BLOCK (COUNT SECTORS) TO BUFFER

LET CUR_BLOCK=1; WHILE (CUR_BLOCK<=513); INCREMENT CUR_BLOCK
BEGIN
  LET SUPER = BUFFER + (CUR_BLOCK * 256)

  /* Check that magic number == 'LEAN' */
  IF (SUPER->MAGIC != LEAN_SUPER_MAGIC)
    DO NEXT LOOP
  ELSE
    CONTINUE

  /* How about the check sum */
  LET CRC = 0
  LET DWORD_PTR = SUPER
  LET I = 1; WHILE (I < 128); INCREMENT I
    BEGIN
      CRC = (CRC SHL 31) + (CRC SHR 1) + [DWORD_PTR]
    END
  IF (CRC != SUPER->CHECKSUM)
    DO NEXT LOOP
  ELSE
    CONTINUE

  /* check primarySuper.  It should equal cur_block */
  IF (SUPER->PRIMARY_SUPER != CUR_BLOCK)
    DO NEXT LOOP
  ELSE
    CONTINUE

  /* log_blocks_per_band must be at least 12
       and not more than 31 */
  IF (SUPER->LOG_BLOCKS_PER_BAND < 12)
```

```
    OR
      (SUPER-> LOG_BLOCKS_PER_BAND > 31)
      DO NEXT LOOP
    ELSE
      CONTINUE

    /* all but bits 1:0 of state should be zero */
    IF (SUPER->STATE > 3)
      DO NEXT LOOP
    ELSE
      CONTINUE

    /* must be version 0.7 */
    IF (SUPER->FS_VERSION IS NOT 0x0007)
      DO NEXT LOOP
    ELSE
      CONTINUE

    /* If we get here, we have found a valid SuperBlock */
    RETURN CUR_BLOCK
  END  // loops back to start until CUR_BLOCK > 513

  RETURN -1
```

There are numerous other checks that may be done to verify further. However, if you verify the items in Listing F-4, you have enough to detect a valid Super Block.

SFS File System Detection
The SFS File System is also fairly easy to detect. The Super Block must be at offset 0x18E in the first sector of the partition, and will contain a Signature and Version fields. Simply check that the Signature field is 0x534653 and the version is either 1.0 (0x10) or 1.10 (0x1A).

Listing F-5: SFS File System Detection

```
LET SFS = (POINTER) 0x018E
IF (SFS->MAGIC != "SFS") OR
        ((SFS->VERSION != 1.0) AND (SFS->VERSION != 1.10))
  RETURN FALSE
ELSE
  CONTINUE

// Found it so return true
RETURN TRUE
```

CDFS/ISO9660 File System Detection

The CDFS File System detection is a little different. There aren't too many items you can check to verify the file system. You may read the first few bytes from sector 16 and verify the ID String and Version number, but this isn't very much.

However, there is one advantage. This file system should only be found on CD-ROM's. Since you have already detected the media type as a CD-ROM, you may then check the few items at sector 16 and assume it is a valid file system.

Listing F-6: CDFS/ISO9660 File System Detection

```
/* Sector 16 is the Primary Volume Descriptor */
IF (PVD->IDENTIFIER != "CD001")
  OR
    (PVD->VERSION != 1)
  RETURN FALSE
ELSE
  CONTINUE

RETURN TRUE
```

There are other checks that you may do. For example, you may check that the Little-endian value matches the Big-endian value of the sector size member, and other checks like this.

Wrap Up

When detecting a file system, be sure to also check for different versions of the same file system. If you find a file system and don't check the version, you may destroy parts or all of the file system if you use a different revision of the file system.

Appendix G – Timestamps

A Timestamp is a way to mark an item with a date and time. It comes from the old postal service act of stamping a letter with a rubber stamp to indicate when it arrived at the station.

Today, digital services use a timestamp to mark the creation or last modification of a file.

A timestamp may be in many different forms, but the issue here is that to be able to pass a file's timestamp to other machines, this timestamp must be a standard known form. Also, when passing files across time zones, via the Internet for example, there needs to me a known way to deal with a different time zone.

For example, if a file is modified and marked in one time zone, then passed to another time zone that is an hour behind, as far as the target system is concerned, the file was modified in the future.

Text Based Timestamps

The ISO8601 specification gives a type of a standard time stamp in the following form.

```
YYYY-MM-DDThh:mm:ssZ
         or
YYYYMMDDThhmmssZ
```

The year is given as four digits, the month and day as two, and the hour, minute, and seconds also as two digits each, with the 'T' used as a delimiter, and the 'Z' indicating Zulu time.

The two halves can be represented in partials, omitting the day and seconds, if desired. However, if the month is omitted, the day must also be omitted. For example, in the following timestamps, the first is correct, but the second would be in error.

```
YYYY-MMTHH:mmZ (correct)
YYYY-DDTHH:ssZ (*wrong*)
```

You must display from largest to smallest and every item in-between must be used. If you use the seconds field, you must use the hour and minutes fields. If you omit the minutes field, you must also omit the seconds field.

The 'T' is used to indicate that the date has ended and the time has started. If you don't omit any parts of the date, then the next field would be assumed the start of the time. However, if you omit the day part of the year and start the time part, the hours field will be read as the days. Therefore, the 'T' character is used to indicate that the date part has ended and the time part starts next.

To correctly display a time across time zones, you can give a time zone indicator. In the examples given, the 'Z' character is used at the end of the string. This is to indicate 'Zulu' time, or a zero offset to Coordinated Universal Time (UTC) time. If you wish to include a non-zero offset, you can use a plus or minus sign and give the hours and minutes offset. For example, if you want to indicate that the time is one hour ahead of Zulu time, use one of the following forms.

```
YYYY-MM-DDThh:mm:ss+01:00
YYYYMMDDThhmmss+0100
YYYYMMDDThhmmss+01
```

Again, if the minutes field of the offset is omitted, zero minutes is assumed.

 In ISO8601, a duration of time is given in the form of:

```
P[n]Y[n]M[n]DT[n]H[n]M[n]S
```

where

```
P2Y6M23DT5H34M22S
```

would give a duration of 2 years, 6 months, 23 days, 5 hours, 34 minutes, and 22 seconds.

Numerical Based Timestamps

A numerical based timestamp is simply a 32-bit or 64-bit number of intervals since a certain time, also called an epoch. The Unix or POSIX style timestamp uses a count of seconds, not counting leap seconds, since an epoch of the first of January 1970, or if given in the ISO8601 form:

```
1970-01-01T00:00:00Z
```

Therefore, if given a 32-bit number of seconds since this epoch, a system can figure the date and time of this number.

However, there are a few drawbacks to this form. This form counts a day as exactly 86400 seconds long. This will lose roughly a single second per year. No big deal, however to be accurate, you must consider roughly one day of the year having 86401 seconds.

Another drawback is that it is only accurate to a second. A file system can modify many files and possibly the same file numerous times in one second. Therefore, you can make two modifications and have the timestamp unchanged, though this is a rare occurrence. To improve this, you can make your interval shorter, say milliseconds instead of seconds from the epoch.

How about another drawback? A numerical timestamp will eventually role over due to the size of memory space it occupies. For example, if the memory used for the time stamp is a signed type, which most Unix style timestamps are, once you reach a value that sets the high bit, you are now well before the epoch, not after. Also, improving the accuracy of the timestamp making the interval smaller, makes this rollover much sooner.

Don't get to discouraged though, if you use a 64-bit timestamp and even use milliseconds, you have 18,446,744,073,709,551,616 milliseconds, which is roughly 584,942,417 years before it will rollover.

Using a millisecond interval and a 32-bit timestamp, this will still give you roughly 50 years before a rollover.

The Unix 32-bit timestamp is signed giving only 31 bits for positive seconds past its epoch of 1970. Therefore, it will roll over in roughly $(2^{31} \div 86400 \div 365)$ = 68 years, or more accurately, the 19th of January 2038.

It is my guess that the signed 32-bit timestamp was so that you could still represent a time before 1970. If a Unix based system uses an unsigned timestamp, it will not rollover until the 7th of February 2106.

Wrap up

Whether you use a text-based form or the numeric form in your file system, is up to you. Each has their advantage and disadvantage. For example, the advantage of the text-based form is that it will be accurate to the year 9,999, where the numeric form, if a 32-bit value is used, might roll over in the first quarter of the 10,000-year period.

The other side of that is the text-based form might use up to 25 bytes to store the time stamp where the numerical form might only use 4 or 8 bytes.

Another advantage to the text-based form over the numerical form is that it will allow time zone offsets where the numerical form does not.

There is another advantage to the numerical form. You can easily tell which file of two or more files is older, simply by comparing the two values. A time stamp of 123,456,789 is more recent than a time stamp of 123,456,780. Therefore, the file with the 123,456,789 time stamp is the newer file, newer by 9 intervals of which might be milliseconds. A larger number means further away from the Epoch, meaning more recent.

Appendix H – Multi-Boot CD-ROM's

This Appendix goes along with Chapter 13 of this book, and explains how to create a multi-boot CD-ROM, the reason you would need one, and the code to create the menu to boot it.

There is a very good reason you might want a multi-boot CD-ROM. One might be that you have a "Lite" install or a "Full" install of a software package. The user could choose either form from the boot menu, and then your boot code would load the correct bootable image from the CD-ROM.

Another would be for multi-lingual installs. Allow the user to choose the language desired and then boot that particular bootable image.

How about multi-platform installs? No need to have a CD-ROM for each platform. You can now let the user choose the platform and then boot that platform's binary image, all residing on the same disc, granted that they all fit on the same disc. However, note that the boot code now must be on the machine booting the CD-ROM, not on the CD-ROM itself.

The Process

The Process to make a multi-bootable CD-ROM, is fairly simple. You place a non-emulated bootable image in the Default/Initial entry in the Boot Catalog. Make sure to mark it as non-emulated, and load to 0x07C0:0000, and be sure to indicate the number of 512-byte sectors to load. When the BIOS finds this entry, it will load the indicated count of sectors to the address given, and jump to it. At this point the BIOS does nothing more.

Your image, now residing at 0x07C000 is executing just as a standard boot sector would. However, there are two advantages, the first being that you no longer have to read in the remaining sectors of your boot code. The BIOS has already done that for you. The second advantage is that you can use the MS Extended Interrupt 13h services to read from the CD-ROM as if it was a hard drive, though do remember that the sectors are 2048 bytes in length.

Once you are at this point, read in the "El Torito" Boot Volume Descriptor to get the Boot Catalog's address, then read in at least one sector from that address.

Verify that the Verification Entry is valid, then read in all of the sections and their containing entries, creating a list of bootable images to show to the user.

 Since you have full control of the machine, and currently reside at 0x07C00, a relatively low address, it does not hurt to read in extra sectors from the Boot Catalog Address. Normally, since a sector can hold about 128 entries, you

only need to read in one sector. However, reading in multiple sectors doesn't
hurt, and uses less code, than checking to see if you need to read in more.

An Example Layout

The figure below shows and example layout of a boot catalog. The Validation Entry, the
Default/Initial Entry, two Sections (three Section Headers), and multiple entries per section.

Figure H-1: Example Boot Catalog

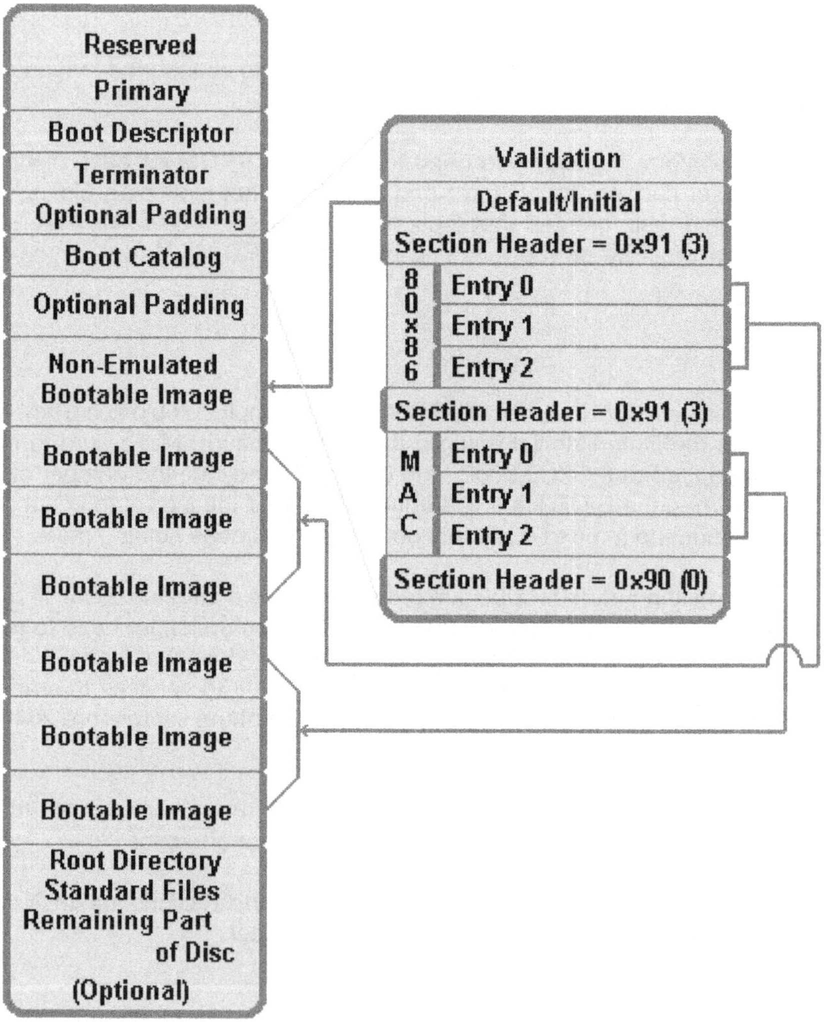

Note that all the images don't have to be in order as they are in the figure
shown. You may place them anywhere on the disk including within the data
part of the disc. An example of this is to have the bootable image(s) within the
data part of the disk, with a root or sub-directory entry pointing to them as
regular files. This way, the image can be booted as well as read from the
standard ISO CD-ROM file system.

Once you have read in these entries and created a list of your own, you may now show
this list to the user allowing them to choose which entry to boot.

The figure below shows an example of a menu system that you might use.

 The source code to this menu system is in the source code repository in the
MAIN\FILESYS\SOURCE\CD_MENU directory.

Figure H-2: Example Boot Menu

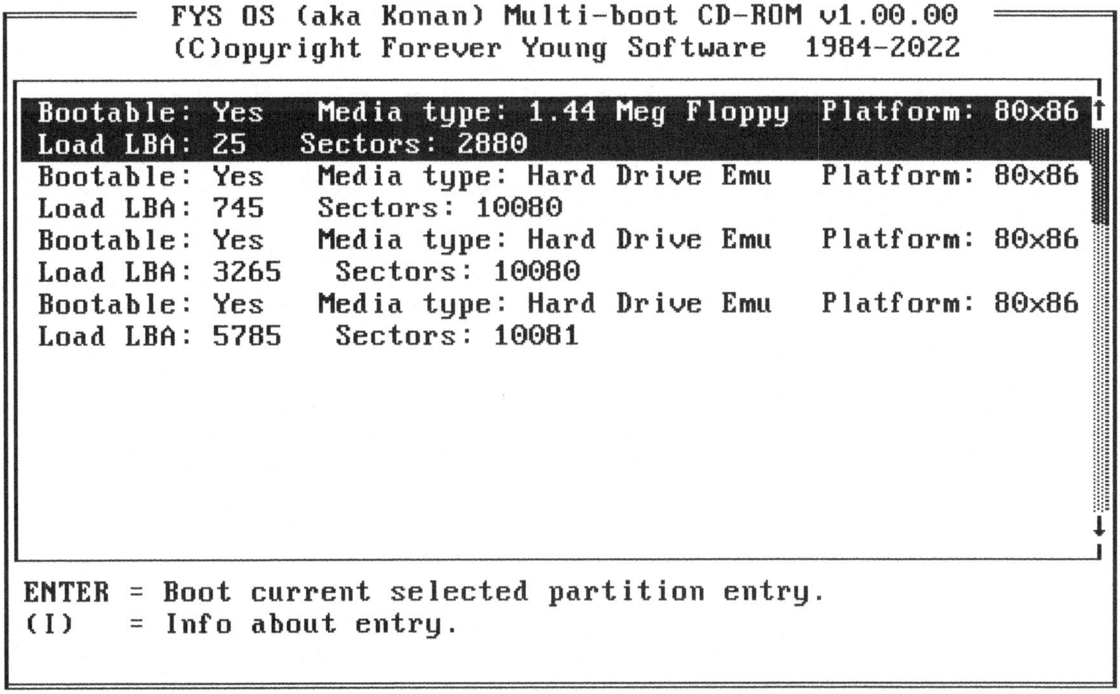

```
    FYS OS (aka Konan) Multi-boot CD-ROM v1.00.00
       (C)opyright Forever Young Software   1984-2022

 Bootable: Yes     Media type: 1.44 Meg Floppy  Platform: 80x86
 Load LBA: 25     Sectors: 2880
 Bootable: Yes     Media type: Hard Drive Emu    Platform: 80x86
 Load LBA: 745    Sectors: 10080
 Bootable: Yes     Media type: Hard Drive Emu    Platform: 80x86
 Load LBA: 3265    Sectors: 10080
 Bootable: Yes     Media type: Hard Drive Emu    Platform: 80x86
 Load LBA: 5785    Sectors: 10081




 ENTER = Boot current selected partition entry.
 (I)   = Info about entry.
```

The Source Code

The source code for the figure shown is an example assembly listing that will boot, load the Boot Catalog, extract the entries from the catalog, and display them to a menu. The user then may select from this menu, press 'I' to get information about this entry, or 'Enter' to boot that entry.

It is written in x86 assembly code, using the NBASM assembler and NBASM IDE found at http:///www.fysnet.net/newbasic.htm. You may modify it to your liking.

Once the user has chosen the image to boot, this source creates the BIOS Int 13h/4C00h specification packet, then calls that service to load and emulate the chosen image.

Emulated Images

For the emulated images, the images of floppies and hard drives, the BIOS uses the CD-ROM to emulate them as a floppy or hard drive. For example, if one of the images in the Section Entries is a 1.44Meg floppy image, the BIOS will emulate a floppy disk and read from this point of the CD-ROM for all 2880 512-byte sectors, using only 720 2048-byte sectors of the CD-ROM to do so.

Since all 1.44Meg floppies have the same CHS values, meaning they all have the same number of cylinders, heads, tracks, etc., the BIOS will know what to do with it.

However, since a hard drive image can be of any length of sectors, you must tell the BIOS what the CHS values are. To do so, you must create a standard MBR with one Partition Entry in the first sector of the image. This is required for the BIOS to load, boot, and emulate the image successfully. Therefore, all hard drive images must have a valid Partition Table in the first sector with a single entry used to describe the size of the disk.

Now your code can use the standard Interrupt 13h disk services to read from the disk, get information about the disk, etc., all acting just as a real floppy or hard disk drive would work, as far as the BIOS is concerned. At boot, the BIOS will give you the drive number in DL. As long as you continue to use this drive number for access to the disk, the BIOS will emulate the drive using the sectors on the CD-ROM as the data.

Wrap up

The only down side to this technique of multi-boot CD-ROM's is that the service 4C00h used to boot and emulate the selected image is not included in some BIOSs.

However, at least with the information in Chapter 13, this Appendix, and the source code mentioned, you will have an idea of how it works, if your BIOS supports this service.

Once built, the `cd_menu.img` file can be copied to sector 22 of the `bootcd.iso` image file, remembering that these sectors are 2048 bytes in size. Also, if you simply copy the modified `cd_menu.img` file to the `bootcd.iso` image file in this manner, remember that it must not exceed three 2048-byte sectors or you will need to completely rebuild the `bootcd.iso` file to give it more room.

Appendix X - For More Information

Where to get the CDROM that is included with this book
The current form of publication does not include a CDROM when publishing a book. However, if you use the contact information at the URL listed below, you can contact the author for a copy of the CD-ROM via the US Postal Service or an ISO image file via email. There is a shipping cost for all CD-ROM's shipped via USPS, however, no cost is added if sent via email.

Where to find more information on this book
For more information, extra documentation, and information on all of the specifications used within this book, use the URL listed below.

Where to get an erratum if one is needed
If and when an erratum is needed, it will be posted to the URL below with dated versions.

Where to get more examples
For more examples and source code, go to the URL below.

http://www.fysnet.net/the_virtual_file_system.htm

Bibliography

One or more of the following sources may have been used for the information for this book, tables and/or figures within it. Also look at the end of Appendix A for more links.

- fnmatch() by Kirk, Doctor Dobbs Journal, September 2008,
    page 38, http://www.ddj.com/architect/210200888
- Lean File System originally by Salvatore ISAJA,
    http://www.fysnet.net/leanfs/index.php
- Simple File System by Brendan Trotter
    https://web.archive.org/web/20170315134201/https://www.d-rift.nl/combuster/vdisk/sfs.html
- Media Descriptor Byte Values
    http://www.win.tue.nl/~aeb/linux/fs/fat/fat-1.html
- Wikipedia: Unix Time
    http://en.wikipedia.org/wiki/Unix_time
- Wikipedia: ISO8601
    http://en.wikipedia.org/wiki/ISO_8601

Contributors

The following list of people (in no particular order) have helped in one way or another, by using their machine as a test machine, sent in bug reports, and/or giving advice in one way or another. I am forever grateful to them. I am truly sorry if I have forgotten to list someone here. If you helped with this book in any way and are not listed, please let me know.

Salatore ISAJA, The Lean File System

The following list of people or groups of people may have directly or indirectly helped in one way or another.

alt.os.development group

Thank you to all,
Ben

Made in the USA
Las Vegas, NV
02 December 2022

60963987R00122